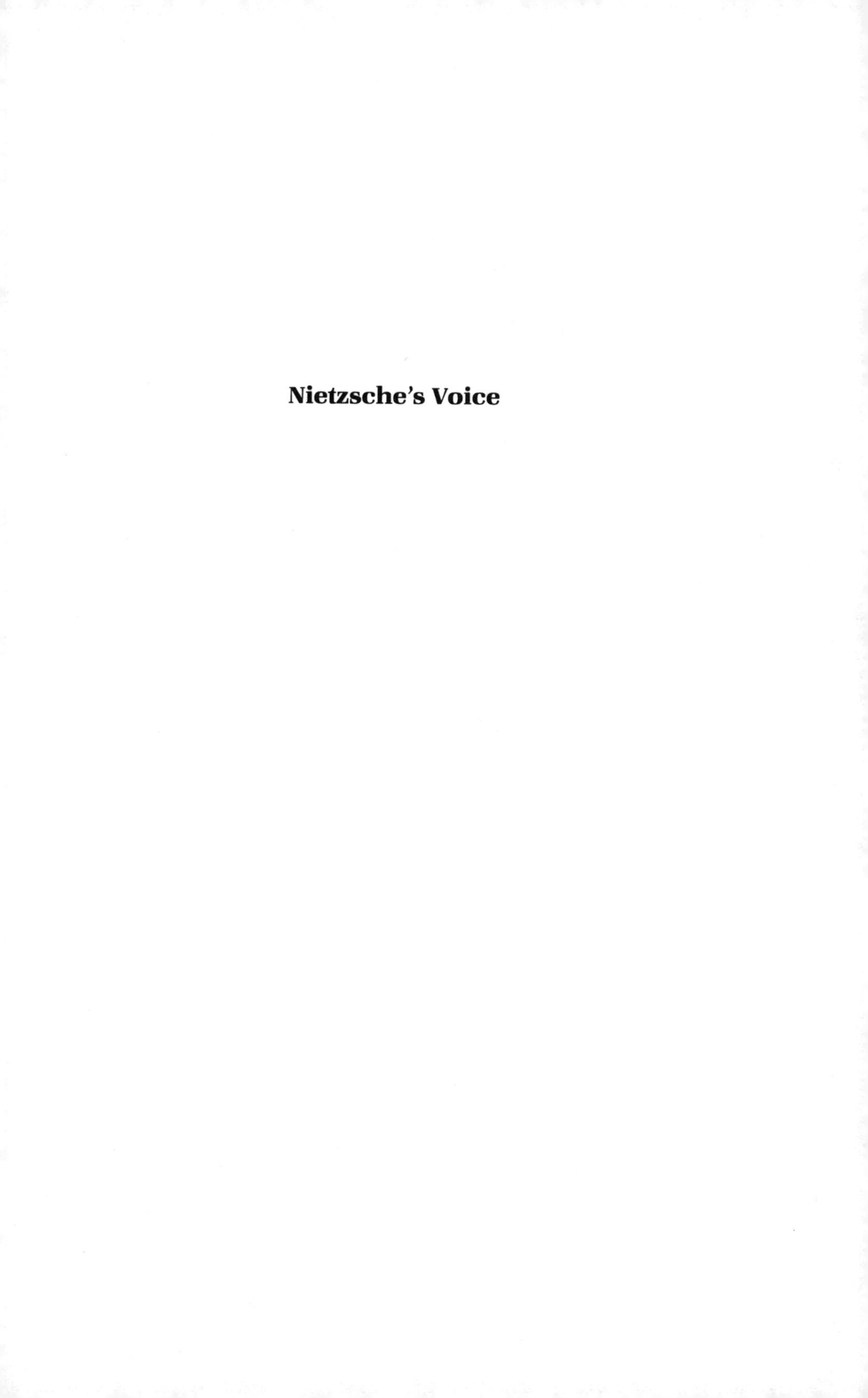

Nietzsche's Voice

BY THE SAME AUTHOR

Wittgenstein and Derrida

HENRY STATEN

Nietzsche's Voice

Cornell University Press

ITHACA AND LONDON

First published 1990 by Cornell University Press.

International Standard Book Number 0–8014–2500–X
Library of Congress Catalog Card Number 90–55131
Printed in the United States of America
Librarians: Library of Congress cataloging information appears on the last page of the book.

♾ The paper in this book meets the minimum requirements of the American National Standard for Information Sciences—Permanence of Paper for Printed Library Materials, ANSI Z39.48-1984.

For Jeri and Joseph

Contents

Acknowledgments

I consider the method of reading employed in this book to be Nietzschean, but I initially had to read Nietzsche's text in a certain way in order then to derive this method from it. The initial orientation I owe to two sources, the work of Jacques Derrida and the teaching of Lonnie Durham. Durham was my teacher when I began graduate work at Minnesota in the late sixties, when he was already purveying an entirely original brand of poststructuralism, a Freudian/deconstructive discourse on desire. This of course was a time when the United States was just beginning to awaken to structuralism. When I discovered Derrida's reading of Rousseau, I understood it in a way that was shaped by what I had learned from Lonnie Durham; and my appropriation of Derrida's method in the present work continues to manifest the influence of that subtle and profound teacher.

To Derrida I am grateful for the overflowing richness of his work. I also thank him for reading a draft of this book and giving me a crucial insight concerning my own voice.

Jeri Schneider has been involved in the writing of this book from the beginning. The basic idea of it germinated in a series of conversations with her, and there is hardly a page in the finished book which she has not helped toward greater lucidity and economy of expression. I believe few authors have the benefit of such acute, sensitive, and sustained criticism as I have received from her.

Josette Price has worked with me on the material realization of the text with unfailing grace and good humor. It has always amazed me what an immense labor it is to transform writing into the material object we call a book, and I am deeply grateful to Mrs. Price for the large share of this labor she has borne in the present case.

And I have gotten unflagging support from an incomparable group of colleagues here at Utah. Brooke Hopkins read an early draft and gave me a much-needed evaluation of the shape the project was assuming. Robert L. Caserio read a late draft and gave me detailed and extensive suggestions for revision, many of which I have adopted. Barry Weller, Lee Rust Brown, Bernard Harrison, and Fred Hagen all read portions of the manuscript and offered valuable suggestions.

Chapter 1 appeared in a considerably different form in *Representations* (Summer 1989); the Appendix, "The Birth of Tragedy Reconstructed," appeared in *Studies in Romanticism* (Spring 1990), a special issue on Nietzsche and Romanticism.

Grateful acknowledgment is made to Random House, Inc., which has granted permission to quote from the translation of Nietzsche's works by Walter Kaufmann and R. J. Hollingdale, published by Random House (Vintage Books). I also thank Viking Penguin, Inc., for permission to quote from *The Portable Nietzsche,* edited and translated by Walter Kaufmann. Copyright 1954 by the Viking Press, Inc. Copyright renewed © 1982 by Viking Penguin, Inc. Reprinted by permission of Viking Penguin, Inc.

I am grateful to the University of Utah for a quarter of leave in 1987 and two quarters of leave in 1988–1989, during which times most of this book was written.

HENRY STATEN

Salt Lake City, Utah

Key to Short Citations

The following are the translations of Nietzsche I have cited. In the case of works cited repeatedly, title abbreviations are given in parentheses. In the case of works divided into sections numbered consecutively from beginning to end, I have cited only section numbers, in Arabic, except in cases where the sections are lengthy and page specifications called for. In the case of works not numbered in this way, I have supplied part or section numbers in roman numerals and, in the case of works with subdivisions, I have numbered these in Arabic. After the semicolon I have cited the page number of the English texts listed below (e.g., *Twi* IX,44;547).

The Antichrist (*Anti*), trans. Walter Kaufmann. In *The Portable Nietzsche,* ed. Walter Kaufmann. New York: Viking Press, 1954.
Beyond Good and Evil (*BGE*), trans. Walter Kaufmann. New York: Vintage Books, 1966.
The Birth of Tragedy (*BT*), trans. Walter Kaufmann. New York: Vintage Books, 1966.
The Case of Wagner, trans. Walter Kaufmann. New York: Vintage Books, 1966.
Daybreak (*D*), trans. R. J. Hollingdale. Cambridge: Cambridge University Press, 1982.
Ecce Homo (*EH*), trans. Walter Kaufmann. New York: Vintage Books, 1968.
The Gay Science (*GS*), trans. Walter Kaufmann. New York: Vintage Books, 1974.

Human, All Too Human (*H*), trans. Marion Faber, with Stephen Lehmann. Lincoln: University of Nebraska Press, 1984.

On the Genealogy of Morals (*GM*), trans. Walter Kaufmann and R. J. Hollingdale. New York: Vintage Books, 1968.

Philosophy in the Tragic Age of the Greeks, trans. Marianne Cowan. Chicago: Henry Regnery, 1962.

Thus Spoke Zarathustra (*Z*), ed. and trans. Walter Kaufmann. In *The Portable Nietzsche.*

Twilight of the Idols (*Twi*), ed. and trans. Walter Kaufmann. In *The Portable Nietzsche.*

Untimely Meditations (*UM*), trans. R. J. Hollingdale. Cambridge: Cambridge University Press, 1983.

The Wanderer and His Shadow, trans. R. J. Hollingdale. In *Human, All Too Human.* Cambridge: Cambridge University Press, 1986.

The Will to Power (*WP*), trans. Walter Kaufmann and R. J. Hollingdale. New York: Vintage Books, 1968.

The following are the German editions of Nietzsche's works I have cited.

Gesammelte Werke Musarionausgabe, 23 vols. Munich: Musarion Verlag, 1920–1929. Cited as "Musarion."

Nietzsches Werke, 15 vols. Leipzig: C. G. Naumann, 1894–1904. Cited as "Naumann."

Nietzsche Werke: Kritische Gesamtausgabe, ed. Giorgio Colli and Mazzino Montinari, 30 vols. Berlin: Walter de Gruyter, 1967–1978. Cited as "*KGW.*"

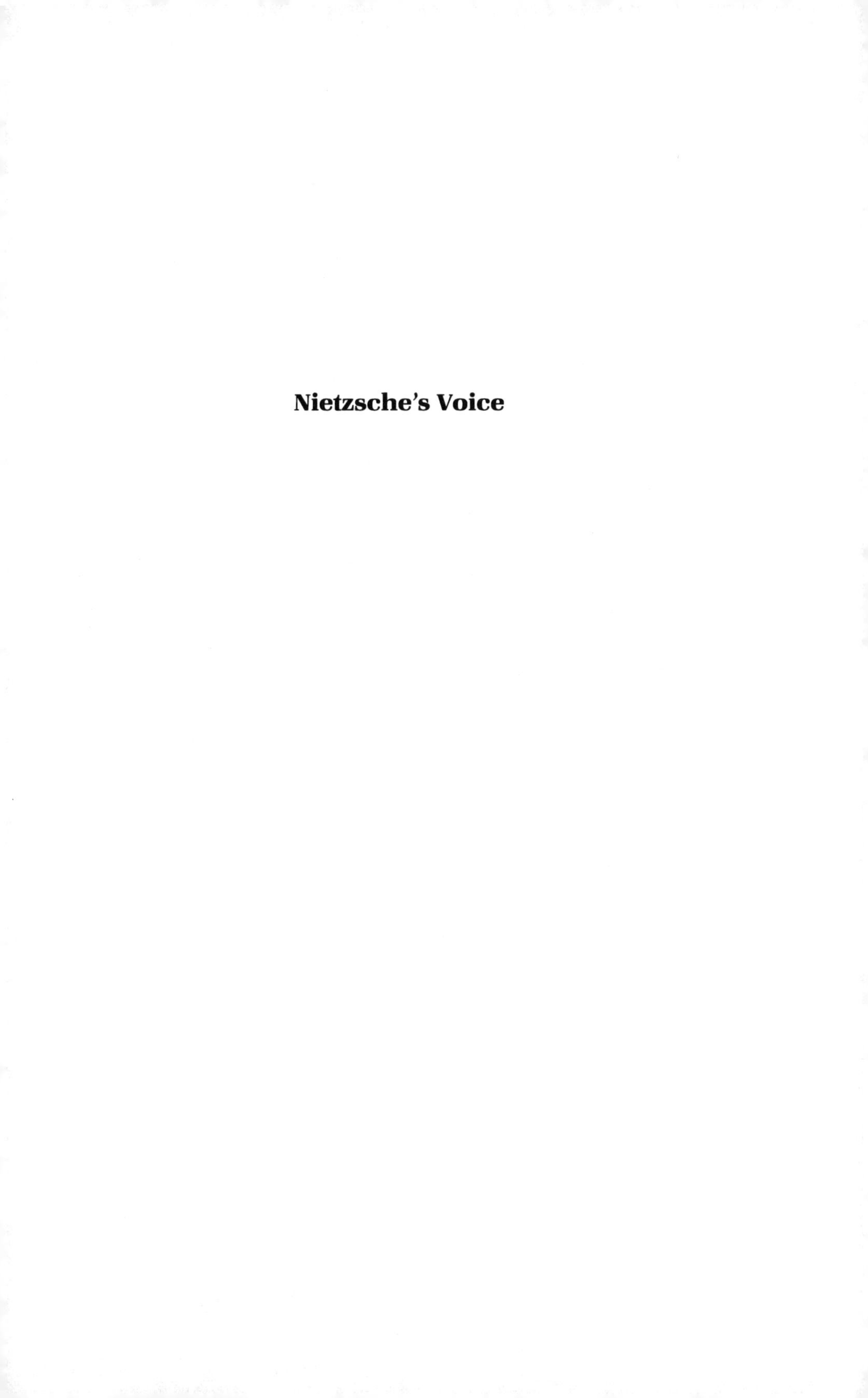

Nietzsche's Voice

Introduction

This book is not a systematic commentary on the canonical *topoi* of "Nietzsche's philosophy." Since my emphasis is on those parts or aspects of Nietzsche's text that most revealingly manifest what I will call its "psychodialectic," some presumptive doctrines, such as will to power, are considered at length, and others, such as perspectivism and eternal recurrence, are slighted.[1] In any case, I am not convinced that the topics made *de rigueur* by the conventions of Nietzsche scholarship are necessarily the most important. The question of pity, for instance, is never long out of sight in Nietzsche's texts, and Zarathustra calls pity his "deepest abyss"; yet this question plays no significant role in any of the commentaries on Nietzsche that I know. Neither do the questions of sadistic and masochistic pleasure, or the relation between Nietzsche's vaunted "master morality" and his misogyny or gynophobia. Are these peripheral or nonphilosophical questions? Even if they were nonphilosophical, this would not necessarily mean that they are irrelevant to strictly philosophical questions. But English-language writers on Nietzsche have characteristically presupposed them peripheral or irrelevant.

"The degree and kind of a man's sexuality reach up into the ultimate

[1] I see little need at the moment for another elucidation of the coherence of Nietzsche's views. Insofar as Nietzsche's thought can be systematized or normalized, this task has now been accomplished with admirable lucidity and rigor for most of the major questions, in particular with respect to eternal recurrence and perspectivism. On the former, the best book I know is Bernd Magnus, *Nietzsche's Existential Imperative* (Bloomington: Indiana University Press, 1978). On the latter, see Alexander Nehamas, *Nietzsche: Life as Literature* (Cambridge: Harvard University Press, 1985).

pinnacle of his spirit," Nietzsche tells us in remark 75 of *Beyond Good and Evil.* In this book I take this remark and others like it very seriously as we pursue our psychodialectical investigation of what Nietzsche calls the "economy" of his soul (*GS* 338). Psychodialectical reading treats the interaction between the libidinal economy of a text and its logical and dialectical structures. It is a form of Nietzschean reading, as mediated by the thought of Freud, Derrida, and Lonnie Durham, thought I consider to be in the tradition of Nietzsche. The method of this book could be considered a form of deconstruction; but it has seemed worthwhile to give the method a distinctive name since "deconstruction" means many things, and rarely if ever (outside of certain of Derrida's works) has it meant what I am calling psychodialectic.[2]

The dialectic between logic and libido is nowhere in Nietzsche's work more clearly visible than it is in *The Birth of Tragedy* and the unpublished texts connected with it. I therefore lay considerably more stress on the significance of these early writings than is common in Nietzsche studies, in particular on the fragments published in the Musarion edition as "The Means Employed by the Hellenic Will in Order to Achieve its Goal, the Genius." These fragments, conceived as part of *The Birth of Tragedy,* provide essential clues to the significance of the image of *sparagmos* in *The Birth of Tragedy,* and also to the way in which *sparagmos* is linked in Nietzsche's text to the questions of sexuality and women. I also freely avail myself of the notes published as *The Will To Power.* Whatever the problems of their relation to Nietzsche's *thought* as a philosophical doctrine, and whether they might be tentative, in process of revision, or relatively finished, the libidinal economy to which they belong is continuous with that of the published texts.[3]

[2]Specifically, the method of this book has a "family resemblance" to Derrida's reading of Rousseau in *Of Grammatology,* trans. Gayatri Chakravorty Spivak (Baltimore, Md.: Johns Hopkins University Press, 1976). Other examples of psychodialectical deconstruction in Derrida's corpus are his reading of Hegel in *Glas,* trans. John P. Leavey, Jr., and Richard Rand (Lincoln: University of Nebraska Press, 1986); and of Nietzsche in *Spurs: Nietzsche's Styles,* trans. Barbara Harlow (Chicago: University of Chicago Press, 1978). On the question of the relation between Nietzsche's "work" and "life," see Derrida's "Otobiographies: The Teaching of Nietzsche and the Politics of the Proper Name," in *The Ear of the Other: Otobiography, Transference, Translation,* ed. Christie McDonald, trans. Peggy Kamuf ("Otobiographies" trans. Avital Ronell) (Lincoln: University of Nebraska Press, 1988), 5–6.

[3]I do, however, refrain from using such of Nietzsche's texts (e.g., his letters) as refer us to the biographical Nietzsche. My reading is therefore, in an expanded sense of the terms, "intrinsic" or "formalist." Some interesting moves in the direction of the exploration of Nietzsche's libidinal economy in its relation to his mother and sister are in Sarah Kofman, *Nietzsche et la scène philosophique* (Paris: Union Général d'Editions, 1979), chap. 8.

Unlike the normalizing interpreters, I do not claim to be excavating what Nietzsche really thought underneath the ellipses, obscurities, ambiguities, confusions, and contradictions, but mapping the textual topography within which all these take place, or take their place. Of course any interpreter is necessarily limited to a selective and partial presentation of Nietzsche's texts; but I have tried wherever possible to track at length their sequential movement, whether within a single aphorism, a connected sequence of aphorisms, or larger swatches of writing in the case of such books as *The Birth of Tragedy, The Genealogy of Morals,* and *Thus Spoke Zarathustra.* Nietzsche's texts are continually transected by heterogeneous forces, and the precise nature of the forces that transect any particular moment of any given text has to be mapped by a precise location of that moment in the texture of the text. For psychodialectical reading there is nothing in the texture of the text that can be isolated as in principle inessential. The "frequent rhetorical excesses" and "ill-considered shots . . . at various targets" which Richard Schacht dismisses as "so much unfortunate static"[4] are integral parts of the movement of Nietzsche's writing. To subtract them is to subtract Nietzsche's signature from his text, to be left with an anonymous patchwork of "views."

I also do not hesitate to speak of "Zarathustra" without distinguishing this textual marker from the one inscribed as "Nietzsche." Textual authority for my inability to distinguish these two markers is provided by Nietzsche's remark that "in all psychologically decisive places" of "Wagner in Bayreuth" one could substitute for "Wagner," without hesitation, "my name or the word 'Zarathustra' " (*EH* IV,4;274). Once this substitution of names has been opened by Nietzsche's text itself, by what principles are we to draw its limits?

But there are stronger reasons why I do not and cannot distinguish a "fictional" character called "Zarathustra" from a "real" one called "Nietzsche." The distinction between a doctrine spoken straightforwardly by a thinker *in propria persona* and that placed in the mouth of a fictional character is significant only where we are confident of the proper identity of the thinker's voice. Insisting on the distinction sounds like a refusal to oversimplify; and yet this refusal may itself be based on a prior over-

[4]Richard Schacht, *Nietzsche* (London: Routledge and Kegan Paul, 1983), xv. Schacht's massive book provides a creditable account of Nietzsche's later thought, though an account of what I am calling the regularizing, patchwork sort. It is aggressively indifferent to Nietzsche's textuality and indulges in a summary dismissal of "certain recent French writers" concerning whom nothing is said but that their "construals" are "inadequate" (xv).

simplification. Thus Gadamer tells us that "it is certainly not right simply to identify Zarathustra with Nietzsche and his discourses (*Reden*) with Nietzsche's philosophy";[5] but he takes it for granted that there is a fixed entity called "Nietzsche" who could or could not be "simply" identified with Zarathustra.[6] Implicit in Gadamer's confidence is an entire metaphysics of the self and of conscious intentionality.

It is precisely this metaphysics that Nietzsche challenges, and not only on the level of argument but also on that of the text, of writing. The voice that speaks in this text splits into a plurality of voices; it tells us with the greatest conviction and sense of authority the most contradictory things. For example, a reiterated championing of authenticity and critique of the actor alternates with a love of irony, concealment, and masks. It is as though the authenticity of this voice consisted in its willingness to pursue any and every possible line of thought to its extreme consequence, and therefore also (perhaps especially) the line that throws authenticity into an abyss from which it can never emerge. Or, alternately, as though this voice were that of a pure impersonator, someone with no authenticity at all, so that he could shape himself *entirely* to whatever persona he adopted, thus become whatever persona drew him the most strongly—and the one that drew him the most strongly, in the end, were that of the *absolutely authentic being*.

Consequently, if I do not distinguish "Nietzsche" from "Zarathustra," it is not because I mistake a fictive voice for that of the philosopher, or because I assimilate the fictive text to the genre of the philosophical doctrine. It is a matter, rather, of calling into play in relation to all of Nietzsche's texts all the resources of reading available to us, both of "philosophical" reading and of "literary" reading. My criticism of Gadamer is thus not that he etiolates his own distinction between philosophical *Lehre* and poetic *Handlung* when he

[5]Hans-Georg Gadamer, "Das Drama Zarathustras," *Nietzsche-Studien* 15 (1986): 1–15; quote from p. 5, my translation. Unless otherwise indicated, all translations are my own.

[6]A cannier and more resourceful investigator of the relation between Nietzsche and Zarathustra is Bernard Pautrat in *Versions du soleil: Figure et system de Nietzsche* (Paris: Editions du Seuil, 1971). Like Gadamer, Pautrat insists that the "sense" of the text cannot be isolated from the "*mise en scène*" of the narration (332) and that Nietzsche is not simply identifiable with Zarathustra (359). But for Pautrat, Zarathustra is not the bearer of Nietzsche's authentic word; rather, he is a stand-in by which Nietzsche can express his nostalgic desire for Being (in the form of the allure of the thought of eternal return). Because the desire is delegated to a fictional or mythic figure, Nietzsche can keep his distance from the fall back into metaphysics that the desire implies (360). Thus Pautrat continues to read Zarathustra as *bearer of Nietzsche's desire,* and the provisional distinction between the real and the fictional remains permeable.

makes the *Handlung* the bearer of Nietzsche's true *Lehre,*[7] but rather that he does not realize that we must extend to the reading of Nietzsche's "philosophical" texts the same kind of "literary" attention that is obviously appropriate to *Zarathustra:* attention to dramatic context, tonal shifts, ambiguities, conflicts between what is said and the motivational forces inscribed within what is said, and the system of entrances, exits, and interactions of personae.

Readers of the manuscript of this book have raised questions about my choice of title. First, why Nietzsche's voice instead of, say, Nietzsche's economy, since the notion of economy plays such a central role in this study? And second, why the singular "voice" instead of the plural "voices"?

I have chosen the figure of voice rather than that of economy because I would like the title to be read as a reference to the address to the present which Nietzsche's text makes. Nietzsche addresses a future that he believes will be able to hear him as his own time cannot; and we are that future. I use the figure of voice to refer to this phenomenon because Nietzsche himself uses it in several crucial passages to which I advert, and also because I want to exploit the metaphoric resources this figure opens, above all that of tone or tonality. Tone is just as much a property of the written text as are grammar and figuration, though it is a more fugitive and less formalizable property, and it is in the tone of a voice/text that the libidinal forces motivating utterance are most clearly revealed, even against the will of the speaker/writer. This is most true when the speaker/writer attempts the most difficult or powerful utterance, or when he or she speaks/writes in the most difficult rhetorical circumstances (see Chapter 1). The crucial point is that *libidinal forces too are textual;* perhaps they *are* the text in its totality and concreteness, and all our other textual categories are their analytical decomposition.

I speak of Nietzsche's voice in the singular because his voice is the index of Nietzsche's economy and the notion of Nietzsche's economy is neither that of his unity nor that of his multiplicity but, one might say, that of the system of transformations of subject positions within the text signed "Nietzsche." One could say that "Nietzsche" is nothing but the as-

[7]In the Lehre of will to power the legacy of metaphysics persists, but the drama of Zarathustra serves as the medium (*vermittelt*) of a different Lehre, the doctrine that says "sing, speak no more"; Gadamer, "Das Drama Zarathustras," 15.

semblage of these subject positions or "voices"; but one could also say that they are all inflections of one voice or masks of one persona. There does not seem to me to be any empirical fact of the matter. Nevertheless, it could be said that Nietzsche's voice is one in the sense that *anyone's* voice is one, in the sense that we identify it by attaching one person's name to it. Beyond that I leave open or "bracket" (in the phenomenological sense) the question of the true nature of its ultimate source. The point is that we identify a certain collection of texts as Nietzsche's, and that we distinguish what we read or hear in these texts from what we read or hear in other collections that bear other signatures. Different readers or auditors read or hear different things in this text; our task here is to consider the shape of the overall phenomenon that allows itself to be heard in these various ways, and to trace the system of forces that gives it this shape.

Only if we treat Nietzsche's text as, to use Nietzsche's term, a "relative unity," however problematic and fractured (as a person is a problematic and fractured unity), can we speak of "contradictions" within it. A true multiplicity of voices could only manifest disagreement, not contradiction.

This last claim brings us to one final objection to the present project which is bound to arise and is very difficult to put to rest. This is the objection that everything I am treating as contradiction in Nietzsche's text is really a function of his "perspectivism," that because he knows that the world has no pre-given form he is free to try out as many and as varied views of each phenomenon as he pleases.

At one level, the "perspectivism" interpretation does in fact account for many of the movements of Nietzsche's text. But here is where the question arises of the *tonality* in which Nietzsche speaks his perspectives—on women and Germans, for instance. Or the privilege he gives to one perspective while suppressing another—the poisonous effects of Christianity as opposed to its curative effects, for instance. Now we would have to supplement the idea of Nietzsche's perspectivism with some notion of him as diagnostician of culture who privileges those specific perspectives he thinks are good for us at this time. But then we must question this diagnosis, which is itself a perspective. For what reason does Nietzsche come to privilege this specific perspective, and to privilege it so massively, as an interpretation of the entire history of his culture? Is it because he thinks it's true? Not if he is really a perspectivist. What, then?

We are thrown back once more on the question of Nietzsche's economy, his *das bin ich*. Something in Nietzsche dictates that he will interpret our history as the conflict between noble and ascetic, and that he will narrate this conflict in an extraordinarily tangled and ambiguous fashion. The notion of perspectivism explains nothing; it refers the heterogeneity of Nietzsche's text back to some perfect originative freedom that would not be subject to the constraints of textuality—constraints I sum up here under the heading of psychodialectic.

1

The Excluding Inclusion

A philosophical text is also a dream text; but it is not only a dream text. Elements of the dream may be read there, at least if the reading is resourceful enough; but the textual laws, the laws of logic and dialectic, that seek to override the dynamics of the dream have a power and efficacy that mark in a decisive fashion the texture of the philosophical text—even if they never succeed in becoming the sole determinant of this texture. Thus in psychodialectical reading we must be as attentive to the logical economy of the text as we are to the libidinal economy with which it interacts. The former provides the channels along which the latter flows, even if these channels are, like the banks of a river, frequently overridden and redirected according to the energies of the flow.

Freud's distinction between ideation or concept and affective/libidinal charge, *Affektbetrag*,[1] is an approximation of the primary contrast at issue

[1]Here, for example, is how Freud makes this distinction in the essay "Repression": "In our discussion so far we have dealt with the repression of an instinctual representative, and by that we have understood an idea or group of ideas which is cathected with a definite quota of psychical energy (libido or interest) coming from an instinct. Clinical observation now obliges us to divide up what we have hitherto regarded as a single entity; for it shows us that besides the idea, some other element representing the instinct has to be taken into account, and that this other element undergoes vicissitudes of repression which may be quite different from those undergone by the idea. For this other element of the psychical representative the term *quota of affect* [*Affektbetrag*] has been generally adopted. It corresponds to the instinct in so far as the latter has become detached from the idea and finds expression, proportionate to its quantity, in processes which are sensed as affects. From this point on, in describing a case of repression, we shall have to follow up separately what, as the result of repression, becomes of the *idea*, and what becomes of the instinctual energy linked to it"; Sigmund Freud, *The*

in psychodialectical reading, though in the case of philosophical textuality ideation and charge are bound together in ways that strictly psychoanalytic reading would not be equipped to identify or disentangle. But, assuming the supplementation of psychoanalysis by the necessary modes of literary and philosophical analysis necessary to psychodialectical reading, we could say that what this sort of reading traces is the character and movement of the libidinal charge with which Nietzsche invests his concepts. Whereas in purely "ideational" terms we can assign a systematically developed (and thus in some sense fixed) meaning to the *concept,* the *charge* is a variable factor that reflects the particular textual and psychological context in which the concept (or its avatars) occurs. By "psychological context" I mean something that is hard to define but whose sense will emerge from the reading presented here. What I do *not* mean is anything that we could find out, say, from Nietzsche's letters, about how he was feeling at the time he wrote this or that. Even if we could reliably establish anything about the mood of some extratextual Nietzsche at the time of a given writing (which I do not believe), we would still have to reckon with the modification of such a mood that the act of writing itself would work; so we are in any case thrown back upon the mood of the writing, the economy of an always textualized Nietzsche.

I authorize this reading of Nietzsche from his own text. It is Nietzsche himself who teaches us to look for the influence on his writing, as on that of any philosophy, of instinct, drive, and desire. "Most of the conscious thinking of a philosopher is secretly guided and forced into certain channels by his instincts," he tells us (*BGE* 3), and a little further on he makes this much-quoted remark.

> Gradually it has become clear to me what every great philosophy so far has been: namely, the personal confession of its author and a kind of involuntary and unconscious memoir. . . . In the philosopher . . . there is nothing whatever that is impersonal; and above all, his morality bears decided and decisive witness to *who he is*—that is, in what order of rank the innermost drives of his nature stand in relation to each other. (*BGE* 6).[2]

Standard Edition of the Complete Psychological Works, ed. and trans. James Strachey, 24 vols. (London: Hogarth Press and the Institute of Psycho-analysis, 1953–1974), 14:152; henceforth cited as "*SE.*"

[2]Throughout quotes from Nietzsche, emphasis is in the original unless otherwise indicated.

"Every great philosophy *so far*": does this mean up to, but not including, Nietzsche's? The suggestion is jarringly at odds with the force of Nietzsche's critique, which teaches us above all to be suspicious of the thinker's pretense at transcendence of the "humanity and animality" we contribute to the reality we perceive (*GS* 57).

Pursuing, then, a "proper physio-psychology" (*BGE* 23), we ask how Nietzsche's drives secretly guide his conscious thinking into certain channels. But in order to approach this question, we have to decide just what the nature of the channels is. Out of the vast diversity of Nietzsche's text, what are we going to select as his "arguments" or "doctrines," and how are we going to set these in relation to each other such that we can then attempt to read their motivating forces?

I am going to privilege a certain set of concepts as the most encompassing framework of this investigation, and I justify my choice in the following way: The concepts in question are structurally privileged in Nietzsche's text as defining the largest or total perspective. There is, Nietzsche tells us, a "large-scale accounting" (*Abrechnung im grossen; GS* 1) that takes stock of the "grand" or "great" economy (*grösse Ökonomie; WP* 291), the "economy of the whole of life" (*Gesamt-Haushalt des Lebens; BGE* 23). This grand economy "is not afraid of high prices, of squandering" (*Verschwendung; GS* 1), it is a spendthrift or potlatch economy, what Georges Bataille calls a "general" economy.[3] Nietzsche often defines the richest, strongest, most noble soul as the one that echoes this spendthrift economy of nature. "A gift-giving virtue is the highest virtue," Zarathustra says to his disciples. "This is your thirst: to become sacrifices and gifts yourselves; and that is why you thirst to pile up all the riches in your soul" (*Z* I,22;186–87). And in notes collected in *The Will to Power:* "It is of the very essence of the rich spirit to squander itself carelessly, without petty caution, from day to day" (77); "the degree to which one loves, spends oneself, proves the degree of individual power and personality" (786; cf. 792, 808, 846).

[3]On general economy and related ideas, see Georges Bataille, "The Notion of Expenditure," in *Visions of Excess: Selected Writings, 1927–1939,* ed. Allan Stoekl, trans. Allan Stoekl, Carl R. Lovitt, and Donald M. Leslie, Jr. (Minneapolis: University of Minnesota Press, 1985), 116–29; idem, "Sacrifice," trans. Annette Michelson, *October 36* (Spring, 1986); 61–74; and Jacques Derrida, "From Restricted to General Economy: A Hegelianism without Reserve," in *Writing and Difference,* trans. Alan Bass (Chicago: University of Chicago Press, 1978), 251–77.

Nietzsche himself in one movement of his economy strives to attain the standpoint of the potlatch economy, to become a soul that would squander itself and thus attain to "gay science":

> To laugh at oneself as one would have to laugh in order to laugh *out of the whole truth*—to do that even the best so far lacked sufficient sense for the truth, and the most gifted had too little genius for that. Even laughter may yet have a future. I mean, when the proposition "the species is everything, *one* is always none" has become part of humanity, and the ultimate liberation and irresponsibility has become accessible to all at all times. Perhaps laughter will then have formed an alliance with wisdom, perhaps only 'gay science' will then be left. (*GS* 1)

These remarks have considerable physiopsychological interest for us. They represent an extraordinary mood, something like a complete release of the tension and anxiety of individuation, a tension with which, as we shall see, Nietzsche is often oppressed. The grand economy is not afraid to squander, and what it squanders is individuals. Therefore, what do *I* matter? "*One* is always none." This is the insight that releases laughter, laughter at oneself: perspective of *The Birth of Tragedy* turned inside-out, Dionysian agony of infinite loss become perfect lightness, because the tragedy of individuation is really the triumph of the whole species, and one can attain the standpoint of the whole.

The concept of the potlatch or grand economy thus marks a limit point in the movement of Nietzsche's text; let us call it the limit of expansion. And there is a certain expansive mood that manifests the attunement of Nietzsche's writing to the grand economy, a mood in which there is no anxiety or reactiveness, in which Nietzsche does not want to react even against those who are reactive: "I do not even want to accuse those who accuse" (*GS* 276).

We will use this concept and this mood as the touchstones of our reading of Nietzsche. Nietzsche's text pulsates between this limit of expansiveness and another limit that is its antithesis—and yet the former regularly modulates into the latter, as though the two were entirely compatible. The very concept of squandering on the level of the whole leads directly to the privileging of what I will call a defensive/appropriative economy on the level of the individual. This move occurs regularly in Nietzsche's text:

> Hatred, the mischievous delight in the misfortunes of others, the lust to rob and dominate, and whatever else is called evil belongs to the most amazing economy of the preservation of the species. . . . This economy is not afraid of high prices, of squandering [*verschwenderische Ökonomie*]. (*GS* 1)

> If, however, a person should regard even the affects of hatred, envy, covetousness, and the lust to rule as conditions of life, as factors which, fundamentally and essentially, must be present in the general economy [*Gesamt-Haushalte*] of life (and must, therefore, be further enhanced if life is to be further enhanced). . . . (*BGE* 23)

> In the great economy of the whole [*grossen Ökonomie des Ganzen*], the terrible aspects of reality (in affects, in desires, in the will to power) are to an incalculable degree more necessary than that form of petty happiness which people call "goodness." (*EH* XIV,4; 329)[4]

There is not necessarily any paradox or contradiction here. Nietzsche reasons that the grand economy requires the reckless expenditure of resources that is caused by disruptive desires, and therefore it must have these covetous and domineering spirits who embody or manifest the potlatch nature of the whole economy—even though they themselves are by no means generous or spendthrift.

But by a curious sort of conceptual contamination or synecdochic slide Nietzsche also ambiguously attributes qualities of the potlatch economy to the self-augmenting economy. It is in large part because he makes this attribution that he can justify his glorification of the defensive/appropriative economy, the one he will most often call "noble." We can witness the slide in progress in this remark from *Beyond Good and Evil,* where the notion of "power that seeks to overflow" can tip as easily in the direction of generosity as in that of Viking "hardness."

> The noble type of man experiences *itself* as determining values; it does not need approval; it judges, "what is harmful to me is harmful in

[4]Notice that the list of affects Nietzsche gives in the first two citations lumps together indifferently the drives of the slave and the noble of the *Genealogy of Morals*.

> itself"; . . . it is *value-creating*. Everything it knows as part of itself it honors: such a morality is self-glorification. In the foreground there is the feeling of fullness, of power that seeks to overflow, the happiness of high tension, the consciousness of wealth that would give and bestow: the noble human being, too, helps the unfortunate, but not, or almost not, from pity, but prompted more by an urge [*drang*] begotten by excess of power. The noble human being honors himself as one who is powerful, also as one who has power over himself, who knows how to speak and be silent, who delights in being severe and hard with himself and respects all severity and hardness. "A hard heart Wotan put into my breast," says an old Scandinavian saga: a fitting poetic expression, seeing that it comes from the soul of a proud Viking. Such a type of man is actually proud of the fact that he is *not* made for pity, and the hero of the saga therefore adds as a warning: "If the heart is not hard in youth it will never harden." (260)

In this and similar passages, Nietzsche manages to weave plausibly together the notions of compulsive gift giving and hardness of heart; but often the characterization of nobility elides even this problematic hint of Zarathustran self-overflowing. For example, in the famous description of a "good and healthy aristocracy" in the following:

> The essential characteristic of a good and healthy aristocracy [note the moralization], however, is that it experiences itself *not* as a function (whether of the monarchy or the commonwealth) but as their *meaning* and highest justification—that it therefore accepts with a good conscience the sacrifice of untold human beings who, *for its sake,* must be reduced and lowered to incomplete human beings, to slaves, to instruments. (*BGE* 258)

On the one hand, nobility is self-squandering; on the other hand, it is self-augmentation. This ambiguity is rooted in the quantitative metaphorics of Nietzsche's physiopsychology, which, like Freud's, functions in terms of drive and discharge. In book 5 of *The Gay Science,* Nietzsche identifies his interpretation of motivation in terms of quantitative economy as one of his "most essential steps and advances":

> I have learned to distinguish the cause of acting from the cause of acting in a particular way, in a particular direction, with a particular goal. The

> first kind of cause is a quantum of dammed-up energy that is waiting to be used up somehow, for something, while the second kind is, compared to this energy, something . . . almost indifferent in relation to the tremendous quantum of energy that presses . . . to be used up somehow. (360)

Some souls have more of this energy at their disposal than others, and Nietzsche translates this differential into the terms of his typology of strength and weakness, richness and poverty, health and decadence. In the translation Nietzsche appears to exploit in a confused fashion the figurality of his initial model: the image of accumulation of drive energy slides easily into images of "richness" and "overfulness," as in Zarathustra's "bless the cup that wants to overflow" (*Z* Prologue;122); and the image of discharge slides into those of "squandering" and "gift-giving." But the dynamics of accumulation/discharge have no necessary relation to Zarathustran self-expenditure, as we see in the case of the noble barbarians of the *Genealogy of Morals*. They are characterized by the ability to discharge their drive energy, but there is nothing self-forgetful or "overflowing" about them; they use their energy to dominate the weak and avenge themselves against transgressions of their personal boundaries. Their economy, in other words, appears to be an extreme form of what Bataille calls a "restricted" rather than a "general" economy (see especially *BGE* 262).

Who then is truly powerful or noble according to Nietzsche, the one who accumulates only to squander or the one who accumulates in order to glorify himself as the purpose and justification of the entire process? And how is it that Nietzsche can move so naturally and easily from one of these conceptions to the other, keeping the contradiction between them in suspension, at times making the restricted economy of certain individuals the telos of the general economy of the whole? What are the patterns of blockage and discharge of Nietzsche's physiopsychological or, as I indifferently term it, libidinal energy as they manifest themselves through the deflections and distortions of his logic and dialectic?[5]

Nietzsche analyzes economies, and his own economy reacts to what he analyzes, affecting the shape of the analysis. Above all, it is in

[5]Though the term "libido" is Freud's, the concept that the term names is familiar to Nietzsche, who identifies the nature of the fundamental drive energy as sexual. See *GM* III,8, discussed below in Chapter 2; also *WP* 805–15, discussed in Chapter 5.

relation to the questions of strength and weakness, health and decadence, and abundance or paucity of physiopsychological energy that we can track the charge of affect with which Nietzsche invests his concepts. His most sustained discussion of these questions is of course in the *Genealogy of Morals,* to which we now turn.

It is very tempting to sum up the movement of history as it is represented in the *Genealogy of Morals* as a dialectical progression from noble barbarian, through the "pregnancy" of "bad conscience" (II,19;88), to the "autonomous" and "sovereign" individual at the end of this process (II,2;59). The autonomous individual is only made possible by humanity's passing through a phase of negation of healthy spontaneity, a phase in which instinct turns against itself and human interiority develops.[6] Humanity is thereby "poisoned" but becomes for the first time a truly interesting and significant phenomenon (I,7;33). And this negation is in turn negated in the lifting of humanity to the higher stage of what Nietzsche in *The Gay Science* calls the "intellectual conscience."

Nietzsche explicitly invites such a reading of the *Genealogy of Morals,* and if the outlines of this dialectical movement are repeatedly lost in the course of the three essays, we can always rectify the divergences and anomalies by assuming that they must ultimately be submitted to the authority of this presumedly dominant pattern. The authority of this pattern would then extend far beyond the boundaries of the *Genealogy,* since the interpretation of the history of morals set forth here appears to provide the key to understanding the most comprehensive structure of Nietzsche's "revaluation of values," a structure into which both Zarathustra's teachings and the diverse "aphoristic" reflections of Nietzsche's other books could be integrated. On this reading, Nietzsche's account of history in the *Genealogy* is compatible with contem-

[6]Cf. the comments on the ascetic "reflection of the will upon itself" by Arthur Danto, in his *Nietzsche as Philosopher* (New York: Macmillan, 1965), chap. 6, esp. 179–80. Though Nietzsche's text clearly seems to invite this dialectical reading, it is not commonly encountered in the commentaries. Philippa Foote's summary statement that "Nietzsche had no place in his ideology for the concept of guilt" sums up the more common view of Nietzsche's moral typology; "Nietzsche: The Revaluation of Values," in *Nietzsche: A Collection of Critical Essays,* ed. Robert Solomon (Garden City, N.H.: Anchor Books, 1973), 164. Gilles Deleuze's influential reading of Nietzsche has strongly reinforced this nondialectical interpretation of ascetic morality; see *Nietzsche and Philosophy,* trans. Hugh Tomlinson (New York: Columbia University Press, 1983).

porary psychological and political liberationism of various sorts; beyond the repressive structures of historical culture lies the promise of a fully "self-actualized" humanity.

On the level of generalization to which our account has so far been restricted, everything looks smooth. But we achieve this smoothness by abstracting from the textual specificity of Nietzsche's writing. Our dialectical reading of the *Genealogy* is in fact based on the same type of abstraction that makes possible Gilles Deleuze's *anti*-dialectical reading. For Deleuze, the distinctions between noble and slave, strength and weakness, and health and sickness resolve into the fundamental distinction between *active* and *reactive,* which are "original qualities of force," and *affirmative* and *negative,* which are "primordial qualities of the will to power."[7] Not only has Deleuze ignored the textual specificity of Nietzsche's writing, as though the truth of Nietzsche's text were a doctrine that happens only incidentally to be strewn about in various books, waiting to be liberated from its embodied state and reconstituted in its abstract coherence, but he has also treated Nietzsche's text as though it were not vulnerable to Nietzsche's own insight that "most of the conscious thinking of a philosopher is secretly guided into certain channels by his instincts."

If we turn our attention once again to the *Genealogy of Morals* and read with an eye to the texture of its textuality and the economy that manifests itself in this textuality, the coherence of its dialectic or antidialectic quickly becomes problematic. This apparent coherence depends on the simple division between a positive essence called "activeness" and a negative essence called "reactiveness" and on the possibility of a correlation between this division and the series of derivative polarities, weakness and strength, health and illness, etc. I waive for the moment the question of the general possibility of dividing the universe into two opposed principles (a metaphysical operation of a classical sort, and thus a very curious one for Nietzsche): even within the system of definitions offered in the *Genealogy* the correlation among pairs will not hold. As soon as the abstract notions of strength, health, etc., and their opposites are concretized in Nietzsche's quasihistorical narrative, the lines of correlation begin to cross in ways Nietzsche cannot control.

Thus in the first essay Nietzsche characterizes the strong, healthy,

[7]Deleuze, *Nietzsche and Philosophy,* 53–54.

noble type in terms of spontaneity in the expression of instincts, and the reactive, slave type in terms of pent-up instinct that results in ressentiment. Strength and health are fundamentally natural, physical attributes: the nobles possess "a powerful physicality [*mächtige Leiblichkeit*], (*GM* I,7;33) and, whenever possible, "go *back* to the innocent conscience of the beast of prey" (I,11;40). The priestly or slave type, in contrast, which is farther removed from natural instinctual vitality, develops the intellectual powers, and thus "a race of such men of *ressentiment* is bound to become eventually *cleverer* than any noble race" (I,10;38). But in the second essay it is the noble type that is given credit for the development of the impersonal, objective eye that creates legal *restraints*. Whereas in the first essay we are told that the nobles can indulge their sudden impulses of rage and vengefulness in an "immediate reaction" and therefore are not poisoned by repressed instinct (I,10;39), in the second essay vengefulness *as such* (not merely repressed vengefulness) is numbered among the reactive feelings ("not only revenge but all *reactive* affects in general" [II,11;74]). Furthermore, we are told that it is in the nature of the strong, active ones to curb revenge, to prevent the instantaneous reactions of the injured by creating "legal conditions" which, note the wording here, "constitute a partial restriction of the will of life, which is bent on power" (II,11;76).[8]

A similar crossing occurs with respect to the question of cruelty. To which series does cruelty belong? To the series natural, strong, healthy, active, or the series unnatural, weak, ill, resentful? Nietzsche strongly implies that it belongs to the former. In sections 6 and 7 of the second essay he gives us his remarkable celebration of the joys of cruelty,

[8]A possible paraphrase that preserves the consistency of Nietzsche's argument here with that of the first essay is as follows: the active, aggressive men are purged of their own vengefulness by indulging it and are thus capable of imposing legal restraints on the *ressentiment*-filled vengefulness of weaklings and decadents. But this interpretation simply slurs the details of Nietzsche's remarks in *GM* II,11. We must be careful of imposing on Nietzsche's remarks here the doctrines of the first essay concerning cathartic vengeance and the origin of ressentiment in physical incapacity to take revenge. The implication throughout this section is not that the vengeful men of ressentiment are impotent to achieve real vengeance but that they *will carry it to extremes*. This entire section makes no sense unless we understand "the senseless raging of *ressentiment*" here as resulting not in imaginary vengeance but in the "violence and capricious acts" which the law condemns. If ressentiment were here based on impotence, it would not be necessary for the ruling power to take "the object of *ressentiment* out of the hands of revenge." Nor is there any hint of the doctrine of cathartic revenge: the "active, aggressive, arrogant" type is treated throughout as antithetical to the reactive type who is overcome by vengeful rage. The violence of the active man is here gratuitous rather than retaliatory—the spontaneous overflow of a boisterous vitality.

which belong to the "most *evil* epochs of the human race" (*GM* II,7;67) (in Nietzsche's laudatory sense of "evil"), when humanity has not yet left behind "the joy and innocence of the animal." He also calls the power to exercise cruelty "a *right of the masters*" (II,5;65). Yet he associates cruelty with revenge, a form of "counterbalancing pleasure" or "compensation" for an injury suffered (II,6;65); and we have seen that Nietzsche in this same essay calls revenge "reactive."

Nietzsche's positive valuation of the concept of a healthy instinctual nobility is so strong that as his narrative unfolds this pole attracts all positive value and repels all negativity. Thus when cruelty is ascribed to the noble ones it is validated as healthy release of impulse; when it is ascribed to the underclasses it is stigmatized as reactivity.

This could just mean that there are two kinds of cruelty; the noble type that is an immediate release and the slave type that is an outlet for pent-up impulses. But we have already seen that in the second essay it is the immediate release of vengeful urges that is stigmatized as reactive.[9] And, even more strikingly, already in the first essay when Nietzsche says that the barbarian nobility revert to the innocence of animals this reversion is a release from a condition in which the nobility have been compelled to repress their instincts: "They compensate themselves in the wilderness for the tension engendered by protracted confinement and enclosure within the peace of society" (*GM* I,11;40).

There remains the difference between those who wield physical power and those who do not, the difference between a society of equals who hold each other in check and the underclass they hold down. But this obvious difference fails to yield the clean typological split between an economy of spontaneous release and one of ressentiment. Both types suffer repression of impulse; both are implicated in the reactive exercise of compensatory cruelty.

At least two stories unfold here. According to one narrative line, the dialectical story sketched earlier, the development of the inward-

[9]Cf. the lengthy analysis of revenge in *The Wanderer and His Shadow* in which, not yet under the spell of his dogmatic typology, Nietzsche speaks of revenge in the service of honor, the nobler type of revenge, as one for which "*Time* is needed—when instead of concentrating on oneself one begins to think about one's opponent, asking oneself how one can hurt him the most" (33); also in *Beyond Good and Evil* where he ascribes to the "ruling group" the "capacity for . . . long revenge" (260).

turned economy is the negation necessary to the development of a higher stage of consciousness or conscience. But according to another narrative line, the one that in fact gives rise to the standard interpretation of this text, there is a nondialectical, natural development of conscience belonging to the noble economy, and this natural development is unnaturally derailed by a perverse form of the inward turn. Noble individuals learn to bind themselves to a "*memory of the will*" through a natural, healthy, "active *desire*" that naturally abrogates its natural, healthy tendency to forgetfulness (*GM* II,1;58), thus bringing forth the "*sovereign individual*" who stands at the end of the "tremendous process" of history (II,2;59). This appears to be the same type of individual who brings forth the restraints of law that bind reactive vengefulness. By creating the state with its laws and binding the instincts of those beneath them, the nobility also creates an "*active* 'bad conscience'" in them, which makes the underclass as well candidates for autonomous selfhood (II,18;87). But this natural process has been perverted, turned from its normal course, by the "moralization" of the concepts of guilt and duty. This moralization, which we see in the third essay is the work of the ascetic priest, "involves an attempt to *reverse* the direction of the development described above, or at least to bring it to a halt" (II,21;91).

In both narratives there must be an account of how humanity goes from quasi-anarchic barbarism to the stage of the ethical autonomous individual. Yet the formation of conscience requires a damming-up of instinct which Nietzsche always interprets as a turning of cruelty against the self. Insofar as this process has the sense of a creative shaping of life, of a lifting of life to a higher stage of development, Nietzsche can give it his approval. Insofar as it corresponds to what he stigmatizes as sickness and weakness, the slave economy, Nietzsche tends to condemn it as mere perversion of nature. One Nietzsche therefore keeps trying to separate the healthy from the sick aspects of the turning inward of instinct, and this Nietzsche tells the story of the natural development of conscience out of the active drives of strong, healthy individuals. Notice in particular the delicacy with which, in the second essay, Nietzsche manages both to assert (in section 3) that only cruelty, the infliction of extreme pain, either by others on us or by us on ourselves, can create a conscience; and also to describe (in section 2) a strong, dominant individual who has formed a conscience apparently without recourse to self-cruelty.[10] But another Nietzsche recognizes, is fascinated by, the paradox of a *sickness that is creative;* understands that the intensification of cruelty against the self which the ascetic priest orchestrates is the necessary condition for the emergence of a Zarathustran type. Within the frame of the narrative that describes the *natural* development of *good* "bad conscience" under the aegis of the noble masters, Nietzsche allows himself to describe the individual of inward-turned instinct as one who has turned the self into a "torture chamber" and then to praise this "animal soul turned against itself" as a divine spectacle, "as if with him something were announcing and preparing itself, as if man were not a goal but only a way, an episode, a bridge, a great promise" (*GM* II,16;85). This torture chamber is both natural and unnatural, depending on which narrative chain we assign it to. It is the "active" bad conscience created by the law-giving masters, therefore natural and right. But it is identical with the ascetic economy Nietzsche describes as a perversion and reversal of nature.

The logic or illogic of Nietzsche's text is embedded within the more complex system of its economy. The text speaks of activity and reactiveness, but the text that so speaks is itself moved by currents of activity and reactiveness. Nietzsche's text reacts against the slave and the ascetic (who are not identical, but whom Nietzsche at times runs together and never definitively distinguishes), condemns them, tries to throw them outside of the boundary that it draws around nature and health. And it swells with praise when the aggressive, noble barbarians pull into sight; all positive value tends to migrate toward them and cluster around them. The logic of the argument becomes ambiguous

[10]Self-cruelty of course characterizes asceticism, and Nietzsche always has to struggle to keep completely distinct the noble and the ascetic economies. The way in which the two tend to collapse together is visible in *BGE* 200, where Nietzsche describes the noble type of Alcibiades and Caesar in opposition to the weaker type of Augustine. (Although Nietzsche does not label the latter type "ascetic," Augustine is the arch-ascetic of Christianity.) Yet he ascribes to the noble type "a real mastery and subtlety in waging war against oneself, in other words, self-control, self-outwitting." In *BGE* 260 we are told that "the noble human being . . . delights in being severe and hard with himself"; and in *Anti* 57 that "the most spiritual men, as the *strongest,* find their happiness where others would find their destruction: in the labyrinth, in hardness against themselves and others, in experiments; their joy is self-conquest; asceticism becomes in them nature, need, and instinct." This war of the self against itself is not mentioned in connection with the noble type in the *Genealogy of Morals,* where Nietzsche tries to keep the opposed types as pure and distinct as possible.

and contradictory as a consequence of the pull exerted by these positive and negative valuations.

Why is Nietzsche so heavily invested in these valuations? If we are not yet ready to answer this question, we can at least identify the structure that conditions the operation of these investments: Nietzsche is implicated within the field he analyzes, the history he narrates is a history to which he belongs, and the economic typology he invents is one that must characterize *him,* he must belong to one or more of the types that play the roles in the history he tells.[11] Is he a master, a slave, or a priest, or perhaps all of these at once, or alternately one and then another?

As it functions within the economy of Nietzsche's writing, the concept of will to power opens out in two directions or communicates with two fields of force. In one direction it opens onto the most supple aspects of Nietzsche's thought, as the key to the question of economy and to the overturning of the moral perspective. In the other direction, it acts as a magnet for Nietzsche's most defensive or reactive impulses and brings out a partiality in his perspective that is fundamentally at odds with the "moraline-free" perspective to which he aspires.

The distinctions between weak and strong, active and reactive, displace the distinction between good and evil, and insofar as they are formulated in terms of quantities and relations of power, the new distinctions seem indeed to be moraline-free. But as they actually function in Nietzsche's text they tend to acquire a moral charge. Nietzsche approves strength and condemns weakness in a way that is structurally identical to moral approval and condemnation, so that the "transvaluation" of the old categories starts to look like their *Aufhebung*. Though good and evil have now been crossed out, the essential charge of moraline has been in a sense transferred intact into the new categories of strength and weakness.

Nietzsche's description of his own economy or instinct manifests

[11]René Girard is the only critic I have found who recognizes the depth and significance of the problem of Nietzsche's implication within the field he analyzes. See Girard's "Superman in the Underground: Strategies of Madness—Nietzsche, Wagner, and Dostoevsky," *Modern Language Notes* 91 (1976): 1161–85.

the character of his attempt at moraline-free evaluation. His stance toward himself is the antithesis of, say, St. Augustine's; instead of judging, condemning, and paring away at his impulses, Nietzsche says he has simply tried to arrange them so that they might all coexist. "Contrary capacities" dwell in him, he says, and he has tried "to mix nothing, to 'reconcile' nothing" (*EH* II,9;254). Such an economy as this is required "for the task of a revaluation of all values." Nietzsche thus stands before himself as he stands before the problem of existence in general, a stance that he describes as "neutrality" or "freedom from all partiality in relation to the total problem of life." He is able to achieve this neutrality or freedom because he embodies both poles of the antinomy of life, being at the same time a decadent and a beginning (*EH* I,1;222). Yet decadence, which together with inaugural strength makes this neutrality possible, is precisely that which it is Nietzsche's project to overcome: Nietzsche's great contribution to the history of knowledge (along with his discovery of the Dionysian) is "seeing morality itself as a symptom of decadence" (*EH* IV,2;272).

Nietzsche, who is neutral because he is *also* decadent (as well as nondecadent) is rarely (almost never!) neutral toward decadence. On the one hand, he tells us that "nothing in existence may be subtracted, nothing is dispensable," which implies that decadence is not dispensable either. On the other hand, he immediately goes on to say that "those aspects of existence which Christians and other nihilists repudiate are actually on an infinitely higher level in the order of rank among values than that which the instinct of decadence could approve and call good" (*EH* IV,2;272), which seems to treat decadence as an unfortunate and undesirable element in existence, a sort of detritus or excrement of the economy of life. Decadence is necessary, it is part of the overall economy (*WP* 40); but decadence is dangerous, it must be fought against because it threatens "the contagion of the healthy parts of the organism" (*WP* 41). Decadence is included within the whole, along with health, only on condition that it be confined behind a boundary that separates it from health; contagion is the leakage of decadence across this boundary. But is not this leakage also a part of the overall economy? Can decadence be segregated away from health? Doesn't the tendency to spread and contaminate belong to the essence of decadence and sickness? If it does, the strategy of excluding inclusion or including exclusion would simply be Nietzsche's refusal or inability really to affirm the great economy of the whole.[12] At one point, Zarathustra admits this inability: "He who would grasp everything human would have to grapple with everything. But for that my hands are too clean" (*Z* III,9;296).

The question I am moving in on is closely related to questions that lie at the center of Alexander Nehamas's admirable book on Nietzsche.[13] No one has tracked with more sustained attention than Nehamas the dialectical intricacies of Nietzsche's texts, and especially the contradictions that seem to call the coherence of all of Nietzsche's thought into question. Nietzsche must somehow extricate himself from the contagion of this decay whose other name is asceticism. Yet the drive to overcome this decay is itself an expression of decadence. It is by the drive for truth that the decadent lies of Platonism and Christianity must be overcome; but the drive for truth is the essence of the decadence of Platonism and Christianity. "We seekers after knowledge today, we godless ones and anti-metaphysicians, we, too, derive *our* flame from the fire ignited by a faith millennia old, the Christian faith, which was Plato's, that God is truth, that truth is divine" (*GS* 344). "If this is so," Nehamas comments, "then in fighting the ascetic ideal Nietzsche (and everyone who follows him) is actually perpetuating it" (130).

This is indeed the conceptual knot that Nietzsche ties, almost so

[12]The issue here is a subtle one. For one thing, it is easy to read remarks such as "every major growth is accompanied by a tremendous crumbling and passing away" (*WP* 112) as expressing acceptance of the totality of the great economy (cf. *WP* 1012). Yet, no matter how minutely he intricates weakness and strength or growth and crumbling he almost always keeps the barrier that distinguishes them from each other in their essence. Growth is essentially growth and nothing but growth, even if decay always accompanies it like its shadow. However applicable this distinction may be in a strictly biological realm, it should be clear how questionable it becomes as soon as Nietzsche tries to apply it to types of *souls* and of *societies*.

A second subtlety, which looks superficially like the first, arises in relation to the type of remark exemplified in *WP* 351, where Nietzsche tells us that "life . . . does not know how to separate Yes from No." Here Nietzsche is addressing the Christian moralist's attempt to separate the yes of goodness from the no of sin; thus yes and no mean precisely the inverse of what they mean in Nietzsche's own system of valuations. And, whereas Nietzsche always insists on a reintegration of the Christian's no into the great yes, this reintegration is almost always the preliminary to Nietzsche's then performing what I call his including exclusion on that which the Christian (according to Nietzsche) had affirmed, because "it is one of life's processes to exclude the forms of decline and decay" (*WP* 339).

[13]Alexander Nehamas, *Nietzsche: Life as Literature* (Cambridge: Harvard University Press, 1985).

tightly that even a god could not untie it. But Nehamas, having pushed this far, having come to the point at which we first begin really to think Nietzsche's text, veers aside and dissolves the paradox. Science is a continuation of the ascetic ideal, so to criticize the ascetic ideal must also be to depreciate science. "But it is not easy," says Nehamas "to see how science can be depreciated without doing more science and therefore without perpetuating it" (133). Nietzsche knows this, and in order to escape the contradiction, Nehamas says, he becomes a "comedian of the ideal," one who does not try "to determine in general terms the value of life and the world." Nietzsche's "solution" is to "fashion a literary character out of himself" such that he gives "value" to his own life in terms of something like the value of literary form (136–37). Nehamas describes the project of self-fashioning in strongly organicist terms. It involves the organization of everything one has done "into a coherent whole" which is "constantly changing, never finally completed" (190). The problem of eternal recurrence is an aspect of this project of self-fashioning, for in order to accept and integrate into a whole every element of the present one must accept "all that has led to it. It is in this sense that one can now say of what has already happened, 'Thus I willed it'" (160). "The eternal recurrence signifies my ability to want my life and the whole world to be repeated just as they are" (191). And none of this has anything to do with truth; it is only Nietzsche's own individual life that he shapes, as an exemplification of the "ideal character" projected by his theories (232). In this way, according to Nehamas, Nietzsche manages to criticize the ideal of truth without engaging in a project of truth that would perpetuate this ideal.

Unlike Deleuze, Nehamas recognizes that we cannot read Nietzsche simply in order to extract a philosophical doctrine. But there is no question of Nietzsche's simply sidestepping the ascetic ideal, as Nehamas claims, by becoming its comedian (although he does that too, it is certainly one of the movements of his text, if not the "solution" of the whole problem) because Nietzsche is himself the embodiment of that ideal. Nietzsche presents the ascetic ideal as a problem, but before he presents it, as he presents it, and as he pretends to move beyond it, he is always driven by it. Nowhere is this knot tied tighter than in the *Genealogy of Morals,* and especially in those sections (III,24–27) from which Nehamas draws the concept of the "comedian of the ideal." A whole book could be written on the textual subtleties of these sections, on the enormous instability of each moment of Nietzsche's argument as he ranges over a series of ambiguous judgments, concealing multiple dialectical inversions in the swiftness of what may look like a straightforward critique of science as an expression of the ascetic ideal. Here I only pause to consider the points that relate directly to Nehamas's interpretation.

What does Nietzsche mean in section 27 when he says that the comedians of the ascetic ideal are "the only ones capable of harming it" (*GM* III,27;160)? In fact, Nietzsche in the preceding section uses the term "comedians" to characterize the most detestable of creatures, who, because they are involved in the "forgery of ideals," create such a "repulsive, ill-smelling, mendacious, pseudo-alcoholic air everywhere." "I should like to know," he concludes, "how many *comedians* of the Christian-moral ideal would have to be exported from Europe today before its air would begin to smell fresh again" (III,26;159). So when Nietzsche speaks of the "harm" these comedians do to the ascetic ideal, he does not mean to praise them; the harm they do leads not to an overcoming of ascetic corruption but to a corruption of its corruption. By one of those movements of progressive subdivision so characteristic of Nietzsche the essence of corruption is here driven into a corner, quarantined as strictly incidental or irrelevant so that the stage can be cleared for the confrontation of heroic magnitudes. Now that the essence of corruption has been displaced from the ascetics onto the comedians of the ideal, Christian-moral asceticism can be treated as a *clean* form of corruption, as cleanliness: "All honor to the ascetic ideal *insofar as it is honest!* So long as it believes in itself and does not play tricks on us!" (III,26;158) And in section 27 he quotes *The Gay Science* 357, in which he speaks of "the transformation of 'the Christian conscience'" into "intellectual cleanliness at any price."

Nehamas, however, plausibly ties the notion of the comedian to a remark in section 25 in which Nietzsche describes art as "much more fundamentally opposed to the ascetic ideal than is science" (*GM* III,25;153–54), and Nehamas derives from this linkage his idea of Nietzsche's project as artistic-literary "comedy" (153–54). But Nietzsche is always deeply ambivalent about the illusionism of art—and that is that case here, where he concludes the paragraph by commenting that "nothing is more easily corrupted than an artist" and that the most common form of this corruption is the placement of art in the service of the ideal. The smell of Wagner is of course very strong here, and as usual in relation to the image of corruption, which belongs to the associative complex of decadence and has tremendous resonance in Nietzsche's text. There is thus good reason for doubting that the concept of the comedian of the ideal can be taken as Nietzsche's self-characterization and as the way out of the Klein bottle of idealism.

Even though Nehamas frames his reading of Nietzsche in terms of the question of style, he treats style as a conceptual category that yields, if not a philosophical doctrine, still a product, the product "Nietzsche as a literary character." Nehamas is no more attentive than Deleuze to the texture of Nietzsche's text, its "written" character across any given expanse of text, as a *sequence* of statements, each of which is generated by (conceptual and affective) forces that accumulate in the statements that precede. These forces exert contradictory pulls on Nietzsche's language, and to read one of Nietzsche's sentences in situ means patiently to disentangle the lines of force that converge on it, thus to undo the formal aspect of unitary sense that the apparent unity of the sentence might give. A more attentive tracing of the movements of Nietzsche's text reveals a Nietzsche who is far more intricately and inextricably implicated within the contradictions he describes than Nehamas will grant, and does so precisely in the movement by which Nietzsche appears to try to set himself apart.

It is not, in the *Genealogy of Morals,* as a comedian of the ideal that Nietzsche claims to oppose the will to truth but as a member of the set he calls "we 'men of knowledge'" (*GM* III,24;148), a set he opposes to the ascetic unbelievers who falsely believe themselves to be "counteridealists."

At this point Nietzsche suggests that the "men of knowledge" somehow do manage to transcend the idealism within which the ascetic unbelievers are still trapped. But it is always a question when we read Nietzsche of who is speaking at any given moment, and never is this more the case than when Nietzsche says not "I" but "we," as in "we 'men of knowledge.'" Let us therefore trace carefully the composition and permutations of Nietzsche's "we" as his discussion unfolds here.

Nietzsche begins section 24 by asking whether the opposition to the ascetic ideal is to be discovered among the "unbelievers." He introduces them in the third person; in the next paragraph he begins to criticize these "unbelievers" as having a *belief* (*Glaube*) in their opposition to the ideal. The stance from which Nietzsche delivers this criticism is that of the "we" he calls "men of knowledge." "We 'men of knowledge' . . . mistrust believers of all kinds"; thus the intensity of faith (*Glaube*) that the unbelievers have in their mission is seen as grounds for the mistrust of them by the "we."

Who exactly is this "we" of which Nietzsche speaks here? The division between his "we" and the "they" he is condemning is a subtle and disturbing one for anyone who hears the resonances of the language Nietzsche uses here in the echo chamber of his work as a whole, for Nietzsche mixes some of his most positively valorized language into his characterization of this "they." In the third paragraph, for instance, he speaks of "their insistence on intellectual cleanliness." calls them "*Antichristen,*" and says that they are the sole incarnation at present of the "intellectual conscience." The problematic implications of Nietzsche's language here and in the succeeding paragraphs are so striking that Walter Kaufmann devotes several long footnotes to the question of exactly whom Nietzsche could be referring to: as Kaufmann says, "the men he speaks of are plainly very close to him" (149, n. 3).

Of course it is possible to smooth out the disturbance, for Nietzsche also mixes elements into the characterization that seem to differentiate "them" from Nietzsche. "They" are "pale," "nihilists," "hectics"—most decisively, according to Kaufmann, "they still have faith in truth" (149, n. 5). Kaufmann's conclusion, which harmonizes with Nehamas's interpretation, seems undeniable. But does it really settle the question about who is "we" and who is "they"?

If we follow the further course of the argument, the general category "scientific opposition to the ascetic ideal" ramifies into various heterogeneous manifestations of which we must keep track if we are not to lose the movement of Nietzsche's prose. It is not according to any strictly logical or dialectical principal that Nietzsche proceeds, but by a logical/dialectical/associative dynamism according to which at times bits break off from a consistent argument and momentarily acquire a life of their own as they magnetize some impulse in Nietzsche's economy. Thus at the end of section 25 Nietzsche slips into a critique of the results of the post-Copernican "self-belittlement" of humanity, including Kant's "victory" over dogmatic theology.[14] Nietzsche ar-

[14]The "self-belittlement" Nietzsche here criticizes appears to be precisely the same phenomenon that he had eulogized as his own task in *Beyond Good and Evil:* "To translate man back into nature; to become master over the many vain and overly enthusiastic interpreta-

gues that the results of this scientific/critical movement have been to strengthen transcendental other-worldliness, which sounds like what he has been arguing all along but is in fact quite different. Up to this point his claim has been that the severe, truth-seeking impulse of science is a form of ascetic idealism, but at this point he slips into the claim that new forms of obscurantism and transcendentalism use science dishonestly as a pretext for their obscurantism. Although Nietzsche calls this also a "*triumph* for the ascetic ideal," his argument at this point strays from his central insistence on rigorous respect for truth as the point of contact between science and asceticism (*GM* III,25;156). Similarly, in section 26 Nietzsche begins with remarks on the "sad, stern, but resolute" attitude of the nihilistic historiographers and then slides into the attack we noted earlier on the "*comedians* of the Christian-moral ideal."

Now, when Nietzsche slides into his attacks on hypocrisy and transcendentalism, the category "scientific critic of the ascetic ideal," which starts out as the disvalued "they" of section 24, becomes, in relation to these dishonest idealists, the relatively higher-valued category (as we saw in his exclamation "All honor to the ascetic ideal *insofar as it is honest*"). But the initial, primary opposition between (they) the unbelievers and (we) the men of knowledge is actually less stable than this secondary opposition, because "they" are described in terms that in other contexts usually apply to Nietzsche's "we." The men of knowledge, on the other hand, are characterized only in terms of their mistrust of all *Glaube*. The men of knowledge are set up here as the group that stands outside of the otherwise all-encompassing sway of the ascetic will to truth. But if we judge Nietzsche's characterization of this group by the standards Nietzsche commonly applies elsewhere, we must be struck by "a certain *impoverishment of life*" (*GM* III,25;154) in that characterization. The only advantage the men of knowledge have is a kind of *negation*, the ability to deny and mistrust—and what they mistrust is nothing less than strength. The strength of faith, to be sure, and faith belongs to one of Nietzsche's most consistently devalued

---

tions and connotations that have so far been scrawled and painted over that eternal basic text of *homo natura* . . . ; to see to it that man henceforth stands . . . deaf to the siren songs of old metaphysical bird catchers who have been piping at him all too long, 'you are more, you are higher, you are of a different origin'" (230). Thus once again Nietzsche is tacitly implicated in what he criticizes in the *Genealogy of Morals*.

categories. But let us not assume this devaluation as a fact of Nietzschean dogma; let us trace, instead, the relational movements of value. Haven't we just noticed that the faith of the unbelievers receives due praise in another context? Furthermore, the affective/intellectual charge that words like "denial" and "strength" bear in Nietzsche's text is so strong that we must be alert to the ways in which this charge tends to override or at least qualify local conceptual meaning.

So let us try to locate Nietzsche's valuation here more precisely. What is the basis of the mistrust of the men of knowledge; what is it that they suspect concerning the faith of the unbelievers? It is "a certain probability—of *deception*" (*GM* III,24;148) (that is, a probability that the unbelievers are deceiving themselves). But then what constitutes the category of the men of knowledge is once again not something that stands outside the will to truth but another manifestation of that same will. The only difference between the ascetics of truth and the men of knowledge is that the ascetics are deceived because they do not know that they still have faith in truth and therefore have not confronted this final involution of the truth project, whereas the men of knowledge (is this a category of one?) do push on to this final confrontation. But pushing on in this way would be a further manifestation of the ascetic will to truth.

In fact, when in section 27 we emerge from the ramifications of the argument and return to "the problem of the *meaning* of the ascetic ideal," Nietzsche folds back the "they" of the unbelievers into his "we": "Unconditional honest atheism (and *its* is the only air *we* breathe, *we* more spiritual men of the age! [emphasis of *we* added]) is therefore *not* the antithesis of that ideal, it is only one of the latest phases of its evolution, one of its terminal forms and inner consequences." Nietzsche is perfectly clear here that *his* project belongs to the "inner consequences" of the will to truth, that the final question that sweeps away the last "deception," the calling in question of the faith in truth itself, is itself an unfolding of the (Christian) will to truth. "After Christian truthfulness has drawn one inference after another, it must end by drawing its *most striking inference,* its inference *against* itself; this will happen, however, when it poses the question '*what is the meaning of all will to truth?*'" And if this is not clear enough, Nietzsche proceeds to restate his point, with his "we" now occupying the slot occupied in the preceding quotation by "Christian truthfulness": "And here I again touch on my problem, on our problem, my *unknown* friends (for as yet I *know* of no friend [so Nietzsche's "we" is indeed a category of one]): what meaning would *our* whole being possess if it were not this, that in us the will to truth becomes conscious of itself as a *problem?*" (*GM* III,27;160–61).

Thus there is for Nietzsche no sidestepping of the contradiction Nehamas describes. The will to truth is called into question by the will to truth itself—and Nietzsche himself is only a vessel in which the will to truth functions as agent ("in us the will to truth becomes conscious of itself"). The will to truth, if it is to be overcome, must overcome itself. "All great things bring about their destruction through an act of self-overcoming," Nietzsche writes in this same section. So the problem of the ascetic will to truth cannot be displaced onto another site; only a further turn of the screw or tightening of the knot of the ascetic ideal will resolve it.

This is all stated as clearly and explicitly as possible in section 27. Nevertheless, in section 28, the concluding section of the concluding essay of the *Genealogy of Morals,* Nietzsche once more characterizes the ascetic ideal in merely oppositional terms, as the will to nothingness which is the simple opposite of a healthy, affirmative will. This is the sense of the ascetic ideal with which most readers of the *Genealogy of Morals* come away from the book: the ascetic ideal as product of the decadent priest. This product has its uses, no doubt, because it saves decadent life from suicidal despair, but it is, in any case, something other, something to which something else can be opposed, for example, life, strength, affirmation, or art.

We thus see here that characteristic movement in Nietzsche's discourse toward and then back away from a recognition of the impossibility of extricating the two sides of life from each other. On the one hand, there is an overall economy that includes both health and decay; on the other hand, Nietzsche cannot deny himself the satisfaction of sounding the note of strong ascendancy over the forces of decay. And the question of the relation between these forces is also the question of Nietzsche's identity.

We have seen the oddly unstable movement of the line that distinguishes "we" from "they" at the end of the *Genealogy of Morals*. How exactly are we to evaluate this instability? Is it really necessary to introduce this complicated machinery of textual economics to account for it? Isn't it quite possible that despite the problematic of caves behind caves of which he speaks in *Beyond Good and Evil* (289), Nietzsche is simply conscious here of what he is doing, that he is playing a very subtle game, calculating very subtle moves around a problem of which he is only too aware? As he demonstrates in this remark from *The Will to Power:*

> If this moral judging and dissatisfaction with actuality were . . . an ineradicable instinct, might this instinct not be one of the ineradicable stupidities and immodesties of our species?
>
> *But in saying this we do that which we censure;* the standpoint of desirability, *of unauthorized playing-the-judge,* is part of the character of the course of things, as is every injustice and imperfection. (Emphasis added; 331)

It could be argued, on the basis of remarks such as this, that far from evading the total character of the economy of the whole, Nietzsche accepts its fatality, knows that he is destined to obey its law of partiality, according to which he must do that which he censures in order to become who he is. It is stupid to desire that things should be different from what they are, Nietzsche says, "but life itself is such a desire!" (*WP* 333). Paradox of part and whole, paradox of *amor fati:* to desire that nothing should be other than it is is also to accept that "life itself," therefore Nietzsche's life, too, is the desire that things should be other than they are. But then are we back where we started? Is there no difference between Nietzsche's style of "unauthorized playing-the-judge" and the moral point of view which he overthrows? Perhaps all the difference in the world: the difference between strength and weakness, the strength of a partial judgment that follows the expansiveness of a yes to the totality of being, as opposed to the constricted partiality of a judgment that stops short of this yes.

But now notice that this reading of Nietzsche's position with respect to the total problem of being reinscribes the problematic terms of decadence and health as the explanation or resolution of the problem. Either there is no difference between Nietzsche's partiality and anybody else's—the recognition that partiality is part of life being only the recognition of a situation to which everyone is equally subject—or there is a special character to Nietzsche's recognition, a character that differentiates his inability to transcend the general conditions of life from that of those he condemns, a character that makes his a transcending nontranscendence. And this character can only be the difference between the will that says yes and the will that says no, which is to say the difference between master and slave, Zarathustra and the ascetic priest, strength and weakness, health and decadence. But it was precisely the valorization of health over decadence that needed to be justified in the first place.

This is not just a logical conundrum. The question concerns Nietzsche's location within the conundrum, his implication in the terms he is manipulating logically or quasi-logically. Nietzsche's above-cited remarks from *The Will to Power* concern the character of his own utterance ("in saying this we do that which we censure"), and in attributing a certain character to "the course of things," he justifies the character of his utterance and thus justifies himself insofar as he is the subject of the utterance. It is once again the question of Nietzsche's "we," of who is speaking in Nietzsche's text and where this subject of utterance is located with respect to the matters of which the utterance speaks. Nietzsche's subject is weakness and strength, and Nietzsche is not neutral with respect to this subject.

But in order to trace the complexities of Nietzsche's implication in his discourse we must return now to the task of mapping the economy of his text. And in order to do this we must now listen to Nietzsche's voice, listen for the way its various tonalities resound in the neighborhood of specific themes, with a special alertness to the note of self-assurance—which is to say, the note that announces Nietzsche's confidence in his own strength.

The authority of any writer depends in a profound way on the quality of self-assurance in his or her prose. But if this is true in general, it is true to an unparalleled degree with Nietzsche. For, on the one hand, the claims to importance his utterance makes for itself are as vast as they could possibly be: Nietzsche speaks to us about the riddle of existence and the fate of mankind, perhaps of being itself. And, on the other hand, there is absolutely no foundation whatsoever for these claims, in the sense of any established or agreed-upon authority to which Nietzsche could appeal. On the contrary, Nietzsche claims to overthrow all of the authority (religious, social, logico-philosophical) that has ever existed. So whatever authority Nietzsche's voice might exercise has to come from this voice itself, its power to convince us to listen to his "unauthorized playing-the-judge" with the kind of attention and respect to which it lays claim.

Of course there are concepts, ideas, arguments, "profound critiques," and so on to be found in Nietzsche's texts, and these have such authority as philosophical arguments have; Deleuze and Nehamas, among others, have shown that Nietzsche's strength along these lines is far greater than has often been supposed. Yet the force of Nietzsche's whole enterprise is to unsettle the canons which would in this way validate that enterprise. It is perhaps the most powerful feature of Nehamas's study that it is framed in terms of the problem of this paradoxical epistemological structure. But behind the epistemological paradox (the truth that truth is deception) lies what I am calling an "economic" problem. The epistemological problem of the conflict between the will to truth and its opposite (it if has an opposite) is a function within Nietzsche's text as a whole of the conflict between decadence and health or weakness and strength. These latter pairs are the macro-oppositions whose charge constantly intervenes in and deforms or deflects the movement of Nietzsche's thought, and whose force must always be calculated in relation to the micro-oppositions that preoccupy the thematics of Nietzsche's text at any given moment. And it is particularly with respect to the question of authority that the charge invested in these macro-oppositions assumes importance, because the stresses on the tone of self-assurance from which Nietzsche's voice draws its authority are most clearly audible when weakness and strength are his explicit or implicit topic.

On the one hand, Nietzsche speaks about weakness and strength; they are his topic, the phenomena out there in the world in which he is most interested. On the other hand, Nietzsche's discourse on power is itself an exercise of power. Because Nietzsche appeals to no instituted authority or canons of demonstration, the constative value of his discourse depends entirely on the persuasiveness of its claim of autarky, or, more precisely, on its enactment of the motions of that very power concerning which it speaks. Where there is no appeal to some additional authority, only the discourse *of* power can be a discourse *on* power.

Yet the power of a discourse is ultimately dependent on an audience; the only power in Nietzsche's writing is whatever power is felt as power by some actual audience at some moment in history. Unlike his barbarians who can demonstrate their strength on their enemies in an irresistible fashion (it being the essence of physical force that it necessarily overcomes weaker force), Nietzsche, as a writer, no matter how powerful, necessarily depends for his effect on the at least provisional receptiveness of his audience. And since his power or authority depends in large part on the self-assurance of his power communicated in the tone and mode of his utterance, the audience that will not listen not only refuses the utterance itself but also saps its energy at the source, weakens it, not only depriving it of its effect but altering its constitution, its tone and mode.

Now, Nietzsche is supremely confident of his power; he knows that he will be read, that he will have an effect—and not just any effect, but the greatest possible. This confidence enables him to take the breathtaking risks he takes in his writing, enables him to address us as from a great height, and is thus precisely what makes a claim on our attention. His power comes from his assurance of his power. At the same time, Nietzsche is afraid no one will listen to him; he fears the lonely echo of his own voice resounding in his ears and doubts whether anyone else will hear it, or whether, hearing it, they will hear it as he intends it to be heard. "Those who live alone do not speak too loud nor write too loud, for they fear the hollow echo—the critique of the nymph echo. And all voices sound different in solitude" (*GS* 182). Yet the effort to reach an unreceptive audience causes the voice to rise: "We say the strongest things simply, provided only that we are surrounded by people who believe in our strength. . . . The mistrustful speak emphatically; the mistrustful also make others emphatic" (*GS* 226). Thus at times Nietzsche speaks loudly, stridently, assuring us of his self-assurance, saying I don't need you—I don't need anybody—and anyway the future is mine, I *will* have readers, that's why I don't care about you.

In the preface to *Ecce Homo* Nietzsche warns us that in order to listen correctly to Zarathustra, what is required "above all" is that we "*hear* aright the tone that comes from this mouth, the halcyon tone, lest one should do wretched injustice to the meaning of its wisdom" (*EH* Preface,4;219). "Halcyon"—this is the tone Nietzsche thinks appropriate to the voice that would utter the most profound wisdom, a tone undisturbed by any of those forces that could mar the calm of its "immortal assurance" (IX,6;305).[15] "Any harsh tone in the throat" is an

[15] "Halcyon" clearly means calm here—and yet Nietzsche the classical philologist must have known that the *halkyon* is, as Homer says, "a bird of much grief (*penthos*)" (*Iliad* 9.563). He probably could not have known that *penthos* "grief" is derived from the same root as is *pathos*—a word that plays a crucial but obscure role in the doctrine of will to power—as we will see. (On *penthos*/*pathos*, see Gregory Nagy, *Comparative Studies in Greek and Indic Meter* [Cambridge: Harvard University Press, 1974], 258–60.)

objection to a man, thus "how much more against his work" (II,10;258); and in the reader, too, "every frailty of the soul . . . even every kind of dyspepsia . . . any cowardice, uncleanliness, secret vengefulness in the entrails . . . all 'feminism', too—also in men—closes the door" to Nietzsche's books (III,3;264). Nietzsche/Zarathustra is above all these things, he has no need of "defensive expenditures," of "energy *wasted* on negative ends" (II,8;252), in general, of all forms of "*ressentiment,*" "anger, pathological vulnerability," and so on (I,6;230). His freedom from all these forms of disturbance gives him the "*instinctive sureness*" of his practice (I,6;231), and this instinctive sureness, this freedom from the need to defend himself, is the calm that resounds in Zarathustra's "halcyon tone."

How are we to read those declarations? The remarks from *The Gay Science* about the "critique of the nymph echo" and the need to be "surrounded by people who believe in our strength" suggest that Nietzsche is very sharply aware of the dangers to his tone of voice inherent in his situation; and in fact the remarks just cited from *Ecce Homo* reveal the same awareness, in the degree to which he must repeatedly assert that he has maintained his control in the face of a difficult situation. Can Nietzsche be so self-deceived as to fail to recognize what is really going on with him concerning a danger of whose general nature he is so intensely aware? Is the tone of his outpourings of self-praise in *Ecce Homo* "halcyon," free from all "defensive expenditure" and "pathological vulnerability"? Does Nietzsche *think* it is? Or has he even tried to achieve such a tone here?

He says that he tells his life to himself, but much of what he says does not sound as though it were addressed to himself. It sounds as though it is addressed to an audience, an audience that in the past has refused to grant him the recognition he deserves. This audience is still not listening, and even if it were listening, he will declare, it could not hear him. Nietzsche addresses this audience, yet he knows that only he can hear the sound of his own voice. And so he tells his life to himself.

But there is a third audience—the ideal reader he imagines awaits him in the future, a "monster of courage and curiosity" (*EH* III,3;264). But then Nietzsche will be dead. His voice will be heard, but only when he can no longer hear himself speak. The sound of his own voice in his own ears and the sound of his voice in the ears of others, these are two things that cannot exist at the same time. Nietzsche's being cannot be confirmed by the response of others to his voice: he hears the hollow echo and speaks mistrustfully and emphatically because he is surrounded by people who do not believe in his strength. There are indeed people alive who can hear the living Nietzsche, but they are elsewhere ("Russians, Scandinavians, and Frenchmen" [XIII, 3;321]). Among those who are closest to him, the Germans, his own people, those whose language he speaks and has transformed, his name "lies buried" under an "absurd silence." Not even his friends really read him, nor do they lift the silence around him (XIII,4;324).

Even those who listen to Nietzsche are unlikely to hear him. Because he speaks "the first language for a new series of experiences," for those who lack his experience (and who doesn't?) "nothing will be heard" (III,1;261).

We must listen to Nietzsche's voice with his immense solitude in mind, hear its tonality as haunted by the critique of the nymph echo. It is all right there to be read in the foreground, the pathos of this voice that echoes unheard, that hears only itself, that reassures itself that it believes in itself and only in this way maintains itself in being: "One has neither heard nor even seen me. I live on my own credit. It is perhaps a mere prejudice that I live." At the beginning of *Ecce Homo* he speaks as though this existence requires confirmation from the credit of others, he must say to them "*Hear me! For I am such and such a person.*" Not only to be heard but to be heard *as* who he is, as Friedrich Nietzsche, whose great danger is that he might be mistaken for someone else ("*Above all, do not mistake me for someone else*" [Preface,1;217]). Later, in a cooler, more ironic tone, Nietzsche dismisses the desire to be heard: "That today one doesn't hear me and doesn't accept my ideas is not only understandable, it even seems right to me." The way Nietzsche continues this remark implies that for him to be heard, rather than establishing his identity, would confuse it with that of someone else: "I don't want to be confounded with others—not even by myself" (III,1;259).

The subtleties of the economic maneuvers that take place between those two remarks reflect the character of the economics of *Ecce Homo* as a whole. In the remark from the Preface there is explicit pathos as Nietzsche cries out to be heard and confesses the dependency of his existence on its recognition by others. In the latter remark Nietzsche slips into a more aloof stance, economizes himself, tells us that he approves of his situation, it is what he wants, it preserves the self-identity of his selfhood in its hiddenness.

Yet this latter move, as transparently self-protective as it is, is also driven by the deepest sort of textual necessity. Nietzsche's self-presentation in *Ecce Homo* is not only a rhetorical front by which he tries to validate his message through an act of auto-authorization, as Charles Altieri suggests;[16] it is also an attempt to represent the enactment of the "thus I willed it" which is the absolute core of Nietzsche's teaching, of his confrontation with the riddle of life. Because *Ecce Homo* is engaged in both of these acts at once, the strain on Nietzsche's prose is enormous. As the enunciator of the teaching of eternal recurrence, Nietzsche is a destiny and his writing carries all the force of that destiny; he can do no other in *Ecce Homo* than declare his yes to his life in its every circumstance, including, perhaps above all, the situation of his utterance with respect to its audience or lack of audience. At the same time, Nietzsche is only a man, and a man in a very difficult rhetorical situation, aware that his audience does not believe in him, tormented by his solitude in such a way as possibly to vitiate the tone of this enunciation which he must deliver before the very audience that he so mistrusts.

The combination of these two circumstances creates an extraordinarily complex rhetorical situation, one that immeasurably complicates the dialectic of rhetorical self-assurance which we traced earlier.

For "thus I willed it" may mean "I assent to what happened, and to the suffering entailed in what happened." Or it may mean "I assent to what happened, and therefore I become master of the suffering, I do not suffer." Is not this latter meaning implied when Nietzsche defines *amor fati* as the ability to "not merely bear what is necessary . . . but *love* it" (*EH* II,10;258)? Later, he makes this implication explicit: "I myself *have never suffered* [emphasis added] from all this, what is *necessary* does not hurt me; *amor fati* is my inmost nature" (XIII,4;324). To suffer is to struggle against necessity, to rebel against what happens to us, try to push it away, say No! No! I don't want this. But if I take the very same event and welcome it, say yes to it, become active with respect to it, perhaps this is liberation from suffering. Illness, lack of recognition, betrayal by one's friends, condemnation to the most total solitude—all of these things would still be, but their sting would be gone if I transformed myself from the passive one who underwent into the active one who chose it all.

[16]Charles Altieri, "*Ecce Homo:* Narcissism, Power, Pathos, and the Status of Autobiographical Representations," in *Why Nietzsche Now?*, ed. Daniel O'Hara (Bloomington: Indiana University Press, 1981).

And yet there is something here that seems unresolved. Nietzsche speaks as though suffering were nothing more than the coloring of an event, something dispensable, so that to will the recurrence of the event is not also to will the recurrence of the suffering. But what then is the essential nature of the event, or of the experience of the event, the essential kernel which one loves in *amor fati*? The suffering involved is precisely what is so hard to will; it seems as though it is the essential point and that Nietzsche is subtly sidestepping it, conjuring it out of existence. This avoidance does not seem to be what the demon had in mind when he announced the eternal recurrence in *The Gay Science* (341) with the promises of the return of "every pain" along with "everything unutterably small or great . . . all in the same succession and sequence."

So it appears that Nietzsche is here falsifying his own insight, using it to justify his pose of autarky and ataraxia.

He is engaging, in fact, in an economic subterfuge of a type that is all too human, perhaps the most human subterfuge of all. Specifically, and ironically, one motivated by what Nietzsche teaches us to call ressentiment, the vengefulness of the impotent against those who have power over them: for example, the vengefulness of a speaker or writer against an audience that ignores him or jeers at him. Ressentiment takes many forms, but it has one most spiritual, most absolute root: if you will not recognize me and thus confer *Dasein* upon me I will make you go *fort,* I will auto-authorize myself and refuse you that same recognition which you deny me, thereby avenging myself against you by consigning you to that nonbeing with which I was threatened by your nonrecognition of me. We thus discover yet a third form of "thus I willed it"—the form identified by Freud in his grandson Ernst, the will that chooses the absence of the other whose presence cannot be guaranteed.[17] And here Nietzsche's circle closes in the most profound way, rejoining in the plurivocality of the "thus I willed it" the will of the Dionysian yes and that of the most abject slave's no. Nietzsche accepts his audience's rejection of him, embraces it, pronounces it right—thus enacting the "thus I willed it" which he announces. But in

[17]Sigmund Freud, *Beyond the Pleasure Principle,* in *SE,* vol. 18. No work of Freud's has been more discussed of late than this. I single out for mention the commentary by Jacques Lacan, "The Function and Field of Speech in Psychoanalysis," in *Ecrits: A Selection,* trans. Alan Sheridan (New York: Norton, 1977), 102–4; and by Jacques Derrida, "To Speculate—On 'Freud,'" in *The Post Card: From Socrates to Freud and Beyond,* trans. Alan Bass (Chicago: University of Chicago Press, 1987).

confirming his identity as the enunciator of eternal recurrence in this way, through acceptance of his absolute solitude, Nietzsche manifests his autarky, his ability to do without an audience (an audience which, at the same time, by the inescapable logic of this economic subterfuge, he continues to address); therefore, *he* rejects *them,* preempts their ability to reject him by having already, since long before, put himself, or found himself, beyond their reach. Long before this or that person could refuse to hear Nietzsche's voice, Nietzsche's ears were already sealed against the entire world, he had made the whole world *fort:* "At an absurdly early age, at seven, I already knew that no human word would ever reach me: has anyone ever seen me saddened on that account?" (*EH* II,10;258).

2

Transcendental Ressentiment

Freud speculates that the "yield of pleasure" the child gets from playing the game of *fort-da* comes from his becoming active in relation to a situation in which he was formerly passive, and that the specific nature of this activity is vengeance. The child avenges himself on his mother for going away by making her *fort,* saying in effect, "I don't need you, see; I don't care if you go away—I'll throw you away myself."

Whatever may be the empirical value or nonvalue of Freud's little allegory, it provides us with an astonishingly rich but also perspicuous picture of an aggressive resentfulness at the core of human subjectivity. When I make the other or the world *fort,* I come into being in the void they leave, I negate their power to negate me, they can no longer turn away from me because I have turned them off. Freud observes that the greater pleasure obviously belonged to the restoration of presence, the return of the spool or of the mother. And yet it was the being-gone (*fortsein*) that was "untiringly repeated as a game in itself" (*SE* 18;15). Freud suggests that the child makes things disappear out of "an instinct for mastery" (*Bemächtigungstrieb:* one might translate, "will to power"), then he suggests the alternate hypothesis of vengeance against the mother (*SE* 18;16). But are these two hypotheses? Isn't vengeance precisely the form of power when *Dasein* assures itself of its autarky by willing the *Fortsein* of the other?

Freud touches on this question here in a way that is both uniquely profound in his writings and also merely momentary. Freud's dominant interest in *Beyond the Pleasure Principle* is in phenomena of repetition, and therefore after sketching the story of the child's vengeance against his mother through a perverse exercise of *Wille zur Macht,* he leaves the idea behind and does not return to it. For Nietzsche, however, this idea stands at the center of his world explication: it is nothing other than what he calls *ressentiment,* the reactive exercise of will, the will that would rather will nothingness than not will, the will of a subject who is powerless to do anything against that which makes him or her suffer and who therefore must "compensate" with an "imaginary vengeance" (*GM* 36), a vengeance in the depths of his interiority, by redefining helpless passivity as a free exercise of will. What Freud identifies in its most primitive moment of articulation as the child's vengeance against the mother who disappoints him by not granting him her presence, Nietzsche identifies in its fullest efflorescence, its expansion into vengeance against the totality of being: "*The World Destroyers*—This man fails in something; finally he exclaims in rage: 'Then let the whole world perish!' This revolting feeling is the summit of envy, which argues: because there is *something* I cannot have, the whole world shall have *nothing!* The whole world shall *be* nothing" (*D* 304).

But Nietzsche is himself, at least in one movement of his economy, one of the world destroyers. Nor is this just an accident of his rhetorical situation in *Ecce Homo:* Nietzsche's complicity with the no of ressentiment is woven deep into the fabric of his attack on that no, and necessarily so, because despite what Nietzsche at times wants to believe, this no does not arise out of an impotence from which some individuals could be or could ever have been exempt. In the memorable image of the "slave revolt in morals" which he paints in the *Genealogy of Morals,* Nietzsche pretends that it is in mere physical weakness that ressentiment is rooted, but in *Thus Spoke Zarathustra* he describes in a more profound account a bondage of which not even the most forceful of humans can be free. He does not call it ressentiment here, but ressentiment is the vengefulness of the impotent, and that is what Nietzsche describes:

> That time does not run backwards, that is his wrath; "that which was" is the name of the stone he cannot move. And so he moves stones out of wrath and displeasure, and he wreaks revenge on whatever does not feel wrath and displeasure as he does. Thus the will, the liberator, took to hurting; and on all who can suffer he wreaks revenge for his inability to go backwards. This, indeed, this alone is what *revenge* is: the will's ill will against time and its "it was." (*Z* II,20;251–52)

The vengeful one in question exercises violence on the world, and Nietzsche elsewhere praises this as mastery and freedom from ressentiment; but forcefulness here is an expression of impotence, a manipulation of objects and other people in such a way as to provide symbolically the feeling of power unavailable in reality. As the child moves his spool, so the violent one moves stones and hurts living beings in order to attain an imaginary compensation for real suffering. We recognize in this imaginary vengeance against time the transcendental form of the situation Nietzsche describes in the second essay of the *Genealogy of Morals,* where he articulates the economics of pleasure and pain upon economics in the usual sense: "An equivalence is provided by the creditor's receiving, in place of a literal compensation for an injury . . . a recompense in the form of a kind of *pleasure*—the pleasure of being allowed to vent his power freely upon one who is powerless" (II,5;64–65). This right to enjoy the pleasure of a compensatory cruelty, Nietzsche says, is a "*right of the masters*" which the creditor, who may stand low in the social order, "for once" gets to taste (65).

"How can making suffer constitute a compensation?" Nietzsche asks (*GM* II,6;65–66), and his answer is that the infliction of suffering is "an extraordinary counterbalancing pleasure." What he does not say, but implies by everything he says in the *Genealogy of Morals,* is that to inflict suffering is a way of taking power by assuming the position of inflictor in place of the position of sufferer. The creditor who enjoys inflicting suffering performs an act with a structure identical (even if one act is real and the other imaginary) to that of the Christian slave who takes vengeance on the powerful by imagining their sufferings in hell. This form of enjoyment is an exercise of power, therefore in its pure form a "right of the masters" which is only copied or caricatured by the creditor and the slave. But we know from *Zarathustra* that even the master when he practices cruelty is engaged in a caricature of mastery; even he is seeking compensation for a suffering against which he is in reality powerless.[1] What we call "real" revenge is just as imaginary or merely symbolic as is imaginary or merely symbolic revenge, because the true master who inflicts suffering is always beyond reach.

Nietzsche tells us all this, but never all in one place, and so he can continue to speak in one place as though he did not know what he says elsewhere. He can continue, as we have seen, to pretend that there are

[1]Cf. *Anti* 589, where Nietzsche describes the barbarians who were conquered by Christianity as "brutalized, cruel people—strong but bungled men" who suffer inwardly from "an overpowering desire to inflict pain and to find an outlet for inner tensions in hostile acts and ideas."

masters, strong, noble, pure ones whose essence is potency, so that "*ressentiment* itself, if it should appear in the noble man, consummates and exhausts itself in an immediate reaction, and therefore does not *poison*" (*GM* I,10;39). The slavish Christian who cannot take physical vengeance must pretend that it is not vengeance at all that is desired but the "victory of God"; the Greeks, however, could openly admit that the "intoxication" of vengeful anger is "sweeter than honey" (I,14;48).

Nothing could be less apt, or more indicative of the idealizing falsification of the idea of the "noble Greek" in which Nietzsche engages, than his attendant quotation of Homer as an antithesis to the dishonest and therefore poisonous vengefulness of the slave mentality. Let us restore the context of the phrase Nietzsche lifts from Homer to remind ourselves that the entire *Iliad* is a story of poisonous, impotent vengefulness. The *Iliad* is the story of "the wrath of Achilles," of a man who is the most powerful of all, but whom cultural restraints force to swallow his rage and to sulk impotently while he nurses thoughts of vengeance. If we read the first chapter of the *Iliad* with Nietzsche's ideas about vengefulness and ressentiment in mind, we cannot help but be struck by the degree to which Homer's theme is precisely the frustration of the powerful by restraints against which mere physical force is powerless. Agamemnon underlines the point when he admits that Achilles is great in physical strength (*karteros*) but then adds that he will take Achilles' girl anyway, to show him how far superior in power (*pherteros*) he, Agamemnon, is (ll.178, 186).[2] Nestor shortly after repeats the same distinction and says that Agamemnon is *pherteros* "because he rules the greater number" (ll.280–81);[3] thus *pherteros,* "better," "superior," here appears to mean superior in political authority.

But even a great king is subject to frustration. As Nietzsche himself emphasizes, the system of restraints among the heroes is reciprocal; but this reciprocality does not, as Nietzsche claims, exempt these warriors from lingering ressentiment. The soothsayer Calchas, when he is about to explain that Agamemnon is to blame for Apollo's ire

[2]The nature of the distinction made here is clear from the context but becomes even more pointed if we accept Emile Benveniste's arguments about the precise sense of *karteros*/*krateros:* "Whereas *kratos* is used exclusively of gods and men, *krateros* can also be applied to animals and things, and the sense is always 'hard, cruel, violent'"; *Indo-European Language and Society,* trans. Elizabeth Palmer (Coral Gables, Fla.: University of Miami Press, 1973), 73.

[3]All citations of the English text of the *Iliad* are from *The Iliad of Homer,* trans. Richmond Lattimore (Chicago: University of Chicago Press, 1951).

against the Greeks, asks for Achilles' protection against the wrath of Agamemnon both now and in the future.

> For a king when he is angry with a man beneath him
> is too strong,
> and suppose even for the day itself he swallow down
> his anger (*kholos*),
> he still keeps bitterness (*koton*) that remains
> until its fulfillment
> deep in his chest.
> (1,ll.80–83)

And Achilles is able to assure Calchas that Agamemnon will have to swallow his anger for good, swearing that no Greek will dare lay hands on him, not even Agamemnon, "who now claims to be far the greatest of all the Achaians" (1,l.91).

The phrase "sweeter than honey" which Nietzsche cites comes from Achilles' regretful speech in book 18 when he acknowledges how wrong and ultimately harmful his nursing of vengefulness against Agamemnon has been to himself. Since his might has been rendered useless to himself or Patroklos by his anger, he says,

> I wish that strife would vanish away from
> among gods and mortals,
> and gall (*kholos*), which makes a man grow angry for
> all his great mind,
> that gall of anger that swarms like smoke inside of a
> man's heart
> and becomes a thing sweeter to him by far than the
> dripping of honey.
> (18,ll.107–10)

Nietzsche's citation thus entirely misrepresents the sense in which the phrase occurs in the *Iliad;* the satisfaction of unleashed vengefulness is not in question but rather the dripping poison of a vengeful anger that is never satisfied and ends in the destruction of Achilles.[4] (The *Iliad* is

[4]The precise tonality and sense in which Nietzsche cites the phrase are eminently arguable, but the meaning seems clear if we place the passage containing the citation in relation to section 6 of the second essay, where Nietzsche explores the deep structure of revenge in terms of the question "how can making suffer constitute a compensation?" Then, in the following sections, having established that vengeful or compensatory cruelty is pleasurable,

a thoroughly ironic work, and Nietzsche, despite what is constantly said about him, is in some very deep sense incapable of irony. It is the structure of this incapacity that we are tracing in this book, the way in which Nietzsche almost always tries to preserve certain forms of purity. "Intellectual cleanliness" is what he calls this incapacity.)

In fact, we recognize in Homer's story of Achilles both levels of the economics of ressentiment described by Nietzsche, the empirical level at which Achilles suffers an actual injury for which he demands compensation and, behind this, the transcendental level at which the injury of time—Achilles' death sentence, sealed at his birth—is the true, ultimate cause of his resentfulness and for which he demands compensation.

The great Achilles weeps bitter tears over his fate, and calls his mother to comfort him:

> Since, my mother, you bore me to be a man with a
> short life,
> therefore Zeus of the loud thunder on Olympus
> should grant me
> honour at least. But now he has given me not even a
> little.
>
> (1,ll.352–54)

---

he proceeds to speak of the joys of cruelty in general. Though revenge is not specifically mentioned in the following remarks, the logical structure of the sequence of his remarks in sections 6 and 7 clearly establishes that vengeful cruelty is an instance of the cruelty-in-general that he here praises: "Let me declare expressly that in the days when mankind was not yet ashamed of its cruelty, life on earth was more cheerful than it is now that pessimists exist. The darkening of the sky above mankind has deepened in step with the increase in man's feeling of shame *at man*. . . . On his way to becoming an 'angel' . . . man has evolved that queasy stomach and coated tongue through which . . . the joy and innocence of the animal has become repugnant to him. . . . Today, when suffering is always brought forward as the principle argument *against* existence . . . one does well to recall the ages in which the opposite opinion prevailed because men were unwilling to refrain from *making* men suffer and saw it as an enchantment of the first order, a genuine seduction *to* life. . . . It is certain, at any rate, that the *Greeks* still knew of no tastier spice to offer their gods . . . than the pleasures of cruelty" (*GM* II,7;67).

In the sentences that follow the remarks just cited, Nietzsche makes clear that he means the Homeric Greeks. These remarks read very much like an expansion of the sense of the earlier passage in which the "sweeter than honey" citation occurred. Both passages thus appear to say that the hypocritical men of ressentiment are, like the noble Greeks, moved by the "enchantment" and "seduction" of causing pain, the "intoxication of sweet revenge," but unlike the Greeks and their poet Homer are incapable of an innocent and spontaneous enjoyment of this pleasure, incapable of acknowledging that revenge is indeed "sweeter than honey." The noble barbarian, of whom the noble Greek is an instance, remains a healthy, ressentiment-free animal because, frankly recognizing the sweetness of revenge, and having the power to do something about it, he acts on his impulse.

His rage against the Trojans in the latter part of the poem, a rage so murderous that nature itself, in the form of the river Scamander, is revolted, is not a joyous act of barbarism but the exaction of a toll of compensatory suffering for Patroklos's death and the death Achilles himself knows he must soon endure. His rage is therefore only a symbolic or imaginary vengeance that has no effect whatever on the real source of Achilles' suffering.

I have gone into some detail concerning the *Iliad* because Nietzsche bases so much of his nostalgic account of ancient heroism on the Greeks and in particular on Homer's depiction of them.[5] To show that Nietzsche has falsified Homer's depiction is to blunt the force of Nietzsche's idealization of noble barbarism, and also to raise questions concerning the forces of Nietzsche's economy that drive him to fantasize in the way he does about the physical force, instinctual freedom, and animal innocence of barbarians.

There is considerable psychoanalytic and philosophical value to Nietzsche's ideal distinction between the active and the reactive individual; but Nietzsche involves himself in unmanageable difficulties when he takes this ideal distinction and tries to realize it in concrete historical form. Elsewhere he acknowledges the possibility of the "interpenetration" of the master and slave moralities: "In all the higher and more mixed cultures there also appear attempts at mediation between these two moralities, and yet more often the interpenetration and mutual misunderstanding of both, and at times they occur directly alongside each other—even in the same human being, within a *single*

[5]In the third essay of the *Genealogy of Morals* Nietzsche writes: "Plato versus Homer: that is the complete, the genuine antagonism—there the sincerest advocate of the 'beyond,' the great slanderer of life; here the instinctive deifier, the *golden* nature" (154).

It is not necessarily an objection to Nietzsche's use of Homer that the Homeric poems create a fictional world only very loosely related to the earlier culture they nominally depict. As Tracy Strong points out, Nietzsche emphasized not that the Homeric poems reflected a real society but that they helped to constitute one, giving the Greeks of the classical period a model of how the heroic life should be lived; *Friedrich Nietzsche and the Politics of Transfiguration* (Berkeley and Los Angeles: University of California Press, 1975), 145–51.

But even granted that Homer helped to create the *ethos* of classical Greece, it is debatable whether his influence is as Nietzsche describes it, at least in relation to the question of ressentiment. Plato in the *Republic* criticizes the Homeric poems precisely because they stimulate ressentiment in the fullest sense as the regretful or resentful chewing-over of experience. Imitation of Homeric models stimulates "that part of us that leads us to dwell in memory on our suffering" (604d; cf. 386a–397) and that is why those are wrong who tell us that "we should order our entire lives by the guidance of this poet" (606e). All citations of Plato are from the Bollingen *Collected Dialogues,* ed. Edith Hamilton and Huntington Cairns (New York: Pantheon Books, 1961).

soul" (*BGE* 260). Notice the combination of higher *and* more mixed, as though higher went hand in hand with more mixed; this is the centrifugal moment of Nietzsche's thought, though most often he argues the opposite.[6] Even here, however, Nietzsche still speaks as though, apart from the mixed forms, there were also in reality pure realizations of these two moral economies. The fascination exerted on his imagination by this idealization is irresistible, and his inability to resist this fascination generates the most remarkable textual effects in the *Genealogy of Morals*.

Our inquiry assumes the shape of a spiral as we return again and again to the sensitive points in the *Genealogy of Morals*, each time articulating with greater precision and depth the immensely subtle psychodialectical movement of the text at these points.

The *Genealogy of Morals* begins with the distinction between noble and slave morality, which is then defined in terms of activity and reactivity or ressentiment. At the end of the third essay, we seem to be still on the same ground, as though perhaps we had only deepened the original analysis: now the no of ressentiment is understood as a no to life itself (though with the complication that it gives degenerate life a reason for living, the project of lacerating itself). Yet in the space between this beginning and this conclusion, the most complex and bewildering series of transformations occurs, such that the original distinction between master and slave is relegated to a position of only the most preliminary significance. In place of this simplistic and tendentious split, the figure who emerges as the real protagonist of Nietzsche's

[6]We find the elements of a formal typology that would have identified what I am calling a "centrifugal" vitality in nineteenth-century culture, as opposed to the "centripetal" vitality of aristocracies that operate according to a restricted economy, in a number of Nietzsche's late remarks. In *WP* 655 Nietzsche even overturns his more usual valuation when he writes that "the greater the impulse toward unity, the more firmly may one conclude that weakness is present; the greater the impulse towards variety, differentiation, inner decay, the more force is present." In *BGE* 262 he distinguishes the "severe, warlike, prudently taciturn men" of the beleaguered aristocracies of the past from the "greater, more manifold, more comprehensive life" that characterizes periods of "young, still unexhausted, still unwearied corruption." And in *BGE* 256 he describes the Romanticism of the mid-nineteenth century, including Wagner, in just such terms, as an era of "an audaciously daring, magnificently violent type of human being" (cf. *WP* 747 and 1015). But it is clear that the centripetal movement, the movement that Heidegger picks up in his analysis of "the Grand Style," is the more frequently visible in Nietzsche's text. Which does not make it the *essence* of Nietzsche's "view."

tale, a protagonist who is neither merely hero nor merely villain, neither merely noble nor merely slave, and all the better qualified as epic protagonist for that, is the *ascetic priest*.

In fact, the ascetic priest confounds the distinction between the economy of the master and that of the slave even before that distinction is established. In section 5 of the first essay Nietzsche describes the aristocratic valuation of good and bad, in section 7 the Jewish inversion of this valuation; but in section 6 we encounter a "highest caste" that is "at the same time the *priestly* caste," an "essentially priestly aristocracy" in which are already introduced the unhealthiness, morbidity, and antisensuality that are the keynotes of the economy of ressentiment Nietzsche will shortly attribute to Christian slave-morality. Whereas the slave can be conceived as the antithesis of the aristocrat, and as originating in another place, the "priestly mode of valuation" branches off from the knightly aristocratic and *then* develops into its opposite (*GM* I,7;33). Aristocracy somehow breeds priesthood within itself. Similarly, we later encounter the new form of the philosopher, who practices "a certain asceticism, a severe and cheerful continence with the best will" (III,9;112). (As we will see, Nietzsche speaks of this economy with considerable good humor and indulgence, very much as though he were speaking of himself, praising his own economy.) This philosopher is the "winged creature" who is in the process of emerging (but has not yet emerged) from the "gloomy caterpillar form" of the ascetic priest (III,10;116).

With this final movement we are on the verge of Zarathustra and the overcoming of nihilism, but what Nietzsche has described is a continuous evolutionary line of aristocrat-priest, historical philosopher, and philosopher of the future in which each new stage develops in the interior of the preceding stage. This complex and fascinating evolution is the dynamic that drives the narrative of the *Genealogy of Morals,* drives it at a deeper level than either of the obvious narrative lines (both of which foreground the gaudy struggle between master and slave), according to which the Zarathustran type is either the ultimate triumph of self-overcoming "master morality" or the third stage in a dialectic that involves as its second stage the negation of master morality by slave morality.[7] But even the underlying narrative which concerns the line of

[7]See my earlier discussion in Chapter 1 on the dialectical progression from noble barbarian to autonomous individual.

descent of the aristocrat-priest domesticates the most powerful pull on Nietzsche's prose, a pull that bends his prose into what is not a progressive narration but an oscillation, in a pattern not unlike that remarked by Derrida in Freud's *Beyond the Pleasure Principle.*[8] For the object by which Nietzsche is fascinated, the object he keeps drawing near and then pushing away, *the ascetic will,* is already fully present in the aristocrat-priest with whom he begins his account, and all Nietzsche's narratives of progressive development entwine themselves around the pulsations of his fascination with and revulsion from this object.

Although Nietzsche does not make a formal distinction between ressentiment as it manifests itself in the ascetic priest and in the slave, and in fact in the first essay conflates the two under the figure of the "slave revolt in morals," it is clear that the character and value of the priestly economy differs essentially from the slave economy. As much as Nietzsche assails the ascetic priest because he "invariably makes . . . *sicker*" (*GM* III,21;142) the sick masses to which he ministers, underneath all the contempt Nietzsche heaps on his motives and methods, the role of the ascetic priest is ultimately to place the "bad instincts" of those who suffer in the service of "self discipline, self-surveillance, and self-overcoming" (III,16;128). As much as Nietzsche pretends to explain the will of the priest as simply rooted "from the first" in "something unhealthy" (I,6;32), and lack of health as a contingent condition, an affliction from which the best and strongest would be free, elsewhere he recognizes that besides the empirical conditions of sickness which strike here and there, there is also a condition rooted in the essential nature of humanity that turns the human will against itself, and that this conflict of itself with itself is the will's struggle for self-overcoming: "Man is . . . *the* sick animal. . . . He, the great experimenter with himself, discontented and insatiable . . . still unvanquished, eternally directed toward the future, whose own restless energies never leave him in peace, so that his future digs like a spur into the flesh of every present—how could such a courageous and richly endowed animal not be also the most imperiled, the most chronically and profoundly sick of all sick animals?" (III,13;121). Nietzsche has just told us two paragraphs earlier that the ascetic ideal comes from degeneration and exhaustion, yet here he derives its sickliness from a "rest-

[8]See Jacques Derrida, "To Speculate—On 'Freud,'" in *The Post Card: From Socrates to Freud and Beyond,* trans. Alan Bass (Chicago: University of Chicago Press, 1987), 301–4.

less energy" that aims at futurity; the self-laceration of ascetic will is the spur of the future which "digs into the flesh" of the present.

Thus Nietzsche here describes the ascetic will as the conquest of transcendental ressentiment. Against the will turned toward the past, raging against its fixity, avenging itself by making others suffer, Nietzsche describes a will turned toward the future, a will that makes itself suffer in order constantly to remake itself.

This characterization is, however, an isolated moment in the *Genealogy of Morals,* and if Nietzsche elsewhere expresses considerable admiration for the ascetic will, it is not for the reasons just described. What he describes here is a self that gives itself up to be rent by time, a self that wills its own suffering in the endless violation of its boundary of selfhood as endless pouring-forth into futurity. But what he describes almost everywhere else, what he admires as power and in power, is autarky, an autonomous, self-preserving selfhood that can impose its will on other selves, as in the case of the noble, or a will even more autarkic than the will of the noble.

Nietzsche discovers in the ascetic priest a transcendental will to power, a will "that wants to become master not over *something in life* but over *life itself* [emphasis added], over its most profound, powerful, and basic condition. . . . We stand before a discord that *wants* to be discordant, that *enjoys* itself in this suffering and even grows more self-confident and triumphant the more its own presupposition, its physiological capacity for life, *decreases*" (*GM* III,11;117–18). The ascetic will is thus the master of the game of *fort-da,* the will that increases its sensation of being by learning to do without the world, willing even the shriveling of the body within which it finds itself.

How can Nietzsche not be fascinated by such a will, how can it not disturb the univocity of the judgment of contempt which he so easily pours out on weakness and sickness? Nietzsche's language seems here to yield involuntarily to a kind of admiration for the phenomenon he is looking at, a phenomenon so dark and questionable that it out-Nietzsches Nietzsche, the one who glorifies in confronting the dark and questionable problems that others dare not face. Here Nietzsche comes up against something he cannot look down on, a paradox that confounds his distinctions between strength and weakness, health and disease: a strength based on weakness, a life that disease makes "more self-confident and triumphant."

Let us now follow the movement of Nietzsche's text as it oscillates or vacillates in its evaluations according to the way in which his subject matter attracts one or another type of charge from him as he writes.

We return once more to the second essay of the *Genealogy of Morals,* taking up the thread of Nietzsche's tale in section 16 of the second essay, where he shows that the condition he had initially stigmatized as that of the slave, the illness of an animal deprived of an outlet in action for its drives, is in fact the universal condition of the human as human, insofar as a human being is an animal who lives in a polis.[9] "Bad conscience" is the illness that follows necessarily from man's being "finally enclosed within the walls of society and of peace" (II,16;84), "the result of a forcible sundering from his animal past" (85). As opposed to the ressentiment of those who are oppressed by Vikings and Romans, civilized people suffer "from lack of external enemies and resistances" and so lacerate and gnaw at themselves (85). There also we are told that this is a condition "pregnant with a future." From Nietzsche's remarks in this section it appears that ressentiment has been superseded as the central factor in his account of cultural development; the condition of cultural frustration of the instincts as a result of civilization itself now appears to be the real problem and ressentiment only an epiphenomenon (although at one point Nietzsche suggests that there are actually the "most various origins" for the "physiological depression" the ascetic priest tries to cure—mixing of classes, climate, diet [III,17;130]). Thus Nietzsche later tells us, in remarks consistent with the analysis in this section, that ressentiment and vengefulness are in reality not at all a consequence of harm endured from an external agent but rather a means of "anesthesia" needed for the pain that is already there, pain that arises from the individual's condition of life within culture. Ressentiment is sought as an anesthetic, but any strong affect would serve just as well as vengefulness to stir up the "orgies of feeling" that mask the underlying pain (III,15;127 and III,20;139–40).

By section 16 of the second essay Nietzsche thus appears to have moved beyond the question of the "slave revolt in morals" into the question of civilization and its discontents. His analysis should logically now proceed to the kinds of matters he in fact will raise in the concluding sections of the third essay: the unfolding of philosophy

[9]This is the empirical condition of all humanity, to be distinguished from the transcendental condition of life, the relation to time, with which Zarathustra is concerned.

and *Wissenschaft* of all sorts as the work of self-overcoming by civilized humanity. But Nietzsche proceeds instead to an astonishing eulogy in which he gives the violent nobility credit for creating bad conscience. It is as though Nietzsche has to maintain a relative differentiation of value between internalized and externalized drive, and when he raises the valuation of the former he must raise the volume on his praise of the latter to a proportionate degree, so that the distance between the two can be maintained. "I employed the word 'state': it is obvious what is meant—some pack of blond beasts of prey, a conqueror and master race which, organized for war and with the ability to organize, unhesitatingly lays its terrible claws upon a populace . . . still formless and nomad" (*GM* II,17;86).

Nietzsche concentrates on these "beasts of prey" almost every kind of virtue that he elsewhere praises in separate types of persons. Not only is this beast one "who can command," "who is by nature master, . . . violent in act and bearing," but he is also artist and mother: "Their work is an instinctive creation and imposition of forms; they are the most involuntary, unconscious artists there are. . . . They exemplify that terrible artists' egoism that has the look of bronze and knows itself justified to all eternity in its 'work,' like a mother in her child." Insofar as bad conscience is good, it must be created by the masters; but insofar as it is bad, it must be stressed that they are themselves free of it: "It is not in *them* that the 'bad conscience' developed . . . but it would not have developed *without* them" (II,17;86–87).

And now, having made violent nobility the cause of the good thing that is bad conscience, having pushed, in a very peculiar fashion and only for the moment, the ascetic priest and the slave out of the picture, Nietzsche allows himself to make an absolutely crucial connection, the full consequences of which he will fail to draw in the rest of the book. I quote at length the remarks from the beginning of section 18 and ask the reader to savor their implications for everything Nietzsche says elsewhere about the slave, the ascetic priest, sickness, degeneracy, and so on:

> Fundamentally it is the *same active force* [emphasis added] that is at work on a grander scale in those artists of violence and organizers who build states, and that here, internally, on a smaller and pettier scale, directed backward, . . . creates for itself a bad conscience and builds negative ideals—namely the *instinct for freedom* (in my language: the will to power); only here the material upon which the form-giving and ravish-

> ing nature of this force vents itself is man himself, . . . and *not,* as in that greater and more obvious phenomenon, some *other* man, *other* men. The secret self-ravishment, this artist's cruelty . . . this uncanny, dreadfully joyous labor of a soul voluntarily at odds with itself that makes itself suffer out of joy in making suffer—eventually this *active* 'bad conscience' . . . as the womb of all ideal and imaginative phenomena, also brought to light an abundance of strange new beauty and affirmation, and perhaps beauty itself.[10]

Even in this remark Nietzsche still clings to the grotesque sentimentality that it is healthier and more noble to inflict suffering on others than to turn it inward; but what is more important is that he utterly breaches the wall he wants to keep between externalized and internalized aggression, because even if internalized aggression is "smaller and pettier," it is still "*fundamentally . . . the same active force*" as the other. And, as we have seen, Nietzsche soon discovers in the ascetic will something that is the farthest possible from a small and petty expression of will to power.

However, Nietzsche has only been able to breach the wall between

[10]Then Nietzsche seems to back away from the strongest implications of what he has just said, ending the paragraph with these words: "After all, what would be 'beautiful' if the contradiction had not first become conscious of itself, if the ugly had not first said to itself: 'I am ugly'?" This sentence seems to imply that the "secret self-ravishment" of the "active bad conscience" is only a negative and preparatory labor, the act of recognizing that "I am ugly" presumably in order then to overcome this ugliness. But Nietzsche has described the force at work here as "form-giving" and as operating on the material of "man himself," the self-reflexive character being the only difference between the active bad conscience and the activity of the masters. If the self-ravishment of bad conscience is form giving, it is more than a negative and preparatory action, though it may include a merely negative moment within it. In that case the "I am ugly" would not be the totality of the function of bad conscience, only its first phase, and Nietzsche need not be reserving the creation of beauty for some later time, post–bad conscience. Our indecision as to the sense of this sentence is indicative of the ambiguity of Nietzsche's thought in general on this point.

We should compare what Nietzsche says here with remarks 225, 229, and 230 of *Beyond Good and Evil,* where he sides unambiguously with the movement of self-ravishment. "In man *creature* and *creator* are united" (225); here he leaves open the question of whether they are united in the *same* man. But he subsequently says that the "seeker after knowledge" forces his spirit to recognize things against the inclination of the spirit, "out of a desire to hurt" its "basic will" (229). And then in a crucial remark Nietzsche unfolds an anatomy of will to power in which he ranges, on one side, the appropriative, incorporative will (which merely "files new things in old files"), the will to ignorance, the will to deception, and the will to the mask, and, on the other side, the "sublime inclination of the seeker after knowledge who insists on profundity, multiplicity, and thoroughness, with a *will* which is a kind of cruelty of the intellectual conscience and fate" (230). This is of course what in the *Genealogy of Morals* he will stigmatize as the ascetic will to knowledge, but here he identifies proudly with this will, the task of which is "to translate man back into nature."

the two forms of cruelty by keeping a hedge between them. What he has described is "active" bad conscience, which implies that he can still identify a bad, passive form of bad conscience on the back of which he can load the reproaches belonging to ignobility. To this identification he now proceeds.

At the beginning of section 19 he concludes the foregoing movement by saying that though bad conscience is an illness, it is so "as pregnancy is an illness," and now he starts a new account of the origin of bad conscience that throws the previous account into confusion. First, going back to the "earlier point of view" of his essay, he returns to the question of debt in order to develop a theory of *Schuldgefühl:* "feeling of indebtedness." Kaufmann and Hollingdale translate *Schuld* as "guilty indebtedness" to capture the double sense of *Schuld,* but since Nietzsche says in section 21 that he has so far "ignored the moralization of these concepts" of *Schuld* and *Pflicht,* it would seem that up to this point *Schuld* would bear only the sense "debt" or "indebtedness." The moralization of which he now speaks seems to be a convergence of the two strands he has traced, of religious indebtedness and bad conscience. The man of bad conscience, the pregnant, actively self-cruel man is said to have "seized upon the presupposition of religion so as to drive his self-torture to its most gruesome pitch of severity and rigor." Consequently, it seems, he ceases to be the artist of the self, the man of "active" bad conscience, because "he ejects from himself all his denial of himself" and projects it outward in the shape of the external reality of a God who condemns him. And now the spectacle of cruelty becomes too "unnerving" even for Nietzsche, and he must "forcibly forbid" himself to gaze too long "into these abysses." For the phenomenon has now ceased to be creative, has become sick in a different sense, no longer as pregnancy is sick but as a "*will* to infect and poison the fundamental ground of things" (*GM* II,22;92–93). And now Nietzsche in his recoil from the ascetic will once more turns to the innocent animal Greeks for the clean air of life affirmation (II,23;93–94).

So at this point, once again with an effusion of extravagant rhetoric, Nietzsche reestablishes the noxious and repellent character of a life-denying economy of cruelty that is turned back on the self and the saliency of the distinction between this and the attractive blond beast (as well as, apparently, the "active" artist of the self). And to refresh his sense of the matter, he begins the third essay with a quotation from

Zarathustra expressing the manly sentiment that "wisdom is a woman and always loves only a warrior." He will not return to his main theme again until section 11 of the third essay. When he does take up once more the question of the ascetic will ("only now . . . do we seriously come to grips with our problem" [III,11;116]), Nietzsche admits that "it must indeed be in the *interest of life itself*" that the ascetic priest exists (117). The priest is no accident, he appears "regularly and universally . . . in almost every age; he belongs to no one race; he prospers everywhere; he emerges from every class of society." With these remarks Nietzsche works himself up to the recognition of the ascetic will as the greatest will to power, power over "life itself." And once again, having reached this recognition, Nietzsche backs away.

He turns to other subjects in section 12, and when he returns to the ascetic will in section 13, he has it once more beaten down to manageable proportions: it is nothing but the last expedient of a "degenerating life" merely trying to preserve itself. Nietzsche does not here grapple with the problem of ascetic will in the profound form that he has posed it in section 11; his characterization of the ascetic priest's will is now amazingly weaker and less interesting (and this will thus easier for Nietzsche to contain). "The ascetic priest is the incarnate desire to be different, to be in a different place" (*GM* III,13; 120). Nothing but escapism! And how is this desire utilized by life? Nietzsche does not even attempt a rigorous derivation of positive from negative: all we get here is a vague reference to how the "power of this desire" chains the priest and "enables him to persuade to existence the whole herd of the ill-constituted."

But now the oscillations become more violent. This time Nietzsche does not even finish the section before the stronger conception of ascetic will surfaces once more: in the next paragraph we encounter the description of "this sickliness" as the future that "digs like a spur into the flesh of every present" (*GM* III,13;121). But immediately thereafter, at the beginning of section 14, we find the healthy once more raised above the tide of contamination: sickliness is normal—"we cannot deny its normality"—and therefore "the higher should be the honor" accorded the healthy and strong, and we should "protect" them from the contaminated "air of the sickroom," because "the sick represent the greatest danger for the healthy" (III,14;121).

Nietzsche now launches one of his most intemperate attacks anywhere in his work on the weak, the failures, the poisonous ones who hate "the aspect of the victorious" (*GM* III,14;122), and "the sick woman especially" (123). We are even treated to this interesting piece of folk insight: "The Bogos say: 'woman is a hyena'" (123). Once again ressentiment is invoked as the simple phenomenon of hatred of the sick against the healthy. As always, we must listen to the *tone* of Nietzsche's voice in order to follow his psychodialectic; we must ask why it becomes so exaggerated, so bombastic. There is no compulsion of thought driving these remarks; on the contrary, the movement of Nietzsche's dialectic has already carried him far beyond the claims he makes here. *Why such rhetoric,* sustained across several pages and building in intensity? "Fresh air! fresh air! and keep clear of the madhouses and hospitals of culture! . . . away from the sickening fumes of inner corruption and the hidden rot of disease!" (125).

Above all, note the change in tone as we move into section 15. It is as though Nietzsche's paroxysm in section 14 has let out the reactive tension aroused in him by the approach to the dangerous subject and he can now approach it yet again. In fact, he now not only approaches once more the question of the ascetic priest but bestows on him an encomium that matches and perhaps even outdoes in its extravagance the earlier one on the violent creators of bad conscience. The accents of Nietzsche's praise in this case are even more significant because this praise runs so much against the grain of what Nietzsche at another and more obvious level of his text has repeatedly asserted. Now Nietzsche reasserts that the ascetic priest "must be sick himself, he must be profoundly related to the sick," and then adds, "but he must also be strong, master of himself even more than of others, with his will to power intact" (*GM* III,15;126). As soon as Nietzsche mentions strength in this way our ears prick up, we know which way the energy has started flowing.

The priest must "defend his herd—against whom? Against the healthy, of course, *and also against envy of the healthy*" (emphasis added; *GM* III,15;126). So the ascetic priest is really the *undoer* of slave ressentiment. He does this by turning the slave's accusation against himself, for the purpose, Nietzsche will tell us in section 16, of "self-surveillance, self-discipline, and self-overcoming" (128). But more, the ascetic priest is "the natural opponent *and despiser* of all rude, stormy, unbridled, hard, violent, beast-of-prey health and might" (126). To "despise"—*verachten*—is to feel contempt; the ascetic priest neither fears nor hates beast-of-prey health and might, he feels contempt for it.

In the first essay, section 10, Nietzsche had ascribed the "affect of contempt, of looking down from a superior height" to the "noble mode of valuation," distinguishing it from the "vengefulness of the impotent"; and precisely this affect now characterizes the ascetic priest. And now Nietzsche's prose can barely find terms adequate to express the virtues of the "new kind of preying animal" that the ascetic priest evolves out of himself in order to make his war of cunning rather than of force against the violent ones. This new, "more *delicate* animal" will have "a new kind of animal ferocity in which the polar bear, the supple, cold, and patient tiger, and not least the fox will be joined in a unity at once enticing and terrifying" (126).

Nietzsche's admiration for power is here caught in the toils of a problem that he never adequately confronts and that makes nonsense of much of what he says about power. In his flight from the sickness of the will that turns against itself, Nietzsche glorifies power as pure physicality. "The true reaction," he has said in the first essay, is "that of deeds" (*GM* I,10;36); the slave and the civilized men are sick because they cannot indulge their aggression and vengefulness in acts of physical violence. This conception leads Nietzsche often to list intelligence among the traits belonging to weakness ("power *makes stupid,*" he declares outright in *Twilight of the Idols* [VIII,1;506]). But in his description of the ascetic priest as bear, tiger, and fox, Nietzsche admits the very real power of a type of man his dogmatic typology classes as "weak." Of course the power of the priest is that of a *pharmakon,* ("when he . . . stills the pain of the wound *he at the same time infects the wound*" [*GM* III,15;126]), but the terms of Nietzsche's description suggest that whatever contempt Nietzsche might feel for weakness, it is certainly not in place here.

Nietzsche now sets off on a new topic that engages his attention from section 16 through section 22: the priest's methods for allaying the pain of "physiological depression" with which his flock is afflicted. Once again, these sections are dominated by the accent of contempt as Nietzsche describes the sickness and bad faith of the masses; but by now the split is very clear between the tone in which Nietzsche speaks of them and the way he speaks of their "shepherd." When he returns to the ascetic will itself in section 23, he begins the new movement that will carry the text from here to its conclusion, concerning the fact that the ascetic ideal has a goal "so universal that all the other interests of human existence seem, when compared with it, petty and narrow"

(*GM* III,23;146). It is no longer the bearer of the ascetic ideal, the priest, who is at issue; Nietzsche is now concerned with the transpersonal force of which the priest is the expression, and once again his language swells with the predicates of strength as he describes the ascetic will in terms of appropriative, assimilative will to power: "It permits no other interpretation, no other goal; it rejects, denies, affirms, and sanctions solely from the point of view of *its* interpretation . . . ; it submits to no power, it believes in its own predominance over every other power" (146), and so on for the rest of the paragraph. We know how this movement ends in section 28, with the striking conclusion about the will that would rather "will *nothingness* that *not* will." But we saw earlier how, before Nietzsche reaches this conclusion, he implicates his "we" with the "they" of the bearers of the ascetic will in a way that confounds any attempt to draw a simple boundary between the two.

What, exactly, does it mean "to will *nothingness*"? Nietzsche gives us an easy answer, or at least an explicit or obvious one, that presupposes a set of positive life-values with which the will to nothingness would be simply and clearly at odds. The will to nothingness is "hatred of the human, and even more of the animal . . . horror of the senses . . . longing to get away from all . . . change, becoming, death," and so on (*GM* III,28;162–63); but nevertheless "man was *saved* thereby, he possessed a meaning." The *pharmakon* of the ascetic priest saves humanity from the "suicidal nihilism" of meaninglessness by poisoning it, making it sicker than it already was, bringing "deeper, more inward, more life-destructive suffering" (162).

Does this answer make sense? In what way can a will to nothingness differ from a "suicidal nihilism"? How can you save humanity from its suffering by inflicting on it a "*more* life-destructive suffering"? At best, the change must be from a quick death to a slow one, from mass suicide by jumping over a cliff to mass suicide by fasting and self-flagellation. Is Nietzsche suggesting that the former is *less* life destructive? But then in what way would the latter have "saved" humanity?

It appears that the machine of Nietzsche's rhetoric, which generates such remarkable effects throughout the *Genealogy of Morals* and rises to a climax here, is now grinding one part of itself against another. Nietzsche's vituperation of the ascetic will must be kept turned up full volume, but this does not entirely harmonize with the other claim Nietzsche must make, that "the will itself was saved" by the ascetic ideal.

Here again is that contradiction Nietzsche keeps stumbling on, of a life turned against itself. In section 13 he had concluded that the idea of "life *against* life" is "a simple absurdity," that even in the case of the ascetic ideal life must be struggling to preserve itself; and he explained the apparent self-contradiction as the desperate expedient of a life that is so exhausted and degenerate that it has to use extreme measures to excite itself back to life. But his conclusion there was that "life wrestles in it and through it with death and *against* death; the ascetic ideal is an artifice for the *preservation* of life"; and a little later, more lyrically and effusively: "The No he says to life brings to light, as if by magic, an abundance of tender Yesses; even when he *wounds* himself, this master of destruction, of self-destruction—the very wound afterward compels him to *live*" (*GM* III,13;121). This description does not sort very well with the condemnation of the will to nothingness at the end. And "exhaustion" and "degeneration" might describe the condition of the masses, but they do little to explain the all-conquering will to power of the ascetic priest concerning which Nietzsche rhapsodizes in section 15 of the third essay.

Here, as in other texts, Nietzsche uses the same formula to speak of a variety of phenomena, and then he confuses matters—often richly and fruitfully—by pretending that he is talking about only *one* thing, but from a variety of "perspectives." Not only does "ascetic ideal" include an astounding variety of phenomena in the *Genealogy of Morals,* it also overlaps in indefinite and shifting ways the concepts of ressentiment, slave morality, and bad conscience. The issue is further confused by Nietzsche's shifting stance toward the ascetic will as expression of weakness or of power. But Nietzsche's own stance toward the ascetic will is most obscured by his oscillation between viewing it in terms of the ascetic priest's self-relation and in terms of the ascetic priest's relation to the masses. When he views it in terms of the former, as we have seen, Nietzsche's admiration begins to overflow the bounds of his official attitude of condemnation, but then he can always shift to the latter in order to touch ground again with that condemnation.

We can introduce some conventional order into the system of Nietzsche's concepts in the *Genealogy of Morals* by distinguishing among three basic phenomena:

1. The will of the ascetic priest as most profound, most spiritual will to power, most fascinating and interesting phenomenon of will in existence, "*ressentiment* without equal" (III,11;117) that tries to take command over the fundamental conditions of life itself.

2. The impotent ressentiment of the slave against those who are strong. This phenomenon also shows itself as the self-laceration of the sense of sin, once the ascetic priest teaches this class of humanity to condemn themselves as the source of their own suffering.

3. The bad conscience which is the inevitable outcome of the cage of culture. This condition resembles the self-laceration of the individual of inward-turned ressentiment because it is also a case of instinct turned inward; but this is a condition "pregnant with a future," it is the womb of humanity's development from an animal and barbarian past into the "*sovereign individual*" who stands "at the end of this tremendous process" (II,2;59). Nietzsche even tells us that the formation of the state happens so suddenly "that it precludes all struggle and even all *ressentiment*" (II,17;86). This line of Nietzsche's thinking crosses with the description of the human being as a creature "whose future digs like a spur into the flesh of every present," even though when he makes the latter remark he appears to be referring to the ascetic priest (III,13;120–21).

Gilles Deleuze considers bad conscience to be simply an extension of slave ressentiment, refusing to recognize that for Nietzsche there is a structure of self-cruelty that is the matrix of futurity and the essential condition for self-overcoming.[11] Only in the case of a certain kind of self-cruelty is the exercise of power anything more than a simulacrum of mastery; only here is there no search for revenge against a cause of suffering that lies outside the necessary conditions that constitute the self as self. "If this is illness, it is so as pregnancy is an illness."

But the ascetic will is not this productive self-cruelty, and Nietzsche is not drawn to it so profoundly in the *Genealogy of Morals* because of its creative power.

Nietzsche is drawn by the ascetic will, and repelled by it. He says no to the ascetic because he wants to *say yes to the body*—the animal, the senses, change, becoming, death. But what he rejects in the ascetic (when he rejects him) is his sickness and decay, which means that in saying no to the ascetic Nietzsche *says no to the body,* change, becoming, death. Sickness and decay are precisely what is bodily about the body,

[11]Gilles Deleuze, *Nietzsche and Philosophy,* trans. Hugh Tomlinson (New York: Columbia University Press, 1983), 128.

at least in the Christian tradition, which always figures the anarchy of desire as corruptibility and bondage to death. Nietzsche pretends to affirm the body and this earth in his affirmation of the strong and healthy, but Saint Paul when he preaches a body of life pursues just the same freedom from the fundamental conditions of embodiment as Nietzsche does in his idealization of strength and health.

Nietzsche thus also *says yes to the ascetic will*, insofar as the ascetic priest, who is in one sense (as contrasted with the self-affirming, healthy animal) an expression of sickness and decay, is in another sense the only one who knows how to become master "over life itself, over its most profound, powerful and basic conditions" (*GM* III,11; 117–18).

We know from *Zarathustra* that the man of physical force rages in vain against these conditions, the tyranny of time and its "it was," the "law of time that it must devour its children" (*Z* II,20;252). Time is the transcendental condition of life, principle of decay and degeneration, law that shatters the autarky of the self, the condition Zarathustra tells us the will cannot master. The will must learn to say yes to time, which is to say yes to the dispersal or spilling of the self in time. But in the *Genealogy of Morals* Nietzsche is repeatedly attracted to the idea of a will that could oppose itself to this violation of autarky, a will that could remain master of itself even in the face of this most fundamental condition of its being and so preserve the substance of the self, prevent its spillage, make it circulate in a closed circuit that flows back into the self once more.

Nietzsche allows himself to dilate on the glories of this economy in sections 5 through 10 of the third essay, attributing the ascetic will he praises here not to the priest but to the philosopher and in this way obscuring that this is indeed still the ascetic will. The philosopher sounds suspiciously like an ascetic priest; he is characterized by "rancor against sensuality" and "affection in favor of the ascetic ideal." Without these, Nietzsche tells us, one cannot be a philosopher, one is only a "so-called" philosopher (*GM* III,7;106–7). Here Nietzsche is at his coyest, speaking in terms that could apply precisely to him, that do apply precisely to him, yet from which he keeps a certain ironic distance. It is, after all, of Schopenhauer that he is speaking, and we know that Nietzsche is not Schopenhauer, that Nietzsche says yes where Schopenhauer says no. But we have seen how complicated are Nietzsche's yesses and nos.

Now, what "*la bête philosophe*" strives for is what "every animal" strives for, "instinctively" (so it is normal, instinctual—therefore healthy?): "an optimum of favorable conditions under which it can expend all its strength and achieve its maximal feeling of power" (*GM* III,7;107). (Notice the image of "expenditure"; we will have to track Nietzsche's imagery of discharge, blockage, saving up, etc.) Therefore, what the philosopher abhors above all is "*marriage*" (Nietzsche does not say "above all," but it is the only example he gives in section 7 and we will see that this is no accident). No great philosopher has ever been married, Nietzsche falsely suggests; it would be comical for a philosopher to marry. The philosopher "does *not* deny 'existence,' he rather affirms *his* existence and *only* his existence, and this perhaps to the point at which he is not far from harboring the impious wish "*pereat mundus, fiat philosophia, fiat philosophus, fiam*" (III,7;108) (Kaufmann furnishes this translation: "Let the world perish, but let there be philosophy, the philosopher, *me*").

Fiam: "let *me* exist, let there be *me*." This is the meaning of the ascetic ideal in the case of a philosopher, this is his "cheerful asceticism" (*GM* III,8;108). Nietzsche now goes on to describe further the conditions of the philosopher's autarky in terms that remind us of Zarathustra and of Nietzsche's own way of life and thus leave no doubt as to his own implication in what he describes. In fact, by the end of the paragraph he has slipped from the "they" of the preceding paragraphs into "we."

> A voluntary obscurity . . . a modest job, an everyday job, something that conceals rather than exposes one; an occasional association with harmless, cheerful beasts and birds whose sight is refreshing; mountains for company, but not dead ones, mountains with *eyes* (that is, with lakes); perhaps even a room in a full, utterly commonplace hotel, where one is certain to go unrecognized and can talk to anyone with impunity. . . . That which Heraclitus avoided . . . is still the same as that which *we* shun today . . . for we philosophers need to be spared *one* thing above all: everything to do with "today." (109)

The philosopher does not need women or world because he has something "growing in him"; he does not expend his energy outwardly because he needs to turn it all back into himself for the benefit of this thing within him; it is a "'maternal' instinct" that drives him. He "assembles and saves up everything—time, energy, love, and interest—only for that one thing." What is ultimately "saved up" is sexual energy, libido: "Every artist knows what a harmful effect intercourse has in states of great spiritual tension and preparation . . . their 'maternal' instinct ruthlessly disposes of all other stores and accumulations of energy, of animal vigor, for the benefit of the evolving work: the greater energy then *uses up* the lesser" (110–11).

The "greater energy" is the energy expended for the artists' or philosophers' work; it is "used up" for the benefit of this work; but all of this is the way in which the artist or philosopher (how did the artist get into this discussion?) says *Fiam* and lets the world go hang.

And even though Nietzsche calls this work energy the "greater energy," it turns out that it is really just the other, lesser energy turned to account, "sublimated" as we would say: "This should by no means preclude the possibility that the sweetness and plenitude peculiar to the aesthetic state might be derived precisely from the ingredient of 'sensuality' (just as the 'idealism' of young girls derives from this source)—so that sensuality is not overcome by the appearance of the aesthetic condition, as Schopenhauer believed, but only transfigured and no longer enters consciousness as sexual excitement" (*GM* III,8;111; cf. *WP* 805, where Nietzsche links the "creative instinct of the artist" and "the distribution of semen in his blood").

The difference between this philosopher's asceticism and that of the ascetic priest is this: the former is a "cheerful" asceticism, the latter is "gloomy" and "serious." Is this a fundamental difference? It seems that both practice the same method of mastery, preserving their substance by keeping it from discharge into the world, other people, a woman.[12]

Yet perhaps there is a fundamental difference. The artist or philosopher brings forth a work, whereas the ascetic priest works only on his

[12]After having described the philosopher's avoidance of sex and marriage as an expression of the will to power and thus a function of what "every animal" strives for "instinctively," Nietzsche (forgetting that he has spoken of the ascetic as having his "will to power intact" [III,15;126]), in section 17 of the third essay, calls the same thing in the case of the ascetic a search for "hibernation" (131), "deep sleep" (133), the attempt to escape the discomfort of "physiological depression": "if possible, will and desire are abolished altogether . . . if possible, no women, or as little as possible" (131). But he seems to feel some discomfort at this reinterpretation of the avoidance of women; he inserts a parenthetical remark in which he now dismisses "the *philosopher's* struggle against this feeling" as "absurd," merely the spinning of ideas, "as when pain is proved to be an error" (131). Here Nietzsche completely ignores his earlier praise of the philosopher's asceticism and the practical measures the philosopher takes; for example, the refusal to marry.

own being, he does not save his energy for the production of a work but uses it to shut down the springs out of which that energy flows. Perhaps this is precisely the difference between a cheerful and a gloomy asceticism. But perhaps, too, the asceticism of the ascetic priest is the pure essence of the same will that drives the philosopher, perhaps the philosopher's will is only a slightly etiolated form of the priest's will. Nietzsche certainly gives us no reason in the *Genealogy of Morals* to think otherwise. The work that grows within is only the reflection of the philosopher's own being, not a real expenditure of his being into the outside, into the world, into time, but a way of avoiding such expenditure, of addressing a postcard to oneself. The logic of Nietzsche's discussion here is entirely that of Diotima's discourse in the *Symposium,* including the theory of sublimation. The production of the ideal work is a way of avoiding the transit of Eros through the body of the female, thus of avoiding mortality, of gaining immortality. Eros is expended, but it is not wasted, as it would be if it were spent on a woman; and the self that gives itself over to this work is in some mysterious way eternalized there.[13] For his part, the ascetic priest may not produce a work that will issue forth from him, but he too uses an object that is himself differed, used as a feedback loop for his Eros—an object called "God." It seems to be part of the logic of the *Fiam* that there must be a circuit of energy through a kind of false outside (even Narcissus has to have his reflection, in order to send his love forth/back to himself).

Or does the cheerfulness of the philosopher mean that there is in his will no ressentiment, that when he says "*Fiam*" the abolition of the world is only an incidental condition, that there is no vengefulness toward the world or other people or women involved? Does Nietzsche believe this? Do we? Do we believe one can say to someone else "Die, cease to exist, it makes no difference to me; on the contrary, I can get along much better without you—even if you still exist, I will act as though you don't"—do we believe one can say this and do so *without any ill will,* without there being a certain spite in the sentiment behind the utterance, a certain satisfaction as of triumph over the one who is dispensed with because unnecessary? Not that we have to say it to another's face; the satisfaction can be an entirely private one. In fact,

[13]"Those whose procreancy is of the body turn to woman as the object of their love, and raise a family," says Diotima; "Those whose procreancy is of the spirit rather than of the flesh . . . conceive and bear the things of the spirit" (*Symposium* 208e–209a); "And I ask you, who would not prefer such fatherhood to merely human propagation?" (209d).

the more private I keep the satisfaction, the more certain I can be that I *really am* independent from this other. "Every spirit has its own sound and loves its own sound" (*GM* III,8;109–110); thus, as long as I can hear myself and feel my self-contained presence I can feel in my very self-enjoyment in solitude the satisfactions of triumph over the other, over the world.

The name of the bondage that the self must break in order to enjoy itself triumphantly in solitude is *Eros,* desire, sensuality. Desire is what makes me spill my "stores and accumulations of energy, of animal vigor" into a boundless and perfidious outside in which I can be endlessly dispersed. The mask of this devouring outside-in-general, the lure by which it draws me into the foolish investments of desire, is some particular object, and for the ascetic the supreme image of this lure is a woman. The task of mastering the "most profound, powerful and basic conditions" of life is in some way, perhaps essentially, bound up with mastering the desire aroused by the woman, with learning how not to spend one's store of energy in that way.[14]

Is there any connection between the ascetic's project of self-preservation and the vengefulness against time described by Zarathustra? What in fact is Zarathustra saying about time and the will's frustration?

There is a traditional problem of time with which we are familiar, which Nietzsche himself evokes in certain other texts and alludes to here, namely, the problem of transience, which receives its original utterance in our philosophical tradition in the fragment of Anaximander. Nietzsche commented on this fragment and also on Heraclitus's reply to Anaximander in *Philosophy in the Tragic Age of the Greeks.* Anaximander, in Nietzsche's interpretation, considered "all coming-to-be . . . a wrong for which destruction is the only penance" (4). Heraclitus, however, affirmed the innocence of the play of becoming. Nietzsche comments that "the everlasting and exclusive coming-to-be, the impermanence of everything actual, . . . as Heraclitus teaches it, is a terrible, paralyzing thought" (5). This traditional conception of the problem of time also plays a role in Zarathustra's remarks. He speaks of "time's covetousness" and quotes those who go

[14]The *locus classicus* of the struggle of the ascetic will with the desire for a woman is of course book 8 of Augustine's *Confessions,* where Augustine sets forth his profound, and profoundly influential, theory of the will in relation to the "bondage" of his need for sex that is the final and most tenacious barrier against the liberation of his will.

mad with the oppression of time as saying: "Everything passes away; therefore everything deserves to pass away. And this too is justice, this law of time that it must devour its children" (*Z* II,20;252).

But the central conception of Zarathustra's insight is not easily translated into the terms of the problem of transience. Here the cause of "the will's gnashing of teeth and most secret melancholy" is called "it was." The will is "powerless against what has been done" (*Z* II,20;251), thus against what has been in a sense eternalized, what now is, as having been, for all eternity; thus it is a "stone" the will cannot move. Even though Zarathustra slides from this conception into the remarks on "passing away" as though it were all the same problem, the "it was" appears, on the surface at least, to be the opposite of passing away; it is what will *not* pass away even though, or rather because, it is past. Is this a confusion or is there a connection here that Nietzsche has merely implied?

What, precisely, is the nature of the will's quarrel with "it was"? We are told that what it wants is to be able to work on the "it was," to move the stone which is frozen in the fixity of the past, to "will backwards." But why, and to what end? Merely in order to put back into flux what has become static? Or is there something else about what is past, something in addition to its pastness, that makes its pastness an injury and deepest cause of suffering to the will?

If what is past were characterized by perfection, if the past moment were one in which desire had been consummated, then there would be cause for melancholy in the pastness of this past, but it would not be of the form Zarathustra describes. The will would not desire to alter the shape of that moment but rather to retrieve it, make it come again. Thus it must be that the will rages against the past because of its imperfection. Zarathustra says, "This is what is terrible for my eyes, that I find man in ruins and scattered as over a battlefield or a butcher-field. And when my eyes flee from the now to the past, they always find the same: fragments and limbs and dreadful accidents—but no human beings" (*Z* II,20;250). The past is the scene of the rending of humanity, its *sparagmos* and dispersal, and Zarathustra's desire is to bring this dispersal back into a whole, perfect unity: "And this is all my desire and striving, that I create and carry together into One what is fragment and riddle and dreadful accident" (251).

The suffering of the will in relation to "it was" comes not from its pastness as such but from its pastness as imperfect, from the fact that the past is given unredeemably as "fragment and riddle and dreadful accident," that the unity and perfection which are all the will's "desire and striving" have always already been utterly violated. What Zarathustra describes is thus the universal structure of desire and of the frustration of desire.

The frustration of desire belongs structurally to the movement of time. The now of my frustration is necessarily the now in which something has already moved away from me or in which a desired fullness has already been denied me; thus the now of frustration is defined in its essence by its relation to a past-now. The recognition of "it was" comes in the instant of that transitional moment in which I find myself cast out from another moment that *just now* promised what is now removed from the grasp with which I reach out for it. The lost now is irretrievable; there may come a future now which will bring another consummation, but the shattered now that is lost is beyond reparation; for all eternity it will remain *that* shattered now. The fundamental structure of ressentiment is rage against the absoluteness of such violation, inability to forgive time for its injury and thus turn toward the possibility that beckons in the future-now like a perhaps faithless lover. There is an economy that once it has tasted time's perfidy can never again fully entrust its substance to the promise of time. Perhaps it is the only economy there is, a restricted economy that must calculate investment and loss; it is a matter of degree. The ascetic is the one who tries to restrict his economy to the ultimate degree.

In the face of the maenad, time, that would rend him unbearably, the ascetic learns self-preservation, the art of the feedback loop that will give him consummation, unity, the closing of the ring, triumph over a world that can never, will never, satisfy the absolute demand of his desire, a world whose appeal to him finds its essential figure in the seductiveness of women, or a woman. A woman who always goes away, or always *might* go away, whose essence is that she always might go away and who therefore even when she is still here violates the unity of the ring, and who therefore must be sent away, made to go *Fort,* so that the ascetic might become fully, inviolably, present to himself in the fullness of his triumph. The aim of the most spiritual will to power is solitude. Universal unity, the unity of the totality, is the allegory philosophy has always used to name the inviolate fullness of the moment of perfectly consummated desire, but in the real absence of this ideal consummation measures must be taken to ensure that the ring of the self can close upon itself.

But if Zarathustra in these passages speaks in terms of the entire history of humanity, we will eventually have to read his yearning for unity in relation to another yearning that also torments him, but to which he can only allude, for example, in his "Night Song":

> Night has come; only now all the songs of lovers awaken. And my soul too is the song of a lover.
>
> Something unstilled, unstillable is still within me; it wants to be voiced. A craving for love is within me; it speaks the language of love.
>
> Light am I; ah, that I were night! But this is my loneliness that I am girt with light. Ah, that I were dark and nocturnal! How I would suck at the breasts of light! (*Z* II,9;217–18)

Zarathustra now repines at the ascetic ring of self-reflected libido to which he is condemned: "But I live in my own light; I drink back into myself the flames that break out of me." At the same time, his solitude is his glory, it is what he wills, what he must will.

3

The Redemption of History

Zarathustra does not speak of his "thus I willed it" in relation to his own longing for love. He speaks of the history of humanity, of his nausea and pity at the imperfection of his species, and this creates a curious ambiguity. The phenomenon of rage against "it was" is not normally directed against such a large and abstract phenomenon as the desolation that is the history of humanity. As Nietzsche comments in *Human All Too Human,* it is only in "very rare cases—when the genius of skill and understanding merges with the moral genius in the same individual" that a person can feel "those pains that must be seen as the exceptions in the world: the extra-personal, transpersonal feelings, in sympathy with a people, mankind, all civilization, or all suffering existence" (157). The will to vengeance against time is normally a case of vengeance for more personal pains than these, and when Nietzsche speaks of the will that moves stones and makes others suffer the reference seems more fitting as applied to this more personal ressentiment than it would be to the transcendental pains of a Zarathustra.

There is not necessarily any contradiction here, for the structure of the injury of time is the same in both cases; Zarathustra's historical pain may be seen as an expanded version of the other, the same pain in a larger perspective. But it is one thing to suffer for all humanity as for oneself, and quite another thing to affirm, to say "thus I willed it," to the suffering of all humanity as to one's own. If I affirm my own suffering, this may be a salutary psychological phenomenon; I might in this way cease to resent and struggle against the injuries of my past and thus take responsibility for my life in a fuller way than formerly. We understand what it would mean to "will backwards" in the case of our personal past. But what can it mean to affirm the past of humanity? How can Zarathustra "redeem" this past from its fragmented and accidental character by *willing* it thus? If "thus I willed it" means that I will the past as just exactly what it was, then my attitude toward its horror may be more relaxed, but how can my willing in any way alter the horror itself, the horror that history was for those who lived it? How can my will revise anything but its own relation to this horror?

Here we touch for the first time on the deepest level of the question of who it is that speaks in Nietzsche's text. For I have been speaking of the will as one speaks of your will or my will, but here is where Nietzsche's strategy of self-occultation crosses the trajectory of his metaphysics. "The will" as psychological phenomenon is an illusion, the conscious simulacrum of a will that does not belong to you or me but to which we belong. The will to power is the will of life itself, according to Zarathustra. "And life itself confided this secret to me: 'Behold,' it said, 'I am *that which must always overcome itself*' " (*Z* II,12;227).

This transpersonal character of the will would seem to resolve the problem I have raised. The personal will would not be able to redeem history; but there is also life's will, the will to power that wields all living things (and nonliving, too, Nietzsche says in his notes), and this will could do what the personal will cannot.

Let us entertain this hypothesis of a transpersonal will for the moment. But then the question arises of why the transcendent will would need to redeem anything. What does the will care?

Nietzsche knows that the will does not care, that it wastes and disperses humankind without aim or purpose. And in fact to experience this wastage or squandering of humanity would be the highest rapture:

> For mankind, as a whole, has *no* goals and consequently, considering the whole affair, man cannot find his comfort and support in it, but rather his despair. If, in everything he does, he considers the ultimate aimlessness of men, his own activity acquires the character of *squandering* [*Vergeudung*] in his eyes. But to feel squandered as mankind (and not just as an individual), as we see the single blossom squandered by nature, is a feeling above all feelings. (*H* 33)

Yet at other times he tells us that this thought is unbearable, that we must concoct values that will act as a barrier against the indifference of the great economy of the whole:

> Imagine a being like nature, wasteful beyond measure, indifferent beyond measure, without purposes and consideration, without mercy and justice, fertile and desolate and uncertain at the same time; *imagine indifference itself as a power* [emphasis added]—how *could* you live according to this indifference? Living—is that not precisely wanting to be other than this nature? Is not living—estimating, preferring, being unjust, being limited, wanting to be different? (*BGE* 9)

For the great indifferent will of life in general, "the exceptions are not the secret aim" (*GS* 109), and the privilege Nietzsche assigns to the exceptional man is an expression of his partiality, of his "wanting to be other than nature."

Gilles Deleuze's entire interpretation of the affirmative will seems to arise within the space of this partiality of Nietzsche's.[1] Deleuze thus denies that for Nietzsche the transcendent will is indifferent. According to him, will to power is affirmative in its essence, and always therefore on the side of the active, noble agents. The negative is as much a "primordial quality" (54) of will to power as is the affirmative, but this negativity is predestined to "transmute itself into an affirmation" (71) because in fact "only becoming-active has being": "becoming-reactive has no being" (71–72). In the eternal return being is purified of the negative; "the small, petty, reactive man will not return" (71). "The negative expires at the gates of being" (190); Zarathustra "passes through" the negative in order to reach the point where it is "vanquished" (191).

Thus in Deleuze's interpretation the indifference of the grand economy gives way to a full-fledged teleology of the positive. He gets rid of everything that is riddle and dreadful accident; on his account this all turns out to be merely the *Dreck* of the system. The eternal return, he says, is "the being of difference excluding the whole of the negative" (190); but we might wonder what the "difference" is in the being of a difference that has purified itself of the negative. Has the negative not always been precisely that which keeps the same from closing on itself?[2]

[1]Gilles Deleuze, *Nietzsche and Philosophy,* trans. Hugh Tomlinson (New York: Columbia University Press, 1983).

[2]For Deleuze what is wrong with Hegelian dialectic is that its motor is the negative, and this is too much negativity for him (*Nietzsche and Philosophy,* 10–12). The essence must be pure affirmation throughout, and the ultimate *Aufhebung* must be not negation of the negation but "affirmation of the affirmation" (186–89). But when Deleuze tries to eliminate negativity altogether, he does so by consigning it to absolute nonbeing—which is to say, he

When he thinks of the triumph of great, noble, terrible leaders, Nietzsche is not erecting a Deleuzian metaphysics but taking refuge from the reign of chance, the dice-throw of Heraclitean becoming, which in this mood he calls "that gruesome dominion of nonsense and accident that has so far been called 'history.'"

> Anyone who has the rare eye for the over-all danger that "man" himself *degenerates;* anyone who, like us, has recognized the monstrous fortuity that has so far had its way and play regarding the future of man—a game in which no hand, and not even a finger, of God took part as a player;[3] anyone who fathoms the calamity that lies concealed in the absurd guilelessness and blind confidence of "modern ideas" and even more in the whole Christian-European morality—*suffers from an anxiety that is past all comparisons.* (Emphasis added; *BGE* 302)

And yet it must be admitted that Nietzsche leaves the door open for Deleuze's reading. It is as though Deleuze's interpretation were the fulfillment of a wish present in Nietzsche's text, a wish Nietzsche cannot quite indulge but which Deleuze indulges for him. Zarathustra does in fact speak of redeeming the past, of fashioning some meaningful unity out of its meaningless fragmentation, and he does not make it clear whether this redemption would be merely in relation to the one who would then view history as redeemed, or whether in some way history in itself would find redemption. The nondistinction between history "for us" and "in itself" leaves open the possibility of the sort of redemptive metaphysics Deleuze reads in Nietzsche.

It is true that Deleuze makes a distinction between the principle of being, *ratio essendi,* and the principle of manifestation, *ratio cognoscendi,* of the world, and this distinction might seem to correspond to that between history in itself and history for us. The essence of the world as temporality, as becoming, is already, according to Deleuze, affirma-

interprets negativity as pure, nondialectical negation. This is not a step beyond Hegel but a quasi-Augustinian metaphysics: the negative as pure nonbeing, all of humanity as sunken in sinfulness ("man is essentially reactive" [64]), positive being as "the being of the whole of becoming" (72), eschatology of final redemption for the elect (the "noble"), and condemnation to nonbeing for the damned ("the small, petty, reactive man [71]).

[3]Is Nietzsche complaining about this? It seems oddly as though he were; though at the same time there is a momentary upsurge of his characteristic malicious satisfaction in the rhetorical embellishment of "and not even a finger". The tone is something like petulant satisfaction, a mixture of complaint and taunt.

tion; affirmation is its *ratio essendi.* But in fact this real essence is hidden from us, we know will to power only in its negative form, its *ratio cognoscendi,* as the will to nothingness (172–73). "We can say that negation has dominated our thought, our ways of feeling and evaluating, up to the present day." But Deleuze confuses his own distinction when he goes on to say that negation, the *ratio cognoscendi,* is in fact "constitutive of man." "And with man the whole world sinks and sickens, the whole of life is depreciated, everything known slides towards its own nothingness" (176–77).

Earlier Deleuze had written in the same vein that "the essence of man *and of the world occupied by man* is the becoming reactive of all forces, nihilism and nothing but nihilism" (169). Negation, which is only the principle of manifestation of will to power, is also said to be the *essence* of "the world," even though the essence is really affirmation and negation is only the way in which this essence is given to our knowledge. How can we understand this except in terms of that most fundamental of metaphysical distinctions, the one most decried by Nietzsche, the distinction between a real, intelligible world (which Deleuze tells us we "think") and a merely apparent world (the object of an apparently limited and ultimately deluded "knowing")? "We 'think' the will to power in a form distinct from that in which we 'know' it" (173); "the negative shoots out from [the affirmative] like lightning, but also becomes absorbed into it, disappearing into it like a soluble fire" (176). Furthermore, "affirmation is only manifested above man, outside man, in the Overman" (177). "Above," "outside," and "over" man and the world he causes to "sicken": this means quite literally that affirmation is *transcendent.* (Nietzsche warns us against these adverbs: "every . . . craving for some Apart, Beyond, Outside, Above, permits the question whether it was not sickness that inspired the philosopher" [*GS* Preface;34]. And if he conceives the overman, he also has Zarathustra say: "All gods are poets' parables, poets' prevarication. Verily, it always lifts us higher—specifically, to the realm of the clouds: upon these we place our motley bastards and call them gods and overmen" [*Z* II,17;240].)

So on Deleuze's reading affirmation is the real, hidden essence of the real world as it really is, and negation is the essence of what Deleuze describes as a temporary, merely apparent world which "shoots out" from and is resolved into the real being that surrounds it and transcends it. For affirmation to accomplish its work of "transmutation" of negative to positive, it merely "relates [*rapporte*] the negative to affirmation in the will to power," thus turning the negative into "a simple mode of being of the powers of affirming" (191). The hinge of Deleuze's entire argument is this mysterious act of "relating" by which the negativity of the world is made to vanish into affirmative being. Whatever this act might be, it is clear that Deleuze interprets Zarathustra's yes metaphysically, as a function of being itself. History would in a sense be self-redemptive; its own hidden essence would reassert itself in the end. This resolves the problem of how Zarathustra's affirmation can redeem history, but Deleuze's solution in order to carry conviction apparently requires faith in a transcendent principle which will do the job for us.

If we reject or find incomprehensible such a solution, does it follow that Nietzschean affirmation is purely psychological? Is history redeemable only "for us" and not "in itself"? Isn't it true that Nietzsche holds that all becoming is will to power and all will to power is affirmative, and does it not therefore follow that Deleuze is right to conclude that for Nietzsche being is self-redemptive?

It is true that for Nietzsche all power is affirmative, but not in a way that yields the Deleuzian drama of the triumph of nobility. The affirmation of the indifferent will is as much beyond positivity and negativity as it is beyond good and evil. This means that negativity cannot be a "primordial quality" of will to power, and there can be no detour of the affirmative will, such that it gives way to a negativity that would be its own delegate or lying representative, in order then to return to itself (the detour described by Deleuze). On the other hand, if there is no detour through the negative, neither does the affirmation of will to power have anything to do with the triumph of the noble, preservation of the higher, and achievement of the *telos*.

But what sort of comfort can we take in such an affirmation, this terrifying affirmation that is identical with indifference, "indifference itself as a power," the process by which mankind is squandered, wasted, dispersed, left as fragment and dreadful accident? Human beings experience this great affirmation as suffering, as "the law of time that it must devour its children."

To learn to call the indifference to suffering and death of the life force in general "affirmation" can only be a way of stimulating an intense form of self-affection; when Zarathustra speaks of redeeming history by an act of will he can indeed only mean history for us.

Zurückwollen, whether it means "to will backwards" or "to will back, to will the Return," must be a realignment of the elements in one's own conscious economy or consciousness of one's own economy. The past moment which violated the positivity of my desire called out from me a negating act of will, an act that condemned that moment and aimed at vengeance against it. Now I must confront this past moment once again and reconcile myself with it, and, beyond this, learn to affirm what was formerly negated. If I can see all willing as will to power and all will to power as affirmation, I can find an affirmation hidden in my former negative willing. This is not the "relating" of one metaphysical principle to another but an awakening to the truth of my deepest desire behind all its masks, detours, and subterfuges: the desire of the self to touch itself, to enjoy the sensation of its being or becoming "at the bottom of every event" and in so doing to achieve "a sense of triumph" in the experience of every moment (*WP* 55).

Yet this explanation resolves nothing; instead, it places us once again at the beginning point of our inquiry. If Nietzsche's or, perhaps, anyone's, desire is fractured in its deepest interiority, if there is always another economic subterfuge, if "thus I willed it" can always conceal an impulse of vengefulness within its affirmation, then the moment of pure affirmation could be conceived only as a regulative idea and the actuality could always begin to decompose under psychoanalytic or psychodialectical scrutiny.

And still our original problem remains. For each of us to redeem our own relation to our personal past and to the past in general might turn us away from nihilism, give us strength, make us affirmers of life. But as regards the past in general this affirmation has not been thought through very seriously or in any detail, either by Nietzsche or by those of his interpreters who blithely tell us that "the eternal recurrence signifies my ability to want my life *and the whole world* [emphasis added] to be repeated just as they are."[4] Here the world appears as a spectacle, an awful spectacle perhaps, but still something judged only in relation to the spectator who unilaterally affirms or denies it. But what about the *inwardness* of this world, the subjectivity of each experiencing being which is itself an absolute origin of the world? Might there not be such a thing as terror so overwhelming that the sufferer

[4]Alexander Nehamas, *Nietzsche: Life as Literature* (Cambridge: Harvard University Press, 1985), 191.

cannot or will not affirm it, and in that case who can affirm it on his or her behalf? We cannot answer this question with any doctrinal generalization about how affirmation must somehow lurk in the deepest heart of all suffering.

So we are thrown back once more to the question of Nietzsche's economy and the impact of history on this economy. We must be careful to qualify the formula concerning the eternal recurrence. It signifies my ability to want my life and the whole world insofar as the world impinges on *me,* insofar as it is hard for *me* to swallow, to be repeated just as they are.

4

Nietzsche's Politics

Nietzsche vacillates between two senses of affirmation, the sense in which it includes and overflows both affirmation and negation and the other sense in which it is opposed to negation. It is this vacillation that makes Nietzsche's political views such an equivocal inheritance for us. The former sense generates a politics of generosity and inclusiveness, the latter a politics of reaction, defensiveness, and exclusion. It is no accident that his work has from the beginning been appropriated by the Right and the Left alike, by anti-Semites and Nazis as is well known, but also, as Hinton Thomas reminds us in an extraordinarily interesting historical reconstruction, by socialists, feminists, and anarchists.[1]

Two valuable books have recently struggled to untangle these two threads of Nietzsche's text in order to liberate from it the force of a political affirmation that would be consonant with contemporary left-liberal ideology: *Beyond Nihilism* by Ofelia Schutte and *Nietzsche and Political Thought* by Mark Warren.[2] (These two books should be read in conjunction with Hinton Thomas's *Nietzsche in German Politics and Society*, so that we may be aware that these are not merely academic issues, that there is nothing arbitrary about the attempt to read liberalism or even revolutionary radicalism in Nietzsche; this is a genuine historical effect that

[1]R. Hinton Thomas, *Nietzsche in German Politics and Society, 1890–1918* (Manchester: Manchester University Press, 1983).

[2]Ofelia Schutte, *Beyond Nihilism: Nietzsche without Masks* (Chicago: University of Chicago Press, 1984); and Mark Warren, *Nietzsche and Political Thought* (Cambridge: MIT Press, 1988).

Nietzsche has had from the outset, one just as real as, if less momentous than, the fascist effect which he has also had.) I concentrate my remarks on Schutte's book because it is overtly polemical, castigating Nietzsche scholarship in general for ignoring the authoritarian bent of much of Nietzsche's thought. I am critical of Schutte's approach, however, precisely because her project in certain ways parallels my own. I think Schutte is right to emphasize the questionableness of Nietzsche's political attitudes, and to remind us how often and at what length Nietzsche descants on politics in a way that must be profoundly repellent to the moral community that Schutte assumes as her audience. These political statements are not just casual or ancillary remarks in Nietzsche's text; they are intimately woven into the texture of his thought in its entirety.

But there is something problematic about Schutte's own stance. She speaks as though there were simply an incorrect morality and a correct one, the incorrect characterizable as inhuman, sexist, and authoritarian, the other just the opposite, so that she can simply display the correct views before our eyes, ticking them off one after the other, and we approve or disapprove on cue.

The question of economy reasserts itself here, expanding to include the scene of Schutte's reading and then also the scene of our reading of Schutte's reading. Who is Schutte, and who are we, that we can recite our moral beliefs in unison? And what authority have these beliefs over certain views Nietzsche expresses which stick in the craw of our moral being?

Our moral beliefs did not fall from heaven and neither are they credentials we can flash like a badge to establish our moral probity. Consider all the rest of human history, including most of the planet at the present moment. What are we to say about this overwhelming spectacle of cruelty, stupidity, and suffering? What stance is there for us to adopt with respect to history, what judgment can we pass on it? Is it all a big mistake? Christianity attempted to recuperate the suffering of history by projecting a divine plan that assigns it a reason now and a recompense later, but liberalism is too humane to endorse this explanation. There is no explanation, only the brute fact. But the brute fact we are left with is even harder to stomach than the old explanation. So Left liberalism packages it in a new narrative, a moral narrative according to which all those lives ground up in the machine of history are assigned an intelligible role as victims of oppression and injustice. There is an implicit teleology in this view; modern Left liberalism is the telos that gives form and meaning to the rest of history. Only very recently is it possible for someone like Schutte to write as she does, with so much confidence that the valuations she assumes will be received as a matter of course by an academic audience, just as much as a Christian homilist writing for an audience of the pious. And only within the protective enclosure of this community of belief can there be any satisfaction in the performance of this speech act, any sense that anything worthwhile has been accomplished by the recitation. When this moral community by means of such recitation reassures itself of its belief, it comes aglow as the repository of the meaning of history, as the locus that one may occupy in order to view history and pass judgment on it without merely despairing or covering one's eyes and ears. There may not be any plan behind history, nor any way of making up their losses to the dead, but we can draw an invisible line of rectitude through history and in this way take power over it. Against the awesome "Thus it was" of history we set the overawing majesty of "Thus it *ought to have been.*"

But our liberalism is something that sprang up yesterday and could be gone tomorrow. The day before yesterday the Founding Fathers kept black slaves. What little sliver of light is this we occupy that despite its contingency, the frailty of its existence, enables us to illuminate all the past and perhaps the future as well? For we want to say that even though our community of belief may cease to exist, this would not affect the validity of those beliefs. The line of rectitude would still traverse history.

It is certainly not my intention to berate liberalism on the basis of a historical relativism that would restrict the validity of moral evaluations to their respective consensual communities. My point is rather that only an implicit confidence in the historically transcendent validity of liberal valuations makes possible the continued belief in and assertion of these valuations, and this confidence is itself made possible by the continued self-reassurance of the valuing community through this same repeated assertion of valuations. But our lever of valuation needs a fulcrum if it is to move history, and the fulcrum which is the valuing community is itself located within history. For a member of this community to confront the absolute historical contingency of the existence of this community, and thus of its *acts* of valuation, may be to experience vertigo with respect to the question of the historically transcendent worth of the values on which these acts of valuation are based. It is the vertigo of the possibility that I might not have been this very moral subject which in fact I am, because my moral stance is the contingent product of this moral community to which I belong, and if I think myself into some other historically constituted time and place I cannot recognize myself there. It is only an accident that I have been born into this here and now, and yet if I had been born into another time or place, it would not have been *I*—if, that is, I am in my being, my essence, *this* moral subject, and not merely the hollow shell of this body which could as easily have housed some murderous barbarian or Nazi. What we since yesterday have come to think of as outrage and atrocity is the normal fact of human history and has rarely interfered with the good conscience of its perpetrators, who could, as Nietzsche says, "emerge from a disgusting procession of murder, arson, rape, and torture, exhilarated and undisturbed of soul, as if it were no more than a students' prank, convinced they have provided the poets with a lot more material for song and praise" (*GM* I,11;40).

I emphasize that I am not arguing a relativist thesis here but commenting on a psychological phenomenon. If the self experiences too vividly the reality of history, history may threaten to overwhelm the boundaries of the sense of self. There must therefore be some economic strategy by means of which the threat of intrusion of the disruptive quantities of energy can be dealt with. I have already described the normative strategy that draws the barrier of a judgment of condemnation across the flood of history. The "most powerful and tremendous nature," on the other hand, Nietzsche says in the essay "The Uses and Disadvantages of History," would not be overwhelmed at all by the historical sense but could absorb all of the past (*UM* II,1;63). Nietzsche aspired to be such a nature, one who could confront the overwhelming expanse of what has been and say yes to all of it. Yet he was always in danger of being overwhelmed by such a confrontation.

This is a purely contingent fact about the economy of the text named "Nietzsche." Is it then no more than a biographical curiosity? What relevance can it possibly have to an analysis of his "political views"? Aren't those views a matter of principle—something that has to be detached from the emotional idiosyncrasies that afflict the thinker? If, on the other had, a thinker's thoughts are not detachable from his or her psychological makeup, then they have no claim on our attention as "thought" at all; they are merely symptoms or expressive phenomena. Yet the pure contingency of the subject is precisely what we must now learn to think, impelled as we are by that current of thought of which Nietzsche is the beginning. To treat Nietzsche's "views" in isolation from the whole psychodialectical economy of his writing is effectively to deny the validity of Nietzsche's critique of idealizing rationality. It makes no sense to give a discursive account of this critique, praising Nietzsche for his achievement, and then proceed to give another discursive account of Nietzsche's "political thought" of the sort one would have given if Nietzsche's critique did not exist. Yet this is routinely done. His views are discussed as though they were propositional entities inhabiting a consciousness that viewed them and was their owner, these entities then being re-viewable by us as the proper objects of our investigation within the overall field called "Nietzsche's thought." These objects could then be manipulated, compared to other objects of the same type, and so on.

In our nonmoral investigation of Nietzsche's economy, instead of putting Nietzsche's "views" on display we want to describe the rhythms according to which they come into play and then disappear, and the patterns of libido, anxiety, and aggression that regulate these rhythms.

Nietzsche cannot bear his vision of the savagery and meaninglessness of history. If he were to view history from a standpoint of humane liberalism, this would be to judge on the basis of sympathy, of a sense of shared suffering, *Mitleid*. This *Mitleid*, derived from Christianity, is the foundation or fountainhead of humane liberalism—it tells me that there is a qualitative parity between persons, that this beggar or this woman or this white middle-class academic feels what I feel (cf. *WP* 765). Even Benthamite hedonistic calculation, for all its apparently abstract and mechanical character, assumes qualitative equality of pleasure and pain across individuals, an assumption unthinkable except against the background of Christian liberal *Mitleid*, which provides the necessary homogenization of subjectivity that makes possible the notion of masses of pleasure and pain quantifiable across entire populations.

Nietzsche is incapable of failing to draw the fullest consequences from such *Mitleid*. If he opens himself to it, he opens himself to an unbearable flood of suffering. We can only judge history if we do not feel too vividly the reality concerning which we judge. Our compassion must not become too real, we must be a bit obtuse or lacking in imagination. If we were to feel in its full reality the grief of even one mother for the child that is slaughtered before her eyes we would not be able to bear it. How infinitely less could we bear even a glimpse of all the enslavements and holocausts of history, to say nothing of the infinitude of private and domestic tragedies and the savagery of the ordinary course of animal nature. What barrier could the moral consciousness erect that would withstand the horror of such a glimpse?

Nietzsche's problem is "economic" here in the starkest sense of the notion, the sense imagined by Freud in terms of the "undifferentiated vesicle" of *Beyond the Pleasure Principle,* whose problem is how to ward off or bind the quantities of disruptive energy flowing into it from outside. That which we call "Nietzsche" is an extraordinarily, almost incredibly, sensitive substance, whose endeavor from beginning to end is to bind the flood of painful stimuli called "life" by becoming the "most powerful and tremendous nature" who could absorb it all. Our concern here is not with Nietzsche's sensitivity as a moral virtue; Nietzsche himself would be the first to argue that there is nothing moral in such a characteristic. But we can understand nothing about the economy of Nietzsche's text if we are not alert to the way in which its movements are motivated by strategies for managing the pain to which this sensitivity makes Nietzsche so vulnerable. Not infrequently these strategies produce a brutal coarseness in Nietzsche's stance; but the object "Nietzsche" or "Nietzsche's thought" is strangely flattened out if we just point to this quality in some of "Nietzsche's views" as though it were simply a moral flaw and the views merely intellectually erroneous.

In order to see the difference it makes whether we do or do not ignore the question of economy, let us take a detailed look at an early essay, originally projected as the second part of *The Birth of Tragedy,* which appears under various names in the various editions of Nietzsche's works. I refer to the text published in volume 3 of the Musarion edition as "The Means Employed by the Hellenic Will in Order to Reach its Goal, the Genius" (hereafter abbreviated as "The Hellenic Will").[3] Schutte has drawn some of her most damning evidence of Nietzsche's reactionary tendencies from portions of this draft which Nietzsche in 1872 turned into an essay called "The Greek State" (one of the "Five Prefaces for Unwritten Books"); Mark Warren, too, draws on these remarks.

Here is Schutte's account of Nietzsche's remarks in "The Greek State":

> [Nietzsche] praised the Greeks for their dependence on slavery, arguing that slavery is required for the flourishing of art and culture. . . . Nietzsche argued in favor of increasing the misery of "toiling men" so as to facilitate for a small number of "olympic men" the production of the

[3]The version of this "essay" published in the Musarion edition comprises (with some differences, mostly stylistic) two fragments published in *KGW,* III 3:347–63 and 175–87. I do not know how the consecutive version published by Musarion was formulated, but it is apparently authorized by an outline drawn up by Nietzsche (*KGW,* III 3:141–42), which provides section headings and the title ("Die Mittel des hellenischen Willens, um sein Ziel, den Genius zu erreichen") used for the consecutive version. As published in *KGW,* it is not immediately apparent that the two fragments form a connected discussion; that is why I have used the Musarion version.

> "*Kunstwelt*." He offers an economic argument for this. . . . Nietzsche takes an elitist stand against labor.[4]

Schutte quotes Nietzsche extensively to support her commentary, and these quotations are chosen in such a way that they do indeed seem to clinch her argument. Warren does not underline the repellent character of Nietzsche's conclusions, but his representation of them is of the same type as Schutte's; it is purely a matter of Nietzsche's premises and conclusions, claims and beliefs.[5]

What these accounts leave out is the tone of horrified fascination with which Nietzsche presents his observations. There is something terrible (*entsetzlich*) mixed with the beauty of nature; to investigate these matters arouses horror (*Schauder*) (Musarion, 3:277). In order that an "unbelievably meager minority" (*unglaublich geringen Minderheit*) of humans might flourish, the slavery of the vast majority is necessary. Our modern nostrums concerning the "dignity of man" and "dignity of labor" conceal the reality that "frightful need compels to labor that consumes the worker" (*furchtbare Noth zwingt zu verzehrender Arbeit*) and perpetuates the suffering of a miserable existence (*elendes Leben*). History shows us that despite occasional outbreaks of compassionate love the same cruelty (*Grausamkeit*) continually reasserts itself, the walls of culture harden once again, and the process is repeated. "Therefore we might compare dominant culture to a victor who reeks of blood, who drags the vanquished along as slaves in his triumphal procession, fettered to his car, their eyes blinded by a beneficent power so that, nearly crushed by the wheels of the car, they still cry out, 'dignity of labor!' 'dignity of human beings!'" (282).

This is not the sort of thing typically said by those who want to make excuses for the way things are. Nietzsche's remarks on the brutal reality underlying culture do not sound like the statements of a conservative apologist; culture is little more than a veneer to Nietzsche in these pages, and there is none of that pious regard for the refinements of culture typically associated with conservative apologetics. Not only does the victor reek of blood, but no matter how high the attainment of culture, the nature of life remains the same.

> The Greeks do not need such hallucinated concepts [as the "dignity of mankind" or of "labor"] because among them it is declared with alarm-

[4]Schutte, *Beyond Nihilism,* 166–67.
[5]Warren, *Nietzsche and Political Thought,* 68, 238–39.

> ing frankness that work is a shameful thing [*Schmach*]—and added on to this is a more hidden and more seldom spoken, but universally living bit of wisdom, that the human thing is an ignominious and miserable nothing and the "dream of a shadow." Work is a shameful thing because existence [*Dasein*] has no intrinsic value. (278)

It should be apparent how inadequate it is to categorize what Nietzsche's reflections express in this essay simply as "an elitist stand against labor." Culture is a beautiful illusion built on the blood of the oppressed; slavery is a "vulture that gnaws at the liver of the promethean advancer of culture" (281). If the forces of history that govern this situation were not inescapable,

> contempt for culture, glorification of the poverty of the spirit, iconoclastic annihilation of the claims of culture would be more than a revolt of oppressed masses against drone-like individuals: it would be the outcry of compassion which would tear down the walls of culture; the drive for justice, for uniform distribution [*Gleichmass*] of suffering, would drown all other ideas [*alle anderen Vorstellungen überfluthen*]. (281)

To get the full resonance of Nietzsche's tone here we need to keep in mind that these passages were originally intended as part of *The Birth of Tragedy,* a text that can be viewed as the nostalgic evocation of the unity of humanity that Nietzsche in "The Hellenic Will" declares unattainable in reality: "Under the charm of the Dionysian . . . the union between man and man is reaffirmed. . . . Now the slave is a free man. . . . In song and in dance man expresses himself as a member of a higher community" (*BT* I;37).[6]

[6]Nietzsche's vision of this Dionysian *communitas* is purely nonpolitical, and it seems clear that he has consciously depoliticized it. In an illuminating essay, Maria A. Simonelli reviews Nietzsche's debt to Creuzer, Welcker, and Bachhofen for his concept of the Dionysian and observes that "Welcker analyzes with clarity and precision the social dimension of the god's cult: Dionysus, in the intoxication that always accompanies his celebrations, infuses courage into the rural populace and makes them able to rebel against the rulers from whom they demand equality and liberty. Of course Welcker is perfectly aware that the Dionysus cult cannot be considered the actual cause of rebellion of a subject class, but it is nevertheless natural that the country populace should attribute to their god everything that they have succeeded in gaining and that they should celebrate him as 'the liberator' and 'giver of equality in a material sense'"; "Alle radici del dionisiaco Nietzscheano," in *Friedrich Nietzsche: O la verità come problema,* ed. Giorgio Penzo (Bologna: Pàtron Editore, 1984), 150–51.

Nietzsche thus does not "praise" slavery as an economic arrangement; he seizes upon it as a desperate expedient in his flight from nihilistic despair at the spectacle of history. Nietzsche is speaking of himself in *The Birth of Tragedy* when he describes the "profound Hellene, uniquely susceptible to the tenderest and deepest suffering," who "having looked boldly right into the terrible destructiveness of so-called world history as well as the cruelty of nature" is "in danger of longing for a Buddhistic negation of the will" (VII;59). We might feel that there is a self-glorifying sentimentality behind these and similar remarks, or that oversensitivity is no justification for the adoption of a reactive stance. But our concern here is not to blame or to praise Nietzsche but rather to map the forces of his economy. To this task we now return.

5

Power and Pleasure

We see in the writings from the early 1870s the earliest expression of the economic dilemma with which Nietzsche struggled to the very end—the problem of how to stomach history as he imagines it, as the totality of affect of suffering humanity, how to keep from vomiting it back up when he tries to swallow it. (This is, incidentally, not a casual image: Nietzsche's references to the stomach are pervasive, and in *BGE* 230 he speaks of "a spirit's power to appropriate" as "its 'digestive capacity'" and adds that "'the spirit' is relatively most similar to a stomach.") There is no God, no meaning behind history. There is this spectacle that we see, and this is life. We can either condemn it because it doesn't measure up to our requirements, or ignore it, or try to work out strategies by which to manage the quantities of pain to which a profound consciousness of history would be subjected. But what has to be accepted is from any human perspective, no matter how nonmoral, a wastefulness and violation beyond measure, and to accept it seems to require what Nietzsche in a note calls "the voluptuousness of the martyr" (*WP* 417), very nearly indistinguishable from the Dionysian experience of *The Birth of Tragedy*.

But as deeply as Nietzsche is moved toward the Dionysian, he recoils from it, tries to take refuge from the immense squandering of life expressed by the Dionysian *sparagmos*. *The Birth of Tragedy* in fact focuses on the necessity of the Apollonian palliation of the unbearable Dionysian reality. Whereas this doctrine of the Apollonian is immediately left behind, there is another form of refuge to which Nietzsche always flees. When history threatens to overwhelm him, he tries to contain the threat, to master it, by betting on the masters, setting the conqueror and the genius on top of the heap where they can give form to the flood of meaningless suffering arising from the struggle for existence. Already by 1871 in "The Hellenic Will" we find his idealization of the masters grounded in what he does not yet theorize as, but clearly describes in terms of, will to power:

> In the indefinable greatness and power of . . . conquerors the observer notices that they are only the medium of a purpose that reveals itself in them yet hides itself from them. Just as though a magic Will proceeded from them, so puzzlingly quickly do the weaker forces attach themselves to them, so marvelously, in the sudden swell of that avalanche of power, under the spell of that creative core, do they transform themselves to an affinity that was not until then present. . . .
>
> Here we see, as the most universal effect of the tendency to make war, an immediate separation and dividing-up of the chaotic masses into military castes, out of which the construction of the "warlike society" arises in the form of a pyramid resting on a most extensive slavelike stratum that lies at the very bottom. The unconscious purpose of the entire movement forces each individual under its yoke and produces also in heterogeneous natures an as it were chemical transformation of their properties, until they are brought into affinity with that purpose. (Musarion, 3:284, 291–92)

Bernd Magnus has argued that it is questionable how seriously Nietzsche finally took the idea of will to power as anything more than a "psychological or organic" principle.[1] But we can see from this early discussion how Nietzsche's thought already gravitates toward the notion of a transcendent will to power that resurfaces in his later ontological speculations.

Nevertheless, since Nietzsche's earlier ontology is strongly Schopenhauerian, the transcendent will in the notebooks from the early 1870s is not a will to power but a will that suffers, an *Urleiden* or primordial suffering. We might thus draw a sharp contrast between the earlier and the later metaphysics of will in Nietzsche's notebooks, the earlier cor-

[1]Bernd Magnus, "The Use and Abuse of *The Will to Power*," in *Reading Nietzsche*, ed. Robert C. Solomon and Kathleen M. Higgins (New York: Oxford University Press, 1988), 226.

responding to the Dionysian and the later to the tyrannophilic aspects of his economy.

And yet there is also a profound continuity between these two conceptions of the transcendent will, a continuity that suggests that Nietzsche's concern is ultimately with something beyond either power or suffering.

In the notes from the period of *The Birth of Tragedy* Nietzsche keeps ruminating the idea that pain is the true metaphysical reality. There is only one metaphysical subject of this pain, therefore the phenomenal pain felt by phenomenal individuals is only a *Vorstellung* of the One True Pain. Sympathy (*Mitleid*) in the usual sense is only a pale echo of the reality of the ultimate ontological unity of all pain. Most important, Nietzsche describes pain as the true self-affection or experience by the self of itself (*Selbstempfindung*). The self alone by itself is aware of itself, keeps company with itself, as pain; pain is true being: *Der Schmerz ist das wahrhafte Sein d. h. Selbstempfindung* (Musarion, 3:333).

Nietzsche's later turn toward joyous affirmation of existence is not, as it may appear to be, radically discontinuous with this metaphysics. Zarathustra will declare that "even if woe is deep, joy is deeper yet than agony" (*Z* IV,19;434), but this is not the mere inversion it seems to be of the metaphysics of pain because "so rich is joy that it thirsts for woe" and "wants agony" (IV,19;435–36). Zarathustra's affirmation is thus a deepening rather than a rejection of the tragic Dionysian. Given the tendency of joy and pain to spill over into each other, the emphasis on one or the other is not as conclusive as it might seem. Joy "wants agony" because it "wants *itself*" (IV,19;436); all affect of whatever sort confirms the *Selbstempfindung* of the "self-enjoying soul [*selbst-lustige Seele*]" (III,10;302).

The notion of self-enjoyment thus in a way names the central problem of Nietzsche's thought from beginning to end. It is the problem of how to think a pleasure that transcends the distinction between pleasure and pain, that may in fact reach the limit of its pleasurableness with the most painful experience possible. In the notes collected in *The Will to Power* Nietzsche repeatedly emphasizes that "pleasure and displeasure are . . . value judgments of the second rank" (*WP* 701), "mere epiphenomena" that follow from the striving after power (702). In this register Nietzsche argues that the opposition between pleasure and displeasure is derivative and inconsequential; pleasure is not the object of striving because both pleasure and pain are comprehended within the increase of power that every organism desires. But Nietzsche also speaks of pleasure as the affect of this all-comprehending phenomenon of increase of power. Pleasure and displeasure are really "false opposites"; pleasure in the deepest sense *includes* displeasure because the feeling of power actually "constitutes the essence of pleasure" (699; cf. 658, 695, 696). And Nietzsche almost always speaks of will to power as self-enjoyment, as the pleasurable *feeling* necessarily experienced by whatever grows in power. "every living thing reaches out as far from itself with its force as it can, and overwhelms what is weaker: thus it takes pleasure in itself" (769); "the whole organism is . . . a complex of systems struggling for an increase of the feeling of power" (703); "the feeling of increase, the feeling of becoming stronger . . . only from this feeling does there arise the will to struggle" (649); "*to feel stronger*—or in other words, joy" (917).

It is in connection with the notion of self-enjoyment that we should understand Nietzsche's description of will to power as "the primitive form of affect" (*WP* 688) and as "a *pathos*" (635). (Notice, too, the strangeness of his calling this most essentially active of principles a *pathos*!) Perhaps the most revealing statement of the way in which the thought of self-enjoyment lies at the root of that of will to power is in *Will to Power* 55:

> Every basic character trait that is encountered at the bottom of every event, that finds expression in every event, would have to lead every individual who experienced it as his own basic character trait to welcome every moment of universal existence with a sense of triumph. The crucial point would be that one experienced this basic character trait in oneself as good, valuable—with pleasure.

These remarks speak of *every* trait of *every* individual; hence they should justify not only the aggressive, appropriative instincts but also those of the inward-turned, ascetic energy, which is also an expression of will to power. But, as we saw in our reading of the *Genealogy of Morals,* this reflexive, self-cruel turn of active will to power gives Nietzsche a headache, and he keeps trying to lift a principle of pure activeness out of the morasses into which his own thought keeps leading him. Thus in the paragraphs immediately following the passage just cited Nietzsche slides away from what he has just called a "pantheistic affirmation of all things" and restricts his affirmation to the triumph of the strong.

Here as elsewhere will to power and self-enjoyment coexist uneasily in Nietzsche's text. Sometimes they function as synonyms, but sometimes the notion of self-enjoyment opens the door to a passive, ascetic, or decadent kind of enjoyment that conflicts with the notion of will to power in its narrower sense as active appropriativeness. This uneasy coexistence persists because Nietzsche never decides whether power is willed as a means to the end of self-enjoyment or self-enjoyment is a pleasure that merely "supervenes," as Aristotle says, on the acquisition of power. In the first case, self-enjoyment would be the real aim of will to power, in the latter the real aim would be power itself. Nietzsche slides from one concept to the other without noticing the difference: "Life . . . strives after a *maximal feeling of power;* essentially a striving for more power; striving is nothing other than striving for power" (*WP* 689).[2] He speaks as though power were simply identical with the pleasurable affect that is the feeling of power: thus, whenever we see power, we know that there must be self-enjoyment; conversely, whenever we see self-enjoyment, we know there must be power. The two concepts redefine each other: we learn something about the nature of power, and also something about the nature of self-enjoyment, by the collocation of the two.

But the matter is not so simple, because even though Nietzsche notionally identifies self-enjoyment with the feeling of heightened power, the divergent semantic domains of the two concepts continue

[2]There is one note in which Nietzsche appears to decide unambiguously the relation between pleasure and power. In *WP* 688 he writes that "pleasure is only a symptom of the feeling of power attained, a consciousness of a difference (—there is no striving for pleasure: but pleasure supervenes when that which is being striven for is attained: pleasure is an accompaniment, pleasure is not the motive—)." The remark is, however, not as conclusive as it may look. In the first place, it is not clear in which sense of "pleasure" Nietzsche is speaking here, pleasure in the ordinary sense, in which case this is merely a restatement of his consistent view that pleasure is only an epiphenomenon, or pleasure in the deep sense, as the self-enjoyment intrinsic to the exercise of power. Since the pleasure in question is that which accompanies "the feeling of power," it seems at first sight that Nietzsche is explicitly demoting the deepest pleasure to the role of mere "symptom." However, the ambiguity is re-inscribed in the phrase "*feeling* of power," which refers us once more to the affect, the *Selbstempfindung* or *Selbstgenuss* that belongs intrinsically to the acquisition of power and which thus is difficult to define as a mere "accompaniment" of that which is truly striven for. Pleasure thus appears to function as the supplement, in the Derridean sense of the term, of will to power: it is added on as something not belonging to the essence of will to power, and yet it is also what most deeply characterizes will to power. The problematic of pleasure and will to power should be considered in relation to the *Nichomachean Ethics* 10.1–7.

in certain crucial contexts to attract divergent analyses from him. The problem arises from the fact that the semantic domain of the concept of power includes the concepts of "appropriation," "overwhelming," "overcoming resistance," and "domination", concepts that turn up frequently in Nietzsche's characterizations of will to power. But these concepts connote primarily a relation to an otherness, a something outside the self, that is appropriated, overwhelmed, and so on. Nietzsche is very strongly drawn to precisely these connotations of power, and this is why the inward turn of the ascetic becomes a problematic and ambiguous phenomenon for him. The ascetic will is a type of will to power, yet in relation to the normative, outward-directed form it seems to be a perversion or pathology. Nietzsche is sometimes able to assimilate it to his normative model by thinking it as a *reflexive* form: it is *self*-overcoming, a *self*-domination, and, especially in *Zarathustra,* Nietzsche can take this reflexive form and think it in a way that goes beyond ascetic ideals. Nevertheless, the idea of power in its simpler, apparently more "natural" form always retains its hold on Nietzsche's imagination, acting like a magnet that draws him away from the more radical investigation of the deepest nature of self-enjoyment.[3]

[3]The couple weakness/power ramifies complexly in various directions in Nietzsche's writing, and because Nietzsche never makes explicit the system of these ramifications he allows himself to exploit inconsistent and contradictory implications of the terms. In the *Genealogy of Morals* Nietzsche emphasizes physical power in its most primitive form as "powerful corporeality," *mächtige Leiblichkeit* (I,7;33), but the concept of physical power is ambiguous. It may refer to any of the following things: (1) The strength of the musculature of an individual person. Even here we would have to take into consideration psychological factors, such as a warlike or timid spirit, and the extension of physical strength through skill with weapons. (2) The efficacy of the physical effort of an individual as a member of a group. Nietzsche always fears the possibility that the weak might be strong by virtue of superior numbers; it seems to him to violate the natural order (*WP* 685; *Twi* IX,14;523). (3) Finally, physical power wielded by one who makes no effort of his musculature at all—or at least no more than is required for the issuing of commands. Caesar and Napoleon are physically unimposing men who have positions of command within a political order. They can release their urges by affecting the material world in whatever way they wish to affect it; yet now the connection with *mächtige Leiblichkeit* has been all but lost. We are now in the realm of intellectual or "spiritual" qualities that make a man a leader. But in Nietzsche's initial split between noble and priestly/slavish economies, intellect and spirit belong to the ressentiment economy, and though Nietzsche does not always hold to this definition he is always drawn to it and repeatedly affirms it (see note 13, this chapter).

Thus, as the notion of healthy physical strength unfolds into its highest and most fulfilled form in the conqueror, it also comes back into contact with that which is its antithesis or deconstructs itself. In *WP* 684 Nietzsche explicitly draws the conclusion that *Caesar is a decadent.* "Among men, too, the higher types . . . are exposed to every kind of decadence: they are extreme, and that almost means decadents! The brief spell of beauty, of

When Nietzsche focuses on power as the aim, he glorifies barbarians and the satisfaction in action of instinctual urges; but when he thinks about self-enjoyment, he generates the more profound analysis of sadomasochistic subjectivity and transcendental ressentiment.

In the latter mood, if Nietzsche is still thinking of "power" at all, it is not as aggressive appropriation but as *capacity,* the possibly decadent active/passive ability to receive into one's sensorium or consciousness the greatest and most intense perceptions—as in the Dionysian experience of *The Birth of Tragedy.* Perhaps the hinge by which Nietzsche swings from the active/passive to the aggressive idea of power is the notion of incorporation (*Einverleibung*), for example in the remark from the essay on history that characterizes the "most powerful and tremendous nature" as having the ability to "incorporate [*einverleiben*] into itself all the past" (*UM* II,1;63). Incorporation may be imaged as a receptive process, but in *The Will to Power* the expansive, incorporative urge is typically seen in aggressive terms, "the will wants to go forward again and again becoming master over that which stands in the way" (696; translation emended). The "simplest case" of such appropriative incorporation is that of "primitive nourishment": "The protoplasm extends its pseudopodia in search of something that resists it—not from hunger but from will to power. Thereupon it attempts to overcome, appropriate, assimilate what it encounters: what one calls 'nourishment' is merely a derivative phenomenon" (*WP* 702; Nietzsche does not use the term "incorporation" in this remark, but he does use it in connection with the same protoplasmic process in *WP* 501 and 656).

Is there not something in this narrowing of the idea of self-enjoyment of what Nietzsche himself had stigmatized in *Daybreak* as the aged thinker's turn toward "coarser and broader means of satisfaction, that is to say . . . the satisfactions of active, dominant, violent, conquering natures" (*D* 542)? In this same work he contemptuously characterizes this crude type of power precisely as *incorporative*—and attributes it to Christianity! "One may admire this *power* of causing the most various elements to coalesce, but one must not forget the contemptible quality that adheres to this power: the astonishing crudeness and self-satisfiedness of the church's intellect during the time it

genius, of Caesar." But Nietzsche neither here nor elsewhere pursues systematically the shattering implications of this conclusion for his theory of morals.

was in process of formation, which permitted it to accept *any food* and to digest opposites like pebbles" (70).

My argument is that the notion of self-enjoyment and that of will to power are partly synonymous and partly in conflict, and that self-enjoyment is in fact the more capacious notion, the one that can include all modalities of the heightened sensation of self, that of the martyr as well as that of the triumphant barbarian. Yet self-enjoyment remains a mysterious notion, since Nietzsche deeply problematizes both the concept of "self" and that of "enjoyment."

We have seen how from the outset, in *The Birth of Tragedy* and related work, Nietzsche oscillates between Promethean receptivity to the suffering of all humanity and flight from this suffering toward a strictly fascist politics. Beginning with *Human, All Too Human* Nietzsche tries to master the ambivalence that results in this oscillation by trying to show that there is no moral difference between *Mitleid* and cruelty, that both are forms of self-enjoyment.

Now, on the one hand, this analysis denies the possibility of any genuine going-outside-the-self or mingling of subjectivities. It is always only our own *Selbstempfindung* that is at issue; our perception of the other, whether we act to inflict pain or to relieve it, is only significant as a means for intensifying our sensation of self. This system is closed and utterly narcissistic. Nietzsche also interprets love in the same way, as a species of desire to appropriate the other and thus increase the self's pleasure in itself.

But, on the other hand, it is only with respect to the other that the self can feel itself, can enjoy the sensations of pleasurable exercise of power. It is really not so much that the other does not exist for us as that ultimately there can be no motivation directed at the other that does not reflect back on the self's enjoyment of itself. Traditional moral thinking is wedded to the illusion that there can be an outflow of energy from the organism that has no ultimate reference back to the self-enjoyment of that organism, an outflow that is an absolute expenditure with no benefit of any kind to the economy out of which it flows. In contrast, Nietzsche suggests that expended energy always has a self-reflexive aspect, no matter what kind of category morality wants to put it into. The categories "selfish" and "unselfish" keep in view only the effect or intended effect on the well-being of others and ignore the dynamics of the economy out of which they originate. When we take this economy into consideration, we see that there is *always* a yield of self-enjoyment, no matter how "unselfish" the act—in fact, the greatest self-enjoyment may derive from the most unselfish acts, as is implied even by such orthodox formulas as "it is more blessed to give than to receive."

Nietzsche does not, however, mean to denigrate all motivation by denying altruism; on the contrary, he wants to declare the nonmoral character and therefore complete innocence of all action (*WP* 362). This is what he in *Human, All Too Human* termed his "theory of complete irresponsibility" (105). "All joy in oneself is neither good nor bad," he declares (103); for "all actions are unconditionally necessary" (133) since our actions result from something like a chemical process that works itself out in our beings until "the most powerful motive decides about us" (107).[4]

Furthermore, the distinction between selfishness and unselfishness rests on another distinction that Nietzsche also problematizes: that between pleasure and pain. So long as this distinction holds, it is easy to define selfishness as pursuit of pleasure and unselfishness as the willingness to undergo pain or forego pleasure on behalf of another's increase of enjoyment or decrease of suffering. But if suffering, and even the most intense suffering, can be a form of self-enjoyment—as in the sadistic and masochistic self-reflections Nietzsche traces—then the foundation for the definition of unselfishness disappears. Nor have the saints and ascetics (for example, Saint Theresa of Avila) ever been bashful about the superiority of their raptures and ecstasies to the mundane pleasures of the "selfish" seekers of well-being; it is really only a very superficial sort of moral thinking that could persuade itself that the notion of "unselfishness" is anything more than a preliminary category suitable for certain pragmatic purposes.

The final complication that throws the orthodox categories of morality into complete disarray is the presence of aggressiveness, cruelty,

[4]This necessitarianism has a psychological coloring that is the opposite of Calvinist predestinarianism; Nietzsche devises it precisely in order to blow away the gloom of guilt and the fear of condemnation. Whereas Calvin's purpose is to persuade humans of their inability to will their own highest good, Nietzsche's is to persuade that we *cannot help but* will whatever it is that fulfills our being's deepest desire. The danger of predestinarianism is always the possibility that it might cause believers to despair concerning whether God wills that they reach the heavenly goal, but Nietzsche's doctrine is intended to make such despair senseless, since each organism is autotelic and autonomic.

or the lust to dominate in various forms of the exercise of virtue. Self-denial may involve the "desire for distinction," the desire to impress on others the pain of their moral inferiority (*D* 30); or it may involve the pleasure of cruelty against oneself. Pity may be a kind of appropriation of the weaker by the stronger, an attempt by exercising generosity to come into contact with the powerlessness of the sufferer and thus to intensify the sensation of one's own power. The complementary category of selfishness disappears along with that of unselfishness, and the entire question of the relation between self and other has to be rethought as a dialectic in which the self finds its reflection in the other and the other is then reflected back into the self.

This is the same dialectic rediscovered by Freud in the metapsychology of 1915 and later.[5] Pain that is experienced as pleasure; the pervasiveness of narcissism; and aggressivity in the dialectic of identifications by which the self is constituted: Freud's articulation of these themes is strikingly parallel to Nietzsche's, but it is more explicit and systematic and can therefore help us to discern the pattern and significance of Nietzsche's articulation.

For instance, in the essay "Instincts and Their Vicissitudes" Freud derives both sadism and masochism from an original impulse toward "the exercise of violence or power [*Macht*] upon some other person as object.[6] From this originally nonerotic heteroaggression develops a second phase of reflexive- or auto-aggression. Freud's evidence for the existence of such a phase is the "self-torment and self-punishment [*Selbstquälerei, Selbstbestrafung*]" of obsessional neurotics (128). From this phase there develops a third phase in which an external agent is sought as the inflicter of torment; this is not masochism proper because a component of erotic excitation arising from pain enters in as

[5]Several writers have recently addressed the question of the continuity between Freud's project and Nietzsche's. There is a thorough, point-by-point comparison of Nietzsche's and Freud's views on drive, the unconscious, and so on in Paul-Laurent Assoun, *Freud et Nietzsche* (Paris: Presses Universitaire de France, 1980). Lucio Russo focuses narrowly on the question of representation in his *Nietzsche, Freud, e il paradosso della rapresentazione* (Roma: Istituto della Enciclopedia Italiana, 1986). Lorin Anderson argues that "all the important themes of *Civilization and its Discontents* are present [in the *Genealogy of Morals*], deployed in the same manner, established in the same relationship to one another," in "Freud, Nietzsche," *Salmagundi* 47–48 (Winter-Spring 1980):3–39, quote from p. 23. All three authors canvas the available evidence on Freud's reading of and attitude toward Nietzsche; the most thorough and to my eyes illuminating discussion of this material is in Russo, chap. 4.

[6]Sigmund Freud, "Instincts and Their Vicissitudes," in *SE,* 14:127.

part of the aim of this urge. Finally, there is the reversal of this structure, in which the subject becomes the sadistic inflicter of pain, which he nevertheless enjoys *masochistically* "through his identification of himself with the suffering object" (129).[7]

Freud's schema is obviously oversimplified, and he later made important revisions of it (above all, the postulation of a "primary erotogenic masochism"). But for our purposes it remains useful as an abstract matrix generating a basic system of logical possibilities, the additional development of which is bewilderingly complex.

Self aggresses other.
Self aggresses self.
Other aggresses self.
Other aggresses other.
Self identifies with other that aggresses self.
Self identifies with other that is aggressed by other.
Self identifies with other that self aggresses.
Self introjects image of other that aggresses self, then self splits into identification with introjected image as punisher and self as punished (with additional possibility of symbolic exchange by means of which punishment of self represents punishment of other who formerly punished—"If you were the child and I were the adult, I would punish you like this" as an internalized scene acted out by a self split against itself).

This is not a complete listing, but it shows how quickly the possibility of a perspicuous overview disappears. Our interest here, however, is not in an exhaustive account of the whole system of possibilities but rather in the basic grammar of this system and its constitutive elements, because Freud's systematic analysis brings out in a perspicuous fashion the dialectic of self-reflection which is mostly implicit in Nietzsche. Mostly, but not altogether; for in two of the less commonly read works of his middle period, *Human, All Too Human* and *Daybreak,* we find the elements of a Nietzschean theory that

[7]On the question of the "turning-around on the subject" of drives, see Jean Laplanche, *Life and Death in Psychoanalysis,* trans. Jeffrey Mehlmann (Baltimore, Md.: Johns Hopkins University Press, 1976), chap. 5. I have been considerably influenced in this book by Laplanche's concept of the death drive as "evacuation" of the entire quantity of energy with which an organism is charged.

strikingly parallels Freud's observations in "Instincts and Their Vicissitudes."

In *Human, All Too Human,* Nietzsche anatomizes cruelty in a way that touches on each of Freud's four phases of the unfolding of sadism:

1. The initial phase of aggression which does not aim at producing pain but only at mastery or destruction: "Now, in nature, we take pleasure in breaking up twigs, loosening stones, fighting with wild animals, in order to gain awareness of our own strength" (*H* 103). "If one does not know how painful an action is, it cannot be malicious; thus the child is not malicious or evil to an animal: he examines and destroys it like a toy" (*H* 104; cf. 81). This form of aggression sounds like the purest physiological expression of what Nietzsche later describes as will to power.
2. Phase of self-aggression as "moral masochism": This is what Nietzsche calls "asceticism," that "rare form of voluptuousness" (*H* 142) by which "man was to feel sinful in all ways and excited, animated, inspired thereby" (*H* 141).
3. Masochism proper (as pain sought from another agent): the martyr. Despite his profound interest in what in *WP* 417 he calls "the voluptuousness of the martyr," Nietzsche does not provide an analysis of martyrdom; whenever he mentions this type of voluptuousness, it is always in connection with the structurally more interesting (because self-reflexive) type of the ascetic (for example, in *D* 113, which we will presently consider).
4. Sadism or the aggression that aims specifically at what Nietzsche calls "empathic" perception of pain inflicted. "Will there be many people honest enough to admit that it is a pleasure to inflict pain?" (*H* 50). "Is the *knowledge,* then, that another person is suffering because of us supposed to make immoral the same thing about which we otherwise feel no responsibility? But if one did not have this knowledge, one would not have that pleasure in his own superiority, which can *be discovered* only in the suffering of the other" (*H* 103).

These observations are scattered unsystematically through *Human, All Too Human,* but in the crucial remark 113 of *Daybreak* Nietzsche develops the same basic set of ideas into a genetic sequence of self-reflections by which sadomasochistic subjectivity is elaborated. In *Daybreak,* Nietzsche does not begin with the innocent aggressivity that aims only at "awareness of our strength" without regard for the affective consequence in the object. Rather, he begins with a heteroaggression that already involves a kind of "empathy [*Mitempfindung*] which is far from being . . . sympathetic [*Mitleidig*]"; at the end of the sequence we arrive at a sadism that has been refined and intensified by a cycle of deepening identifications with the other.

Phase 1 is the "striving for distinction." We make others suffer in order to "impress" our image on their souls; our pleasure in their pain lies in our perception ("empathy" without "sympathy") of their recognition of our being in the depths of their own.

Phase 2 involves the ascetic or martyr. This phase comes at the end of a "long scale of degrees." The ascetic or martyr "feels the highest enjoyment by himself enduring . . . precisely that which . . . his counterpart the *barbarian* imposes on others." Man is now "split asunder into a sufferer and a spectator . . . there is only one character burning and consuming himself." Both the barbarian and the ascetic experience "unspeakable happiness at the sight of torment."

Phase 3 is the divinization of the ascetic disposition. There is the idea of a "loving god" who creates "suffering men" so that the god (or the ascetic who adopts this godly perspective) can then suffer from "ceaseless torment at the sight of them, and thus tyrannize over himself."

Phase 4 is sadism proper, in accord with Freud's definition. Nietzsche describes it as "doing hurt to others in order thereby to hurt *oneself,* in order then to triumph over oneself and one's pity and to revel in an extremity of power!" Compare Freud: "When once feeling pains has become a masochistic aim, the sadistic aim of *causing* pains can arise also, retrogressively; for while these pains are being inflicted on other people, they are enjoyed masochistically by the subject . . . through his identification of himself with the suffering object."[8]

Freud's investigation concerns the development of (erotic) sadism and masochism in childhood; Nietzsche's is more in a Hegelian vein, a quasi-historical phenomenology of sadomasochistic spirit. This difference between them is most visible in Nietzsche's phase 3, which integrates into the dialectic of self-reflection conjectures concerning the complex intellectual structures of historical religions. But both Freud and Nietzsche are engaged in a redefinition of the roots of

[8]Freud, "Instincts," *SE,* 14:128–29.

subjectivity, a redefinition that replaces the moral problematic of selfishness with the economic problematic of what Freud would call narcissism. If Freudian narcissism is not precisely identical with Nietzschean self-enjoyment, it nevertheless demarcates a field of phenomena the analysis of which by Freud has the closest affinity with that performed by Nietzsche. For narcissism in its fullest Freudian sense encompasses the whole field of libidinal economy: the transit of libido through other selves, aggression, infliction and reception of pain, and something very much like death (the total evacuation of the entire quantum of excitation with which the organism is charged).[9]

In what way does the field of this problematic differ from what Nietzsche first calls self-enjoyment and then focuses more narrowly as will to power? It seems there is a crucial difference, that will to power leaves out the essentially erotic character of libido, its fundamentally *sexual* nature.

But do we know what we have said when we use the terms "erotic" or "sexual" to describe the character of the fundamental drive energy in Freud? Very attentive reading of Freud's later works shows how confused are his attempts to keep eros separate from aggressiveness and the death drive, so much so that Laplanche is driven to conclude that "the death drive is the very soul, the constitutive principle, of libidinal circulation." And Leo Bersani argues that "we don't move *from* love *to* aggressiveness in *Civilization and Its Discontents;* rather, love is redefined, re-presented, *as* aggressiveness."[10] Think of Nietzsche's representation of primitive will to power in terms of appropriation of the other through incorporation and then compare these remarks from Freud's "Group Psychology and the Analysis of the Ego":

> Identification is known to psycho-analysis as the earliest expression of an emotional tie with another person.
>
> It behaves like a derivative of the first *oral* phase of the organization of the libido, in which the object that we long for and prize is assimilated by eating and is in that way annihilated as such. The cannibal, we know,

[9]The problematic toward which I can only gesture here is perhaps probed most profoundly by Freud under the heading of *the dominance of the pleasure principle*. What is the relation between this dominance and the prevalence of what Freud calls narcissism? A triangulation that I cannot perform here is called for between these two terms and Nietzsche's "self-enjoyment."

[10]Laplanche, *Life and Death,* 124; Leo Bersani, *The Freudian Body* (New York: Columbia University Press, 1986), 21.

has remained at this standpoint; he has a devouring affection for his enemies and only devours people of whom he is fond.[11]

And if Freudian libido contains a strong element of aggression and destructiveness, Nietzschean will to power never takes place without a pleasurable excitation that there is no reason not to call erotic. That physical pleasure in aggressiveness which Nietzsche describes, that "strong excitement" (*starken Erregung*) it produces (*H* 104), that "high tension" (*hohen Spannung*) in the feeling of self-enjoyment (*BGE* 260), are these not what Freud identifies as sexual in nature?[12] Nietzsche himself mainly reserves the characterization of "voluptuous" for the more refined forms of (sado-) masochistic subjectivity, those associated with asceticism and its derivatives. But in several notes, mostly from the year 1888 (*WP* 805–15), Nietzsche speaks of love and sexual desire in terms that suggest its extremely close relation to will to power. In *WP* 809 he equates "desire" (*Lust*) with "the feeling of strength" (*das Gefühl der Kraft*). And in *WP* 815 Nietzsche tells us that "the force that one expends in artistic conception is the same as that expended in the sexual act," and concludes that "there is only one kind of force"—*es gibt nur eine Kraft*. These notes are continuous with the remarks on the sublimation of the sexual drive in the *Genealogy of Morals* which we have already examined.

I am not arguing that will to power is really sexual, or that it means the same as "libido." I am concerned, rather, to show that these terms are unstable, that our object of investigation must be not the entity supposedly named by a term but the range of values, only loosely indicated by each term, across which thought must move if we are to understand the complex system of conceptual dynamics within which these terms function.

The notion of self-enjoyment leads Nietzsche into a profound exploration of sadomasochistic subjectivity, one in which he recognizes the

[11] Freud, *SE,* 18:105.

[12] "There are present in the organism contrivances which bring it about that in the case of a great number of internal processes sexual excitation arises as a concomitant effect, as soon as the intensity of those processes passes beyond certain quantitative limits. . . . It may well be that nothing of considerable importance can occur in the organism without contributing some component to the excitation of the sexual instinct"; Freud, *Three Essays on the Theory of Sexuality, SE,* 7:204–5.

fluidity of sadomasochistic affect, the interchangeability of subject positions that is involved in the relation between sadist and masochist. In *Daybreak* 113 we see a first sketch of the reading of history that Nietzsche will unfold in the *Genealogy of Morals,* as the development from barbarians who hurt others to ascetics who hurt themselves; but he does not yet in *Daybreak* 113 distinguish the barbarian and the ascetic as antithetical types. On the contrary, he treats them here as variants of a single structure or pieces of a single puzzle:

> The striving of distinction is the striving for domination over the next man. . . . There is a long scale of degrees of this secretly desired domination, and a complete catalogue of them would be almost the same thing as a history of culture, from the earliest . . . barbarism up to the grotesqueries of over-refinement and morbid idealism. . . . At the end of the ladder stands the *ascetic* and martyr, who feels the highest enjoyment by himself enduring, as a consequence of his drive for distinction, precisely that which, on the first step of the ladder, his counterpart the *barbarian* imposes on others on whom and before whom he wants to distinguish himself. The triumph of the ascetic over himself, his glance turned inwards which beholds man split asunder into a sufferer and a spectator, . . . this final tragedy of the drive for distinction in which there is only one character burning and consuming himself—this is a worthy conclusion and one appropriate to the commencement: in both cases an unspeakable happiness at the *sight of torment!*

One might read in this "unspeakable happiness at the *sight of torment*" a development from Nietzsche's earlier analysis of the Dionysian tragic experience, that protomasochism in which "pain begets joy" and "ecstasy may wring sounds of agony from us" (*BT* III;40). But, as opposed to the celebratory tone of *The Birth of Tragedy,* here Nietzsche takes some ironic distance from the type of self-enjoyment that transforms pain into pleasure. By the time of the *Genealogy of Morals,* this ironic distance has split into a condemnation of ascetic masochism and a celebration of barbarian cruelty, as Nietzsche tries to extricate from the dialectic of sadomasochism an autonomous essence of pure self-reflecting selfhood. Thus in the *Genealogy of Morals* Nietzsche speaks of the self-affirmation of the noble subjectivity as though it were a pure self-affection, one that does not have, or hardly has, to take a detour through its reflection in the base selves by contrast with which it defines itself as noble: "it acts and grows spontaneously"; "looking away" from the lower orders, the noble self guards itself "against a real knowledge" of them and thus has only a "pale, contrasting image" of them "in relation to its positive basic concept" (*GM* I,10;37).

Yet Nietzsche's analysis in *Daybreak* 113 confirms what we found in our earlier reading of the *Genealogy* in Chapter 2, that only the ascetic who has internalized the scene of torture achieves the full autonomy of a will to power that is not dependent on a world or other human beings. The barbarian who tortures, and whom Nietzsche wants to see as the truly powerful one, is dependent on the transit of his substance through *another* subjectivity, where it could always be lost; for example, entangled in the meshes of a slave cunning that knows how to use its weakness to overpower the master. Nietzsche knows as much about the power of the slave as Hegel does, but in his tyrannophilic phase he cannot reconcile himself to what he knows, cannot gaily grant the slave a place in the dialectical *commedia* of the whole. If Nietzsche tries again and again to constrict the notion of self-enjoyment to the feeling of power, with power defined as active appropriation, as cruelty without an admixture of masochism, this is at least in part because of a certain anxiety, the fear that the strong will not prevail, that the power of the slave will overflow the whole.

Now, whereas in the period of *The Birth of Tragedy* Nietzsche, under the influence of Schopenhauer, had glorified an expansive, even cosmic, receptivity to the being of others and Promethean self-expenditure on their behalf, in *Human, All Too Human* and *Daybreak* he begins his reinterpretation of morals by a critique of that receptivity and self-expenditure called pity (*Mitleid*) which Schopenhauer had treated as the root of all moral feeling. Nietzsche now praises as "the highest gratification of the feeling of power" (*D* 18) a form of affect that he describes as the most egoistic or self-affirmative possible. This upward revaluation of cruelty has a significant critical and dialectical force in relation to the cultural moment at which it emerges; but at the same time it manifests a kind of contraction of Nietzsche's being, an attempt to pull back together and reinforce the boundaries of a self that had spread itself too thin in the earlier glorification of Dionysian martyrdom.

Nietzsche is attracted to cruelty in its nondialectical form because it is economical, a good investment, one that promises to preserve and augment the being of the cruel one. The one who inflicts suffering forces the sufferer to turn toward him and grant him an absolute recognition; he thus appropriates the substance of the sufferer as mirror of his own being, the sufferer reflects him back to himself with an intensity and inevitability which belong only to the being of the inflicter of pain. "One hurts those whom one wants to feel one's power, for pain is a much more efficient means to that end than pleasure," Nietzsche says in *The Gay Science;* "pain always raises the question about its origin while pleasure is inclined to stop with itself without looking back" (13). The "pathos of distance" and the distinction of rank order that Nietzsche loves to praise are variants of this striving to impress one's being violently on the substance of the other: "If one did not have this knowledge [that another person is suffering because of us], one would not have that pleasure in his own superiority, which can *be discovered* only in the suffering of the other" (*H* 103). Nietzsche's fullest exposition of the nature of this motivation for cruelty is once again in *Daybreak* 113.

> The striving for distinction keeps a constant eye on the next man and wants to know what his feelings are: but the empathy [*Mitempfindung*] which this drive requires for its gratification is far from being harmless or sympathetic [*Mitleidig*] or kind. We want, rather, to perceive or divine how the next man outwardly or inwardly *suffers* from us, how he loses control over himself and surrenders to the impressions our hand or even merely the sight of us makes upon him; and even when he who strives after distinction makes and wants to make a joyful . . . impression, he nonetheless enjoys this success not inasmuch as he has given joy to the next man, . . . but inasmuch as he has *impressed* himself on the soul of the other, changed its shape and ruled over it at his own sweet will.

As Nietzsche recoils from the expansiveness of the Dionysian his pity becomes nausea, fear of contamination and violation of his being by the touch of those same masses of humanity whose suffering he feels so deeply; and he seeks to fortify himself by an affirmation of ascendant life that tends to become a celebration of isolation, cruelty, and appropriativeness.

Let us try to identify the structural properties of Nietzsche's text that facilitate the ambivalence of his affirmation of strength. On one side there is cathectic energy, the movements of which are regulated by the economic law enunciated by Nietzsche, according to which self-enjoyment is the individual's only demand. This self-pleasure principle determines that conscious cathexis will invest those self-representations that allow individuals to take the greatest pleasure in themselves. This idea is the basis of Nietzsche's unmasking of morality: thus pity, which masks itself as an altruistic and morally good act, is really a form of self-enjoyment. On the other side we have the conceptual structures (moral, religious, philosophical) in which are durably instituted the pathways along which this libidinal narcissistic energy can flow. The structure of the pathways may be such that it makes self-deception easy or nearly inevitable, as in the case of Christianity, which gives the weight of divine authority to its moral misrepresentations of libidinal economics.

In the case of Nietzsche, whose whole project is directed at the unmasking of such misrepresentations, the structural snare within his thought is hidden from him because it is also the weapon he uses to combat the self-deception and nihilism of his civilization. This weapon, his affirmation of ascendant life, becomes for Nietzsche the bearer of a *double investment* that gives it what we could call a cathectic ambiguity or bipolarity. On the one hand, this affirmation requires strength, to affirm ascendant life is to *be* ascendant life; on the other hand, and folded under the first meaning so as to be invisible or at least evadable, to affirm ascendant life *may be* to act under the spur of fear or anxiety, to attempt to protect oneself against the threat of decay, suffering, the permeation of self by the being of the all-too-many, and this affirmation may thus be the mask of some *insufficiency of strength,* of some nonidentity with ascendant life. Nietzsche's self-regard is seduced by the positive face of this affirmation: he can represent himself to himself as courageous, rich, overflowing, while at the same time he defends, preserves, economizes himself by means of the economic maneuvers proper to the disguised second face.

Nietzsche slips from his "pantheistic affirmation of all things" (*WP* 55) to a partial, economizing affirmation of strength and cruelty by a line of reasoning so plausible that he does not notice his own sleight-of-hand. Suffering is the great objection to existence; in order to affirm existence, Nietzsche must affirm this suffering and all the dark forces that cause it. Pity stands in the way of this affirmation; Nietzsche himself is prey to this affect and is the disciple of the great pitier and glorifier of pity, Schopenhauer. But Nietzsche sees that pity leads to negation, to a refusal that life is worth living; the apostles of pity are enemies of life. On behalf of pity, they have slandered much of existence, and in fact the strongest, most flourishing part of existence, the beasts of prey and the conquerors and tyrants. The apostles of pity are wrong to affirm only part of existence, the suffering part, for this partial affirmation ends in total negation, negation of the real world in favor of a compensatory fantasy world, and we *must affirm the whole,* the suffering-causing part as well. "Everything that the good call evil must come together so that one truth may be born" (*Z* III,12;312).

But when Nietzsche affirms cruelty, the urge to dominate, acquisitiveness, and so forth, he slides insensibly into a nostalgic naturalism which he erects as a normative model. Look at the eagle and the lamb, he says—it is *natural* for the eagle to eat the lamb (*GM* I,13;44–45). Dominance of the weak by the strong, that is how it is in life; if we are to affirm life we must affirm how it is, we must affirm this dominance. At precisely this moment, Nietzsche slips into the perspective of dominance, because it is the strong and dominating who affirm how it is and the weak and dominated who say no. The eagle says "I have nothing against these lambs" but the lambs have plenty against the eagle. The lambs are excluders and deniers, the eagles affirmers and includers. Therefore it seems as though to be an affirmer means to have the perspective of dominance, to be an eagle. But there is a very crude equivocation here, passed off as a joke: "We don't dislike them at all, these good little lambs; we even love them: nothing is more tasty than a tender lamb" (*GM* I,13;44). The acceptance of the lambs by the eagles is their acceptance as prey, as something to be appropriated—it is not the acceptance of their lamb-being, their lamb-subjectivity and lamb-perspective. The lambs are "good" (to eat) but they are inferior, nay-saying, and weak, and their weakness cannot be affirmed as such, in the indifference of a being that draws all its consequences at every moment, in the lamb as much as in the eagle, but only as that which is the rightful prey of the eagle. And this drives Nietzsche into an intolerable contradiction; he is now compelled to draw a normative boundary around the weakness of the lamb, declaring that since weakness is the nature, the intrinsic essence, of lambhood, it is unnatural, unhealthy, decadent, perverted for "lambs" under any circumstances to triumph over "eagles." But when he tries to apply the normativity of lamb and eagle relations to human beings, Nietzsche is obliged to admit that the perversion is the rule, the strongest-by-rights turn out to be the weakest, accidents are continually happening, the strong are sometimes delicate (*WP* 684) and sometimes stupid (*WP* 950), the weak are incredibly tenacious and cunning, and what's more, they gang up on the strong.[13] "Strange though it may sound," Nietzsche marvels in a note from 1888, "one always has to defend the strong against the weak" (*WP* 685), and this thought is one of the most persistent throughout his work.

Nietzsche's perspective, which should be the perspective of the whole, slips into one part of the whole he looks at. He identifies the perspective of dominance and then assumes it as his own, and sometimes he recognizes his partiality but other times continues to believe that he is affirming the whole.

It is all very well to speak of "creative positing" as Nietzsche does: "To *posit a goal* and mold facts according to it; that is, active interpretation and not merely conceptual translation" (*WP* 605). But Nietzsche is not satisfied with his tyrannophilia as a mere creative positing and tries over and over to find an *immanent justification* for it, something in the nature of things that grounds his positing and makes it something more than a positing. He tries to deduce it from the character of the whole and thus to call it "natural" while at the same time he recognizes that nature is indifferent to our positings. We could demonstrate this with any number of passages in which Nietzsche moves immediately and with no sense of contradiction from the claim

[13]Nietzsche almost always associates intelligence and cunning with weakness, as in this passage from *Twilight of the Idols:* "The species do *not* grow in perfection: the weak prevail over the strong again and again, for they are the great majority—and they are also more *intelligent*. Darwin forgot the spirit (that is English!); *the weak have more spirit*. . . . Whoever has strength dispenses with the spirit. . . . It will be noted that by 'spirit' I mean care, patience, cunning, simulation, great self-control, and everything that is mimicry" (IX,14;523). (Notice "everything that is mimicry"; we will return to the question of mimicry in relation to Nietzsche and the Dionysian.) But in *WP* 544 he considers cunning an index of *organic superiority:* "Increase in 'dissimulation' proportionate to the rising order of rank of creatures. It seems to be lacking in the inorganic world—power against power, quite crudely—cunning begins in the organic world; plants are already masters of it. The highest human beings, such as Caesar, Napoleon . . . , also the higher races (Italians), the Greeks (Odysseus); a thousandfold craftiness belongs to the essence of the enhancement of man." This conception of human greatness calls fundamentally into question the basic dichotomies of the *Genealogy of Morals*. See also *BGE* 257: "In the beginning, the noble caste was always the barbarian caste: their predominance did not lie mainly in physical strength but in strength of the soul." By "strength of soul" Nietzsche means here that they were "more *whole* human beings" and this means "more whole beasts." He is here trying to attribute some form of *esprit* to the barbarians without contaminating it with mentality.

of "the absolute homogeneity of all events," from "how everything . . . moral is identical in essence with everything immoral," to the claim that "everything decried as immoral is . . . higher and more essential" (*WP* 272).

"How does the part come to sit as judge over the whole?" he asks (*WP* 331), and he replies that this is just how it is, that's how the whole works, it brings forth creatures like us who need to posit values. Nature is indifferent but we are part of nature and we are not indifferent, therefore it is natural not to be indifferent. So far so good. But Nietzsche cannot stop there, for he wants to justify not valuation in general but rather one specific set of valuations, to show that the eagle is *nature's* choice, we naturally choose the eagle, and nature, which is not in itself choosy, nevertheless chooses through us when we do so. "The *order of castes,* the supreme, the dominant law, is merely the sanction of a *natural order,* a natural lawfulness of the first rank. . . . Nature, not Manu, distinguishes," Nietzsche declares in *The Antichrist* 57 (a passage that, however, in another of those Nietzschean turns whose structure we have been tracing, names "the most spiritual men" as "the *strongest,*" those whose "joy is self-conquest" and in whom "asceticism" becomes "nature, need and instinct").

Of course there are all of those weak or degenerate or perverted ones who do *not* make the same choice as Nietzsche, so the question arises as to how we know whose choice resonates with that of unchoosing nature. Nietzsche claims his is a choice of strength, of what affirms and furthers life and inspires faith in life. Yet in his tyrannophilic mood what Nietzsche chooses is a form of beleaguered, endangered life, so that he must constantly fret that "monstrous fortuity" and the numerous cunning weak ones will overcome it (*BGE* 203). His choice does not accomplish what he claims it should, because it is only under special circumstances that hardly ever occur (and which certainly have not occurred for a long time) that this strong life flourishes: "The man of antiquity . . . alone has hitherto been 'the man that has turned out well'" (*WP* 957). Instead of overflowing confidence in life, we are given reaction, paranoia, and nostalgia for antiquity. It is very suspicious that it is almost always *in illo tempore* that health and strength are located, almost never in *this* world that Nietzsche inhabits. Nietzsche claims to affirm this world, yet he finesses the issue by affirming a version of this world that is really *another* world, long ago and far away, and perhaps a world that never was.

6

"The perfect woman tears to pieces . . ."

We traced in the last chapter the most general outlines of the psycho-dialectic in Nietzsche's text by means of which the man of heroic violence acquires his privilege. Nietzsche's text is pervaded by a fear of the power of the weak, a power against which he must fortify and rigidify the boundaries of strength. But this fear, this "anxiety that is past all comparisons" (*BGE* 203), seems disproportionate, exaggerated. Why should any flagging in Nietzsche's energy result in such a violent contraction of his economy?

In *The Gay Science* 3 Nietzsche presents the expansive noble economy as an expression of a superabundance of *Eros* in the Freudian and Platonic sense of the term:

> The higher type is more *unreasonable,* for those who are noble, magnanimous, and self-sacrificial do succumb to their instincts, and when they are at their best, their reason *pauses.* An animal that protects its young at the risk of its life, or that during the mating period follows the female even into death, does not think of danger and death; its reason also pauses, because the pleasure in its young or in the female and the fear of being deprived of this pleasure dominate it totally: the animal becomes more stupid than usual—just like those who are noble and magnanimous.[1]

[1]Here, as repeatedly in Nietzsche, one hears the echo of Diotima's discourse, addressed to Socrates in Plato's *Symposium:* "Haven't you noticed what an extraordinary effect the breeding instinct has upon both animals and birds, and how obsessed they are with the desire, first

At such moments, Nietzsche can view with equanimity the abandonment of the individual to the great species-drives. But it is precisely this same abandonment from which Nietzsche must take refuge in the contractive phase of his economy.

We begin now to pursue the libidinal elements in Nietzsche's tyrannophilia; that is, the connection of this tyrannophilia with the ascetic gynophobia the lineaments of which we traced in the *Genealogy of Morals,* a gynophobia that stands at the opposite pole from the erotic superabundance described in the remark just cited. In order to do this, we return to "The Hellenic Will," an essay in which the energies that agitate Nietzsche's economy emerge in an even more uncontrolled and revealing fashion than in any published text. In our earlier look at this text we considered mainly the affective coloring of Nietzsche's argument for the necessity of slavery. Now we are in a position to track the types of libidinal investment that move his arguments here, especially in relation to an incoherence or contradiction that arises at a crucial moment. We will then see how the structure of this contradiction is echoed in *The Birth of Tragedy.*

In "The Hellenic Will" Nietzsche assails the notions of equal rights and of the dignity of labor as "transparent lies" on the grounds that the vast majority of humans are motivated by nothing more than the bare drive of self-preservation, whereas "dignity" only enters in "where the individual goes completely beyond himself and is no longer compelled to produce and labor in service of the continuation of his individual existence" (Musarion, 3:279). The mass of individuals has no dignity because mere *Dasein* has no value in itself; all other existence is merely a means toward the end of the rare, exalted individual who is the "tip of the pyramid of appearance" (276), the genius. The genius alone can bestow dignity on human life because through him the one will achieves its goal of "self-glorification in works of art" (287). The Dionysian genius understands that he is the "purpose and goal" of the "chaos of suffering and self-rending" existence (301). All other individuals can achieve a degree of dignity only by becoming the means (*Mittel*), the instrument (*Werkzeug*) of the genius. At the same

to mate and then to rear their litters and their broods, and how the weakest of them are ready to stand up to the strongest in defense of their young, and even die for them, and how they are content to bear the pinch of hunger and every kind of hardship, so long as they can rear their offspring?" (207a–b).

time, however, that the genius (also the military genius [292]) makes others instruments of his will, he himself remains only an instrument; but there is something in geniuses (*etwas ist in ihnen;* emphasized in original) for which the cosmos stages its performance (286). In order to propagate the flower of genius, nature brings forth the instrumentality of the state, which is an arrangement for the protection and care of the genius individual (286); and this function was performed in the most consummate way by the Greek state. The Greek state compelled egoistic individuals to sacrifice themselves to the achievement of the great state-sponsored art works (286–87). In the modern state, however, the egoistic, non-self-transcending instincts of certain individuals have transformed the state into the means (*Mittel*) for the pursuit of their own purposes. But when the true function of the state is undermined in this way, humanity ceases to fulfill its ontological vocation as vessel of a higher purpose (288–92). All that is left is the meaningless struggle for survival of egoistic individuals whose bare *Dasein* is empty and meaningless.

Once again here we encounter a tension between two possibilities of actualization of a single concept, or, as we can say with equal justice, two concepts that are put in play with a single word. The word or concept is *der Einzelne*—the individual. There are two kinds of individuals, one the "aim and final purpose" (*Zielpunkt und letzte Absicht*) of nature, the other the degradation or ruin of this purpose. The good individual lords it over everybody else, he is the highest expression of individuation, but only because of "something in him" of which he is the instrument. The bad individual is bad because he is *too much of an individual*—he does not submit to a higher will, does not make himself a *Werkzeug*.

Nietzsche is trying to steer between two alternatives, either of which would nullify the life-justifying transcendence he wants to define. The individual who is an end in himself, without reference to a higher will, is meaningless; but on the other hand the individual who is merely a tool is *no individual at all*. The genius is at the same time instrument and end, *Werkzeug* and *Zielpunkt*. He fulfills the goal of a universal will, but he is preserved in his value as individual, it is as individual that he fulfills the universal/transcendent goal. If the individual pursues merely individual goals, the universal goal is effaced; if he pursues only a universal goal, the individual is effaced. Therefore Nietzsche requires the coincidence of the individual goal with the universal.

But how can the individual fulfill a universal goal and do it *as individual?* That is, how can he be *preserved* in the fulfillment? Doesn't self-preservation belong to the individual precisely as nonservant of a transcendent goal? This reflection, which disturbs the whole structure of valuations that is the main line of the argument in "The Hellenic Will," is, according to Nietzsche, the Greeks' own reflection. To the Greeks the creation of art came "just as much under the same dishonorable [*unehrwürdig*] concept of labor as any vulgar handicraft," and it made them feel something like *shame*. *Shame* enters in for the Greeks wherever the human being is only the instrument (*Werkzeug*) of manifestations of will which are "infinitely greater" than the human in the "isolated form of the individual [*Einzelgestalt des Individuums*]" (Musarion, 3:279–80).

Thus the Greek, who most fully perceives the deep workings of the will and most perfectly fulfills its aims, justifying existence by transcending mere individuality, is ashamed of the productive act by which he brings into being the artwork that is the "redemption" (*Erlösung*) aimed at by the will, and it is *because* the will transforms him into mere instrument of its transcendent powers that he is ashamed. "The delighted amazement over the beautiful did not blind him to the way it comes into being [*sein Werden*]—which appeared to him, like all becoming [*Werden*] in nature, as a violent need [*Noth*], as self-pressing-forward into being [*Sichdrängen zum Dasein*]" (3:279–80).

This is a very strange moment in Nietzsche's text.

When Nietzsche introduces the concept of shame, he is leading up to the next paragraph where he speaks of the shame of slavery that lies hidden beneath the lovely visage of artistic culture. Yet Nietzsche could make his point about slavery without allowing shamefulness to overflow onto the art that is supposed to justify it or making the transcendent principle itself the source of shame. *Wherever the form of the individual as individual is overwhelmed by infinitely greater forces, there is shame.* What could be more strangely at odds with the principle that only the individual who serves these forces can justify an existence that is otherwise meaningless? It is as though at this moment Nietzsche had confused the instrumentality of the genius with that of the slave, forgotten that this instrumentality is supposed to be consummation rather than negation of the individual.

How does this come about?

Initially, through the reflection that the creation of art, too, requires *Arbeit* and therefore is contaminated with some form of the activity that characterizes slavery. According to Plutarch, who, Nietzsche says, speaks with "the instinct of the ancient Greek," the noble Greek did not wish to be a Phidias or Anacreon, regardless of how much he might admire their works, because of the labor involved. But when the "compelling force" (*zwingende Kraft*) of the artistic "drive" (*Trieb*) worked in him, he had to create and submit to the *Noth* of *Arbeit* (Musarion, 3:279). It is really *Zwang* and *Trieb* that are the origin of the shameful, and *Arbeit* itself only shameful because rooted in *Trieb,* the all-powerful drive (*allmächtigen Trieb*) to *Dasein* that moves stunted plants to drive their roots into soilless rock (277–78). This is the same *Trieb* that Nietzsche will praise in *The Gay Science* as "noble," in the example of the animal "that during the mating season follows the female even unto death" (*GS* 3): but here Nietzsche tells us that the noble Greeks regarded the sexual *Trieb* as shameful. "As a father admires the beauty and talent of his children, but thinks with shamed reluctance of the act by which they came into being, so it went with the Greeks. . . . The same feeling, with which the process of begetting [*Zeugungsprocess*] is regarded as something shameful, to be concealed, . . . the same feeling veiled the coming into being of the great works of art" (280–81).

On the one hand, there is will as drive, as the compelling pressure of the need to exist, *sichdrängen zum Dasein,* thus as the sordid struggle for existence of stunted plants, the ugly necessity of slave labor, and the shameful process of begetting—in general, all of the material conditions of existence, everything having to do with the body and its needs. On the other hand, there is will as what aims at redemption from the shame of existence, as creator of the illusion of art by means of which the horror of existence is kept from overwhelming the desire to live and life-negating nihilism is kept at bay (Musarion, 3:302).

Now, the major movement of Nietzsche's thought in these fragments is undoubtedly toward the goal of Dionysian negation of individuation (*Vernichtung der Individuation* [304]). The condition of individuation is the source and foundation of all suffering and evil and thus something "objectionable" (*verwerflich* [303]). The value of the genius individual is that he transcends the mere drive to existence and produces the mirror of art in which the primordial suffering (*Urschmerze*) can see itself and thus achieve redemption (275). There is, as Nietzsche himself was to recognize, a strong Hegelian tint to this structure. The individual is the negation of the primordial unity; the artistic and, above all, the tragic vision is the negation of this negation. There would thus not necessarily be any contradiction in the fact that will manifests itself both as the shameful and as transcendence of the shameful through the instrumentality of the shameful. But, although this dialectic structures Nietzsche's overall account, it does not do so systematically. Nietzsche does not strictly control each emerging thought according to the restricted form of the textual economy called "Hegelian dialectic," and as a consequence there arise, as always in Nietzsche's text, those associative buddings that open the argument to the forces of the larger and more chaotic economy called "Nietzsche." His initial distinction was between the sordid *Trieb* of individuals who aim only at their own existence and the transcendent activity of individuals who have been freed from the struggle for self-preservation. But now he tells us quite precisely that the creative and procreative drive is shameful "despite the fact that in it the human being serves a higher goal than his individual preservation" (280). Thus there intrudes into the orderliness of the dialectic of transcendence this moment in which we are told that wherever the forces of will overflow the boundary of form of the individual, his *Einzelgestalt,* there is disgrace (*Schmach*) and shame (*Sham*): transcendence itself is shameful.

Of course it isn't exactly "Nietzsche" who says this. He tells us that it is the Greeks who felt this way. But Nietzsche gives no Greek source at all for the idea that the feeling of shame attended the begetting of children, and in fact there is a very prominent Greek source that directly contradicts him. In Plato's *Symposium,* Diotima informs us that the *Trieb* behind procreation is the desire for immortality, and that this same *Trieb* manifests itself in the creations of the intellect, all the way up to the purest philosophic contemplation of the ideal. Far from being shameful, the erotic drive is the mediator between the human and the divine. An even stronger refutation of Nietzsche's claims comes from Plutarch himself, whom Nietzsche cites concerning the shame of artistic labor. In his *Dialogue on Love* (*Erotikos*) Plutarch engages in a lengthy panegyric of the divinity of Eros and praises sexual union with a lawful wife as "the beginning of friendship" (*philia*) and the source of "respect and kindness and mutual affection and loyalty" (*time kai kharis kai agapesis allelon kai pistis*).[2] So Nietzsche's

[2]Cited from *Plutarch's Moralia,* vol. 9, trans. Edwin L. Minar, Jr., F. H. Sandbach, and W. C. Helmbold (Cambridge: Harvard University Press, 1961), 427. Nietzsche's remarks may have been suggested by the terms in which an earlier speaker in the dialogue, Protogenes,

attribution is highly arguable, and if he introduces it so peremptorily, it manifests the economy of his text and not the compulsion of respect for intellectual history.

This economy is shaped by Nietzsche's fascination with the image of the Dionysian *sparagmos,* an image that functions in a paradoxical fashion but does so so openly that commentators have to my knowledge never probed its paradoxicality. Dionysus torn apart represents the tearing apart of the primal unity and the coming into being of individuals; Dionysus reborn represents the *Vernichtung* of individuation and the return to the primal unity. Coming into being as an individual is torment, ceasing to be as an individual is bliss. But the image of the torment of individuation is the tearing apart of an individual, and the image of the bliss of ceasing to be is the rebirth of that individual.

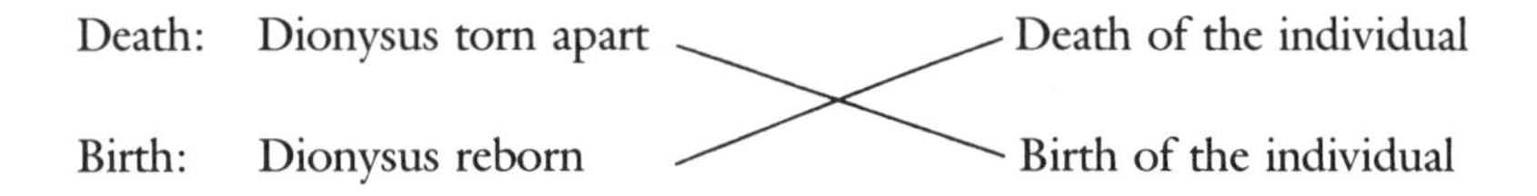

Of course it is a commonplace of mystery cults and mystics that we "die into eternal life," but the ambiguity in the story of Dionysus Zagreus plays a crucial role in Nietzsche's text, one that he never fully controls. The chiastic relation of the symbol to its significance provides him with a structure along which the flow of a double investment can circulate endlessly.

Now, Dionysus is not an individual in the sense that he is a member of a multiplicity; he is the image of the totality, the universal individual. Yet the myth can only perform its symbolic function if Dionysus takes on himself the aspect of contingent individuality. The myth must represent the horror of individuation, and thus the image

---

speaks of pleasure in sex with a woman: "When the impulse (*horme*) that drives us to this goal is so vigorous and powerful that it becomes torrential and almost out of control, it is a mistake to give the name love to it. . . . The appetite for woman . . . however well it turns out, has for net gain only an accrual of pleasure in the enjoyment of a ripe, physical beauty" (316–17). But the speaker identified as Plutarch refutes this view at great length. The underlying issue in the debate is the question of whether sex with a woman can involve anything more than mere lust (*epithumia*), and Plutarch's reply is that it can and should involve *eros.* Nietzsche chooses Protogenes' view that it is only *horme,* drive; but Plutarch attributes this view to "ill-tempered fellows, who had never fallen in love" (417).

it uses must be one that arouses horror; and the only image that arouses the adequate horror is that of the rending of a contingent individual.

The horror of *sparagmos* is, however, the antithesis of the horror of individuation; one is horrified by it precisely because one so intensely does not want one's individual existence to end. Of course there exists a profound religious or metaphysical logic by which we could resolve this antithesis, but I want to insist on the difficulty that needs overcoming because it racinates deeply in Nietzsche's text.

The image of *sparagmos* acquires for Nietzsche a certain privilege as figure of violation of the essence of singleness, of the boundary of form that constitutes the embodied self. This essence is expressed by the term *Individuum,* and *sparagmos* is the violent dividing up of the in-dividual. But the thought of the *Einzelgestalt* of the individual has an essential place in Nietzsche's text, in his thinking about humanity and in his own stance toward the world. Nietzsche is himself *einzeln* in every sense of the term, as individual, as single, separate, and isolated.

The early writings on tragedy and genius suggest what the character is of the libidinal charge with which Nietzsche invests the *sparagmos* of Dionysus Zagreus. The utmost image of the unbearable pain and horror of existence is that of the absolute dispersion of the self, the violent rending of the *Einzelgestalt* of the individual. The little death of the act of generation, which Nietzsche tells us is shameful because it too violates this *Einzelgestalt,* thus echoes the major death of *sparagmos.* In the image of *sparagmos,* death supervenes as violence from outside; in that of sex, death is the internal upsurge of *Trieb,* a drive that Nietzsche does not call *Eros,* though he describes it in terms close to those used by that same Diotima whom a few pages later in the same essay Nietzsche names as an example of the greatness of Greek women. The reality symbolized by the image of the Dionysian suffering is, however, fundamentally that of the internal upsurge; for Nietzsche in *The Birth of Tragedy* the image of the torn Dionysus is the visible figure of the internal surge of natural *Trieb.*[3] The Dionysian Greek, unlike the noble Greek who sees shame in sex, "sees himself changed, as by magic, into a satyr," and the satyr is "a symbol of the sexual omnipotence of nature [*geschlechtlichen Allgewalt*] (*BT* VIII;61), "the image of nature and its strongest urges [*stärksten Triebe*]" (65).

[3]See the Appendix, "*The Birth of Tragedy* Reconstructed."

Nietzsche does not mention this erotic *Triebkraft* when he speaks in sections 2 and 4 of *The Birth of Tragedy* of the mixture of "pleasure, grief, and knowledge" (*BT* IV;46) which issues in Dionysian cries, but the image is patently orgasmic, yet still with the sense of the death that such ecstatic transport carries within it: "Ecstasy [*Jubel*] may wring sounds of agony from us. At the very climax of joy [*Aus der höchsten Freude*] there sounds a cry of horror or a yearning lamentation for an irretrievable loss" (IV;40). (Kaufmann's translation here conveys a sexual connotation ["ecstasy," "climax"] not so starkly conveyed by Nietzsche's German, but his translation acknowledges that same undertone of meaning to which I am calling attention.) The excess (*Uebermass*) of nature that issues as transport and agonized cries is the affective state for which the vision of the suffering Dionysus is the only adequate objective correlative, and tragedy itself is thus also "the objectification [*Objectivation*]" (VIII;65) of the Dionysian state which is the overwhelming of the form of the individual by the upsurge of *Trieb*.

Two attitudes, one phenomenon: the noble Greek (whom Nietzsche in *The Birth of Tragedy* terms "Apollonian" without mentioning the question of sexual shame) sees as shame the same rupture of the *eidos* of the individual which the Dionysian reveler celebrates. The Apollonian "apotheosis of individuation" knows "but one law—the individual, i.e., the delimiting of the boundaries of the individual, *measure* in the Hellenic Sense" (*BT* IV;46). The rupture of this boundary is imaged as the rending of the visible body of Dionysus, but it is really the essence of self as conscious and sensitive being that is at issue. The artist in the *Rausch* (rapture) of creation or the natural man in the *Rausch* of procreation run the risk not of actual death but only that something within them will overwhelm the boundary of their conscious selfhood. This something has the character of a pressure or impulsion and its effect in the most extreme case is to throw the self outside itself, into a state of self-forgetfulness, transport, ecstacy, "annihilation of the ordinary bounds and limits of existence," oblivion of the personal memory (*alles persönlich in der Vergangenheit erlebte*) constitutive of the identity of the individual as such (VII;59).

Nietzsche fears this experience, this absolute and potentially irrecoverable expenditure of self. Insofar as he thinks the thought of his own annihilation as *Einzelne,* it is as the madness of overwhelming *Trieb* resulting in *sparagmos* that he thinks it. And insofar as there is an element of hysteria in his economy, it is in relation to this thought, because hysteria is the unmeasured and uncontrollable reaction to the threat of annihilation, of the explosion of the boundary of definition that holds the self identical with itself. If Freud defines hysteria (strictly speaking, anxiety hysteria) in terms of the fear of castration, this is only one image more of *sparagmos* as objectivation of an internal threat, the threat of uncontrollable *Trieb* which bears within it the "yearning lamentation for an irretrievable loss." This is how Freud redefines castration anxiety and the fear of death in a discussion the results of which have been largely neglected.[4]

[4]Sigmund Freud, *Inhibitions, Symptoms and Anxiety, SE,* 20, chaps. 7–10. The loss to which Freud traces the primal lamentation is that of the mother. When it misses its mother, the child becomes anxious and eventually "helpless" in the face of "a growing tension due to need." It is this "economic disturbance caused by an accumulation of amounts of stimulation which require to be disposed of" that is the "real essence of the 'danger'" both in separation from the mother and in castration anxiety. Castration anxiety, like the anxiety of separation from the mother, is "a fear of being separated from a highly valued object," and in fact one which is valued precisely because it signifies connection with the mother. "The high degree of narcissistic value which the penis possesses can appeal to the fact that the organ is a guarantee to its owner that he can be once more united to his mother—i.e., to a substitute for her—in the act of copulation. Being deprived of it amounts to a renewed separation from her, and this in its turn means being helplessly exposed to an unpleasurable tension due to instinctual need" (*SE,* 20:139). The fear of death is, analogously, the ego's fear of being abandoned by the agency that internalizes the image of the parents, the super-ego. The threat of destruction by some external danger reproduces the infantile situation in which the child finds itself unprotected, helplessly exposed to need, and the affect of fear is primarily a response not to the danger itself but to the feeling of the absence or anger of the one who protects and punishes. Freud declares that castration anxiety and the fear of death "signify in a certain sense a separation from the mother" (151), and this discussion would seem to be the inspiration for the Lacanian doctrine of castration as separation from the mother. In relation to Nietzsche, the striking significance of Freud's theory of separation anxiety is that it identifies (at least momentarily) as the basis of castration anxiety and the fear of death the "cathexis of longing" for the mother and the "economic disturbance" aroused by the fear of solitude, of being left utterly alone.

Yet there is a curious indecision in Freud as to whether the essence of castration anxiety is this original separation-fear or whether this original fear is only a sketch of the fear that will become (at least for men) the *real thing*. Freud's discussion is obscured by the lingering presence of the question of birth anxiety as original prototype of all separation fear; he has an odd difficulty in letting go of this theory (proposed by Rank on the basis of an earlier hint by Freud himself), and under cover of his complicated wrestling with this theory we can miss the significance of the other thesis concerning separation from the mother. Thus Jean Laplanche and J.-B. Pontalis argue that "every page of *Inhibitions, Symptoms and Anxiety* bears witness to Freud's wish to disassociate himself from Rank's argument," and then conclude directly from this that "his constant concern in this work of synthesis is to replace the castration complex in its literal sense at the very centre of clinical psychoanalysis"; "Castration Complex," in *The Language of Psychoanalysis,* trans. Donald Nicholson-Smith (New York: Norton, 1973), 58. I take it that this judgment is also ultimately that of Lacan. (Contrast the work of John Bowlby, who has placed separation anxiety at the center of his own psychoanalytic theory; see especially *Attachment and Loss, Vol. 2: Separation* [New York: Basic Books, 1973].)

Nietzsche is thus not being merely figurative when in *Ecce Homo* he confesses his sexual hysteria: "May I here venture the surmise that I *know* women? That is part of my Dionysian dowry. . . . They all love me. . . . Fortunately, I am not willing to be torn to pieces: the perfect woman tears to pieces when she loves.—I know these charming maenads" (III,5;266). There is a similar association in *Beyond Good and Evil*: "Fear and pity: with these feelings man has so far confronted woman, always with one foot in tragedy which tears to pieces as it enchants" (239). Here woman is almost synonymous with tragic *sparagmos*. To enter into an erotic relation with a woman would be to risk the irretrievable dispersal of his *Einzelgestalt:* but how can Nietzsche say that this is part of his "Dionysian dowry"? Dionysus is precisely the one who *is* torn to pieces. Not by maenads, of course, but it is curious that Nietzsche should adduce his unwillingness to be torn to pieces in the context of his claim to be Dionysian.[5] Just as curious as the almost complete absence of maenads from *The Birth of Tragedy,* given that the cult of Dionysus was so predominantly identified with female worshippers. Nietzsche ignores this, laying the emphasis instead on the chorus of (male) satyrs. This is, as Silk and Stern say, a "striking omission"—so striking, I think, that it qualifies as an instance of repression.[6] It is as though, if Nietzsche is going to allow full imaginative and emotional play to the thought of the Dionysian *sparagmos,* he can only do so by repressing any thought of its relation to women. Of course this relation is encoded in the references we traced to *Trieb* and sexuality, but the direct connection of women and *sparagmos* is never made explicit, even when Orpheus and the maenads are mentioned in section 12, for there the "maenads" are the all-male court of Athenians that figuratively tore Socrates to pieces.

And if the mere omission of the maenads from *The Birth of Tragedy* is not enough evidence that something is being avoided here, then consider that in the "The Hellenic Will" Nietzsche assigns women a role the *inverse* of the maenadic, a role specifically as maintainers of measure and boundary and as preventers of the tendency of a unity to fly to pieces. Woman is eternally self-identical (*ewig Gleiche*) and in this way sets a boundary to everything measureless (*alles Maasslose be-*

[5]It was of course Orpheus, not Dionysus, whom the maenads killed. But, as M. S. Silk and J. P. Stern point out, "Nietzsche does not distinguish between the 'regular' cult of Dionysus and Orphism (or his interpretation of Orphism)"; *Nietzsche on Tragedy* (Cambridge: Cambridge University Press, 1981), 175.

[6]Ibid., 173–74.

grenzt), to that which goes beyond itself and is excessive (*das Auschreitende, Ueberschüssige*). What can this excessive, unmeasured being be but that of men? So if man naturally explodes himself, it is not toward the female that he does so (as was implied in the earlier remarks about the shamefulness of procreation); on the contrary, the female is what draws a limit to man's self-negating outflow, restores the spent one (*das Verbrauchte*) as does beneficent rest (*wohltätige Ruhe*) (Musarion, 3:296). Further, in a political image that curiously echoes, while inverting, the image of the sparagmatic maenads, Nietzsche says that

> in Greece there was one never slumbering concern: that the frightfully overcharged political drive [*Trieb*] should splinter into dust and atoms [*in Staub und Atome zersplittere*] the little political entities, before they could reach their goals. . . . Above all it is the Pythia, in which the power of woman to supplement [*compensiren*] the State made itself apparent more clearly than it has ever again done. That a people so split up [*zerspaltenes*] into little tribes and communities nevertheless was in its deepest foundation *whole* and in its fragmentation [*Zerspaltung*] only accomplished the task of its nature: for that the wonderful phenomenon of the Pythia and of the Delphic oracle stood as surety, for always, so long as the Greek being still produced its great works of art, it spoke out of *one* mouth and as *one* Pythia. . . . The Pythia was the clearest expression and the common center of all the accessory devices which the Greek will set in motion in order to arrive at art; in her, the truth-speaking woman, the political drive [*Trieb*] regulated itself, in order not to exhaust itself in self-laceration [*Selbst-zerfleischung*]. (298–300)

Here is woman as principle of unity, as what keeps a body from tearing itself to pieces. Of course there is not literally a body in question here but rather the cultural or spiritual unity of ancient Greece; yet the resonance of the *Zersplitterung, Zerspaltung,* and *Zerfleischung* mentioned here with that of the Dionysian *Zerstückelung* and *Zerreisung* of a very few pages later is very strong, and since the "overcharged political *Trieb*" belongs exclusively to men, the mystical political body is very clearly a masculine body. Nietzsche is thus here fantasizing woman's power as the opposite of that as which his fear, and the Dionysus cult, pictures it.[7]

[7]Nietzsche's characterization of the nature of women in these pages is all the more striking when we consider that Bachhofen, one of his principal sources on the Dionysian, had said precisely the opposite concerning the feminine principal. According to Maria A. Simonelli's

But even though the violent rending of the form of the individual is what Nietzsche most fears, the goal he exalts in the writings on tragedy is the negation of individuation. On the level of Nietzsche's explicit argument, the tearing of Dionysus is horrible because it signifies not the death but rather the coming into being of the individual. The rebirth of Dionysus signifies *the end of individuation,* a return to the womb of being. Yet it is sex and the getting of children just as much as the tragic work of art that guarantee this rebirth:

> That nature has bound the arising of tragedy to these two fundamental drives of the Apollonian and Dionysian may count for us just as much as an abyss of reason as the arrangement of this same nature which binds reproduction to the duplicity of the sexes. . . . The common mystery is, of course, how out of two hostile principles something new can arise in which the conflicting drives appear as a unity: in which sense reproduction, just as much as the tragic work of art, may count as a guarantee of the rebirth of Dionysus. (Musarion, 3:304–5)

Thus Nietzsche's greatest hope and greatest fear are bound together in a complex of imagery that uses the same figures to represent now the hope, now the fear. To explode the boundaries of the isolate, conscious self, to defend these boundaries against the threat of explosion: Nietzsche's fear and hope circulate along the chiasmus of the Dionysian sacrifice and its reversible signification in such a way that he can accomplish both of these at once, accomplish each by means of the other.

Nietzsche never ceases this movement, the ambivalence of which is traceable just as vividly in the writings on will to power as it is in *The Birth of Tragedy*. The individual is nothing, as individual he matters only as an expression of forces that transcend his individuality. The individual who *is* an expression of such forces, however, *does* matter as individual, because he is more than individual, because he is *ausschrei-*

summary, Bachhofen's "earthly-feminine" principle "rejects every limitation," and the Dionysian cult, which favors "the return of feminine life to savage aphrodisian naturalism," tends toward "the progressive dissolution of political organization"; "Alle radici del dionisiaco Nietzscheano," in *Friedrich Nietzsche, O la verità come problema,* ed. Giorgio Penzo (Bologna: Pàtron Editore, 1974), 153. Nietzsche, we could say, takes the feminine out of the Dionysian and the Dionysian out of the feminine.

tend, ueberschüssig, constantly overflowing his own boundaries; but because this individual is precious, because he justifies the rest of the species, the boundary of his self-overflowing self-identity must be kept intact, preserved against the *sparagmos* of self-transgressing drive.

7

The Exploding Hero

Nietzsche works a radical reduction of all evaluative hierarchy. There is only force and becoming, new centers of force are continually forming and constantly falling apart or being incorporated into new constellations, and in all this there is nothing to blame or praise. All becoming is innocent, the throw of the dice of the divine child. This thought is summed up in Nietzsche's dictum that "becoming must appear justified at every moment (or incapable of being evaluated; which amounts to the same thing)" (*WP* 708).[1] But in "The Hellenic Will" we find a telling variation of this formula: "From that vast viewpoint of the Primal Unity *the genius is achieved in every moment,* the whole pyramid of appearance perfect all the way up to the top" (emphasis added; Musarion, 3:275). This image is unstable; it suggests a transcendent leveling of all becoming, and yet it does so in terms of a valuable part ("the genius") that justifies a pyramidally structured whole. A few lines later, the instability resolves into the declaration that for "the Universal Eye [*Weltauge*]" the genius is "the tip of the pyramid of appearance" (276): the exceptional individual is the end or *energeia* of humanity that fulfills its essence and justifies its existence.

Is it un-Nietzschean to say that the powerful individual "fulfills the essence" of humanity? But then how are we accurately to characterize whatever it is that Nietzsche thinks as the consummation embodied by

[1]Cf. *WP* 55: "Can we remove the idea of a goal from the process and then affirm the process in spite of this?—This would be the case if something were attained at every moment within this process—and always the same."

the superior individual? From the earliest to the latest writings, Nietzsche continues to reiterate his belief that there are higher human beings who are *more valuable* than the mass and *for whose sake* the mass exists and may be sacrificed. We have seen how he expresses this idea in 1871 in terms of the artistic genius; Nietzsche later drops the aesthetic metaphysics, but the rest of the thought remains unchanged. In a note from the 1880s he writes the following: "The basic phenomenon: countless individuals sacrificed for the sake of a few [*um weniger willen*], to make them possible— One must not let oneself be deceived; it is just the same with peoples and races: they constitute the 'body' for the production of isolated [*einzelnen*] valuable individuals, who carry on the great process" (*WP* 679). The superior few are *that for the sake of which,* a phrase which in classical Greek is *toû heneka* and which is Aristotle's set phrase for what we call "final cause." There is a teleology of the isolated superior individual in Nietzsche's thought, early and late.

Nietzsche continually deprecates the importance of self-preservation, most commonly when he carps about Darwinism (which he understood so crudely), treating it as a drive subordinate to the drive for power, for self-expansion. This drive for self-expansion is the mark of health and strength; only the weak would be satisfied with merely preserving themselves. Yet Nietzsche has a very strong tendency to preserve within the outline of the expansion the identity of the being that expands. If self-preservation is not the aim, it is because of the static nature of such a condition, because the self that only preserves itself loses the intense sensation of self; if, conversely, an organism disdains preservation as its aim, if it aims at growth and expansion, this is precisely so that it may preserve its sensation of itself: "Our pleasure in ourselves tries to maintain itself by again and again changing something new *into ourselves*. . . . To become tired of possession means tiring of ourselves" (*GS* 14).

In this contractive or self-preservative movement of his economy Nietzsche tries to recuperate even the process of procreation by defining it as something that maintains (while expanding) the boundary of individuation: "The tremendous importance the individual accords to the sexual instinct is not a result of its importance for the species, but arises because *procreation is the real achievement of the individual* and consequently his highest interest, his highest expression of power (not judged from the consciousness but from the center of the whole individuation)" (emphasis added; *WP* 680).[2] The distinction Nietzsche makes here between the

[2]It is this contractive, restricted moment of Nietzsche's economy that provides Heidegger

consciousness of the individual and his *Zentrum der ganzen Individuation* is a fascinating one, and in a way focuses the most elusive problem of the later work, the question of *who* wills in will to power. Nietzsche calls this an "absurd question" because "the essence itself is power-will and consequently feelings of pleasure and displeasure," but the question arises all over when he then adds "Nonetheless: opposites, obstacles are needed; therefore, relatively, encroaching units [*Einheiten*]" (*WP* 693). The fact that the "encroaching units" are only relative does not at all dispel their character as units, thus as identities with a boundary of identity, thus as something that can in some way remain itself across change. But then how far are we, really, from the "subject" that Nietzsche supposedly "deconstructs"? In *WP* 643 Nietzsche worries that "mere variations of power could not feel themselves to be such: there must be present something that wants to grow and interprets the value of whatever else wants to grow."

Something that wants, and something that interprets on the basis of that desire: isn't this just an instinctual or affective subject in place of the old conscious, rational subject, *desidero* in place of *cogito,* as Lacan says in the case of Freud? This is a radical enough revision of the concept of the subject, but it does not go nearly so far as Nietzsche wants to go. He wants utterly to undo the substantial or essential presence of a subject of any kind, wants there to be left only waves of will to power perpetually overflowing themselves: "no subject but an action" (*WP* 617). "One may not ask: 'who then interprets?' for the interpretation itself is a form of the will to power, exists (but not as a 'being' but as a process, a becoming) as an affect" (556). Nietzsche knows that the notion of an *Einheit,* the unified self-identical singularity of the individual, is the core of the substantialist metaphysics he criticizes, both the essence of the substantialization of the ego and the bridge from this to the derived substantialization of the world: "We have borrowed the concept of *Einheit* from our 'ego' concept—our oldest article of faith. If we did not hold ourselves to be *Einheiten,* we would never have formed the concept 'thing'" (635). An

---

with the evidence with which he supports his attempt at containment of Nietzschean *Rausch.* Heidegger thus tells us that "for Nietzsche, *rausch* means the most glorious victory of form"; *Nietzsche,* vol. 1, trans. David Farrell Krell (San Francisco: Harper and Row, 1979), 119. This victorious form, which Nietzsche calls "the grand style," manifests "the *protective* mastery of the supreme plenitude of life" (1:126). Thus we must distinguish between the exposure to absolute loss of self, absolute self-squandering, and what Heidegger means when he says that "in order for the real to *remain* real, it must . . . simultaneously transfigure itself by going beyond itself, surpassing itself in the scintillation of what is created in art" (1:217).

Einheit, Neitzsche continues, is just the same as an "atom"—*a-tomos:* literally, in-dividuum, that which cannot be cut into pieces—a thing "whose effect remains constant," which is thus calculable by mechanistic theory. As opposed to this theory, Nietzsche now posits a world in which there are no *Einheiten* "but only dynamic quanta, in a relation of tension to all other dynamic quanta: their essence lies in their relation to all other quanta." But then, as we have seen, in remark 693, which dates from the same period (March–June 1988), he adds his "nonetheless": opposition and overcoming require "relatively, encroaching *Einheiten.*" The crucial word here would seem to be "relatively": isn't a *relativist* metaphysics fundamentally different from a *substantialist* one, and wouldn't then Nietzsche's *Einheiten* be something else altogether from the type of unity he criticizes?

This is one of those places where it is possible to stash away a considerable cathetic investment in the nook of a slight conceptual obscurity. Even a purely relative *Einheit* can be thought only in terms of some boundary of identity. In a world of continual becoming, this boundary would be continually shifting; but then we must ask, at what point does a given *Einheit* cease to be and a new one come into being? At one extreme of possibility, we could say that *Einheiten* are absolutely instantaneous, that there is a fresh panoply of beings at every new "now" of eternal time. But in what sense could one then speak of "appropriating," "becoming stronger"? Who or what is it that would grow, appropriate, satisfy its will to power? If there is to be a sensation of growth, there must be a *substratum* of change.

Of course Nietzsche scholarship constantly repeats as a self-evident item of doctrine that there is no unified subject of will to power, that will to power has to do with the play of forces, that there is no relation between Nietzsche's "will" and Schopenhauer's, and so on.[3] And yet there is an obvious problem here that is being ignored. Let us make it as obvious as possible. Consider this diagram:

[3]As examples of the sort of account I am criticizing (which is practically universal), see Michel Haar, "Nietzsche and Metaphysical Language," and Alphonso Lingis, "The Will to Power," both in *The New Nietzsche,* ed. David B. Allison (New York: Dell, 1977).

A is an object (or an organization of forces constituting a "relative *Einheit*") at a point in time *x*; the arrow indicates the direction of time; *B* is another object (or "relative *Einheit*") at time *y*. Now, let *Einheit A* grow in power over time, such that at some moment (indicated by the vertical line) it "surpasses itself," transgressing the boundary of its self-identity. At time *y* we now find a new *Einheit B* that is the resultant of the growth of *A*. Object *B* is stronger than *A* but cannot enjoy the feeling of increase over *A* because *B* has not increased: *A* increased and at a certain point lost its identity, became a new entity *B*, as a consequence of the increase. So long as it remained self-identically *A*, it could enjoy the feeling of its increased power. As soon as the chain of self-identity is snapped, however, and a new "relative *Einheit*" with a new *Machtzentrum* arises, we start all over with a new subject which cannot experience itself as having surpassed itself because it is a new self, not the one that was surpassed. Only if it retained some sort of "memory" of its previous state could it feel that it had increased; in that case it would retain some form of identity with the previous state and no radical self-surpassing would have taken place. If, in contrast, we ascribe the *pathos* of increase not to the entities *A* and *B* but to the will to power of which they are manifestations, then either will to power is self-identical as the substratum of the metamorphosis of *A* to *B* or once again we face a break in the process of increase such that the resultant magnitude of will to power cannot enjoy the feeling of growth over the initial magnitude.

The problem arises from Nietzsche's insistence that will to power is an affect, a feeling, a pleasure, a pathos. Without this *Selbstempfindung* of will to power there would be no need to ask about the link of identity between successive magnitudes. But once will to power is defined as an enjoyment of the self, the question becomes urgent of the *threshold* beyond which one organization of forces with a relative identity *A* becomes a different organization of forces with a relative identity *B* which has forgotten that it was once *A*. This threshold is called death and was imaged by the early Nietzsche as Dionysian *sparagmos*. Of course death is no problem if we say that self-identity is an illusion, that there are only multiplicities. But then we must also drop the notion of the pathos of self-transcending will to power.

The usual way of getting past the difficulty I am raising is to argue that for Nietzsche *Einheiten* are not really given in the world at all but are relative only to interpretations. A beautifully articulated argument of this form is offered by Nehamas, who claims that Nietzsche is not offering "an alternative to the metaphysics of substance and accident" but rather trying "to show that the world has no ontological structure" and that therefore the stable objects of the world are constituted by interpretive processes manifesting the will to power of the interpreters.[4] But this argument leaves a residual difficulty which bears the full weight of Nietzsche's dilemma: what is the identity of the entities whose interpretations constitute the entities of the world? Nehamas presupposes the identity of the interpreter as something relative to which interpreted objects become defined: "Each way of dealing with the world manifests the will to power of those who engage in it as at the same time it arranges this indeterminate world into a definite object" (97). But aren't interpreters also *Einheiten* in the world who should then also be treated as merely relative to other interpreters' interpretations? Nehamas evades this conclusion; for him "the unity of the body provides for the identity that is necessary, but not at all sufficient, for the unity of the self" (181), and he argues that this further unity of the self is something that can be achieved, the "goal" at which Nietzsche aims (182). Poststructuralist writers, on the other hand, commonly take for granted that Nietzsche utterly shatters the unity of the self. Nehamas seems inconsistent in exempting the body and the self from the otherwise universal ontological indeterminacy of objects; but the utter dissolution of the unity of the self leaves us with the problem I am raising, of how it would then make any sense to speak of the *feeling* of increased power.[5]

Nietzsche wants to have it both ways when he writes, "No subject 'atoms.' The sphere of a subject constantly growing or decreasing, the center of the system constantly shifting" and then adds in the same paragraph, "No 'substance,' rather something that in itself strives after greater strength, and that wants to 'preserve' itself only indirectly (it wants to *surpass* itself)" (*WP* 488). What is this elusive "in itself" that

[4]Alexander Nehamas, *Nietzsche: Life as Literature* (Cambridge: Harvard University Press, 1985), 96–105.

[5]Cf. J. Hillis Miller, who after dispersing the self into a multiplicity is obliged to recognize that a "fiction of selfhood" must be reinstated as the subject of the act of interpretation by which the self is deconstructed; "The Disarticulation of the Self in Nietzsche," *The Monist* 64 (April 1981): 260–61. The deconstructive view is countered strongly by Stanley Corngold in "The Question of the Self in Nietzsche during the Axial Period (1882–1888)," in *Why Nietzsche Now?*, ed. Daniel O'Hara (Bloomington: Indiana University Press, 1981), 55–98.

preserves itself in order to surpass itself, or perhaps preserves itself even as it surpasses itself?

It is tempting to accuse Nietzsche of having fallen back into a form of transcendental idealism with the doctrine of will to power. This will that is the substratum of all change, that transcends the obliteration of all individuals and continues to affect itself as it overflows the boundaries of all selves, isn't this quite clearly a *metaphysical subject?* Here the specter of Schopenhauer returns to haunt Nietzsche's latest work as it did his earliest. There are certainly important adjustments: Nietzsche affirms the ultimately joyous nature of the whole enterprise, and he makes will more dynamic when he makes its urge a drive toward "becoming more" rather than toward mere self-preservation. But these are superstructural adjustments with respect to the question of Nietzsche's attempt to overcome "Platonism." If Platonism (i.e., metaphysics in general) is characterized by the split between a merely apparent reality and a true one, then it seems as though Nietzsche's concept of will to power occupies at best an ambiguous relation to metaphysics. True, its essence is "becoming" rather than "being," but this is ambiguous, too, as Heidegger makes us aware.[6]

If will to power is to be an "affect" and a "pathos," as Nietzsche says, if its will is to affect itself with the sensation of its self-overcoming, then it must be a metaphysical subject. And if it is unconscious, if it does not form *Vorstellungen* of its desire but is in its essence *pure urge,*

[6]"In the thought of will to power, what is becoming and is moved in the highest and most proper sense—life itself—is to be thought in its permanence. Certainly, Nietzsche wants Becoming and what becomes, as the fundamental character of beings as a whole; but he wants what becomes precisely and before all else as *what remains,* as 'being' proper, being in the sense of the Greek thinkers. Nietzsche thinks so decisively as a metaphysician that he also knows this fact about himself. Thus a note that found its final form only in the last year, 1888 (*WM,* 617), begins as follows:

Recapitulation

To *stamp* Becoming with the character of Being—that is the supreme *will to power.*

"We ask: Why is this the *supreme* will to power? The answer is, because will to power in its *most* profound essence is nothing other than the permanentizing of Becoming into presence.

"In this interpretation of Being, the primordial thinking of Being as *physis* advances through the extreme point of the fundamental position of modern metaphysics, thus coming to its completion. Rising and appearing, becoming and presencing, are in the thought of *will to power* thought back to the unity of the essence of 'Being' according to its initial and primordial meaning, not as an imitation of the Greek but as a transformation of the modern thinking of being to its allotted consummation"; Martin Heidegger, *Nietzsche,* vol. 3, trans. Joan Stambaugh, David Farrell Krell, and Frank A. Capuzzi (San Francisco: Harper and Row, 1987), 156.

this is also what Schopenhauer had said about the will. Here it is necessary to read those unpublished notes from the period of *The Birth of Tragedy* in which Nietzsche struggles with the question of the blindness of the will (e.g., Musarion, 3:236–38), but it is also necessary to read Schopenhauer, who does not say what Paul de Man in his influential reading of *The Birth of Tragedy* implies that he says.[7]

I am not primarily interested in debating the cogency of Nietzsche's doctrines; I am trying to identify the trace left on Nietzsche's discourse on will to power by the movements of that fear and desire the lineaments of which we discovered in the writings on tragedy. All of Nietzsche's writing is exploratory and experimental, and his unpublished notes are obviously so to an even greater degree. We thus cannot conclude anything definite about his doctrine from these notes; but, as with the "The Hellenic Will," we can follow in the movement of his explorations the various kinds of charges that motivate them. This procedure is also not affected by the possibility that Nietzsche is positing fictions that he knows to be mere fictions, or that his positings hover in a space of undecidability in the fashion described by de Man. Whether language is performative or constative, or whether it oscillates undecidably between the two, it is always a network of cathectic pathways, no matter how repressed or sublimated or cunningly disguised. And in Nietzsche the repressions and disguises are very thin because his explicit themes are the abstract structures of libidinal economy: storing-up, blockage, and discharge of "animal energy"; self-preservation, self-dispersal, self-enjoyment.

The crux of our problem is this: the Nietzsche who tells us that units, atoms, and monads do not exist (*WP* 715), that there is only a "millionfold growth" each of whose impulses has a "sphere of power" that is "continually changing" (*WP* 704), why does this Nietzsche also hang on so insistently to one privileged constellation of forces, the type of the stronger, "more valuable" human individual? Why does the boundary of the skin that outlines the visible *eidos* or *morphe* of a biological human individual endow all the preceding moments with

[7]Paul de Man, "Genesis and Genealogy (Nietzsche)," in *Allegories of Reading: Figural Language in Rousseau, Nietzsche, Rilke, and Proust* (New Haven: Yale University Press, 1979), 79–102. See the fuller discussion of this point in the Appendix, "*The Birth of Tragedy* Reconstructed."

value and significance?[8] Why is a group of human beings when they "conspire together for power" (*WP* 636) not just as much a significant constellation of force as an individual? "Individualism is followed by the formation of groups and organs," Nietzsche writes in *WP* 784, "related tendencies join together and become active as a power; between these centers of power [*Machtzentren*] friction, war, recognition of one another's forces." And in *WP* 284 he attributes to the group the same predicates he usually reserves as honorifics for the "noble" individual: "The herd is, in relation to the outside world, hostile, selfish, unmerciful, full of lust for dominion, mistrust, etc." These remarks follow with perfect logical consistency from the doctrine of will to power: groups, herds, organizations of individuals are *Machtzentren* and "every center of force—and not only man—construes all the rest of the world from its own viewpoint" (*WP* 636). Thus there is no principled reason why biological individuals should be privileged over groups as centers of power, especially when we consider that Nietzsche sees the biological individual itself as a collection of drives and affects, a "multiplicity of subjects, whose interaction and struggle is the basis of our thought. . . . A kind of aristocracy of 'cells'" (*WP* 490).

[8]Nietzsche's investment in the preservation of the precious individual is analogous to that aspect of his aesthetics which lends itself to Heidegger's privileging in (one of) his reading(s) of Nietzsche of "the Grand Style," the style that involves "the subjugation and containment" (*Bewältigung und Bändigung*) of "chaos and the rapturous" (*des Rauschhaften*); *Nietzsche,* 1:126. (Note the linking of "chaos" and "rapture.") We should keep in mind the whole problematic of *sparagmos* and the grand economy as we read Heidegger's remarks on *form:* "Form, *forma,* corresponds to the Greek *morphé*. It is the enclosing limit and boundary, what brings and stations a being into that which it is, so that it stands in itself: its configuration. Whatever stands in this way; what the particular being shows itself to be, its outward appearance, *eidos,* through which and in which it emerges, stations itself there as publicly present, scintillates, and achieves pure radiance. . . . Form defines and demarcates for the first time the realm in which the state of waxing force and plenitude comes to fulfillment. Form founds the realm in which rapture as such becomes possible. . . . *For Nietzsche rapture means the most glorious victory of form* [emphasis added]" (1:119).

Of course, Heidegger emphasizes that this process is "not the mere subjection [*Bezwingung*] of chaos to a form" (though we just saw him speak of the *Bewältigung* of "chaos and the rapturous"), but instead that "mastery which enables the primal wilderness of chaos and the primordiality of law to advance under the same yoke, invariably bound to one another with equal necessity" (1:128). This bow in the direction of the essentiality of *force* as well as *form,* however, seems merely formal, the de rigueur recognition that the formality of form must not become a dead rigidity. The momentary statement of equality between chaos and law (unconvincing enough in itself, for how can chaos and law be *equal* once there is *form?*) quickly disappears in the reaffirmation of the containing power of law: "Art is not only subject to rules, must not only obey laws, but is in itself legislation. Only as legislation is it truly art. What is inexhaustible, what is to be created, is the law" (1:130).

And yet Nietzsche's thought is pervaded by a sense of conflict between these two levels of organization, a paranoia about the tendency of the power of the group to overwhelm the power of the superior individual. "The strongest and most fortunate are weak when opposed by organized herd instincts, . . . by the vast majority. . . . I see how the lower preponderate through their numbers, their shrewdness, their cunning" (*WP* 685). In this mood, Nietzsche is forced to the conclusion that there is a conflict of interest between "the power of a species" and that of "its children of fortune, of strong members." The power center of the strong individual is intrinsically hostile to the development of larger constellations of power, a different "center" that is no longer the center of the collectivity that is a biological individual but instead that of a transindividual collectivity. Nietzsche approves of this reticence of the "born 'masters,'" he sees it as part of their nobility, their difference from the intrinsically weak ones who overcome them with their numbers and their cunning;

> The strong are as naturally inclined to *separate* as the weak are to *congregate;* if the former unite together, it is only with the aim of an aggressive collective action and collective satisfaction of their will to power, and with much resistance from the individual conscience; the latter, on the contrary, *enjoy* precisely this coming together—their instinct is just as much satisfied by this as the instinct of the born "masters" (that is, the solitary beast-of-prey species of man) is fundamentally irritated and disquieted by organization. (*GM* III,18;136)

This remark seems to show that there is *another* will operating here, a larger will, that of a collectivity. Why doesn't Nietzsche consider this possibility? Once again, what is so special about the form of the individual that it should function as such a privileged center of power? And how is such a privilege to be reconciled with the idea that what a center of power wants in wanting more power is "to *surpass* itself" (*WP* 488)?

The expression "to surpass itself" is cited from one of the notes in

[9]In one note, the disharmony between the law of the species and that of the exceptional individual even leads Nietzsche to postulate that these individuals are actually *decadent:* "They are extreme, and that almost means decadents" (*WP* 684). The thin membrane that separates the *extreme* from the *decadent* is one that is constantly in danger of permeation in Nietzsche's text.

The Will to Power, but it is in fact a rare formulation in that collection, where the habitual statement of what will to power wills is "accumulation," "appropriation," "overwhelming," and so on. We get this same general sense of will to power in *Beyond Good and Evil* and the *Genealogy of Morals.* In *Zarathustra,* however, the formulas for will to power are "overcome yourself" and "create beyond yourself":

> I love him who wants to create over and beyond himself and thus perishes. (I,17;177)
>
> To be the child who is newly born, the creator must also want to be the mother who gives birth and the pangs of the birth-giver. (II,2;199)
>
> And life itself confided this secret to me: "Behold," it said, "I am *that which must always overcome itself.*" (II,12;227)
>
> No violent will can attain the beautiful by exertion. . . . When power becomes gracious and descends into the visible—such descent I call beauty. And there is nobody from whom I want beauty as much as from you who are powerful: let your kindness be your final self-conquest. (II,13;230)
>
> And he who wants to create beyond himself has the purest will. (II,15; 235)
>
> Thus I am in the middle of my work, going to my children and returning from them: for his children's sake, Zarathustra must perfect himself. (III,3;273)

Nietzsche assimilates the two conceptions by passing from the notions of growing and becoming more into that of self-surpassing, which hovers ambiguously between the notion of something that is surpassed-yet-preserved and the notion of something that perishes in the transition and thus yields to something new and radically other. In *Zarathustra,* there is no such ambiguity (at least not until the end of book 4, which I discuss in Chapter 9): the reiterated message is *bring forth and perish* (even if just what it means to perish remains in a certain obscurity). One is an image of conquest, the other of creation; and the privileged image and condition of possibility of all other creation is *procreation,* pregnancy and childbirth.[10] This prevailing conception in

[10] Of course the concept of pregnancy, like any other, can be recuperated for purposes of self-preservation. In the third essay of the *Genealogy of Morals,* as we saw, pregnancy became the

Zarathustra is also stated, somewhat anomalously for this work, in *Twilight of the Idols:* "That there may be the eternal joy of creating, that the will to life may eternally affirm itself, the agony of the woman giving birth *must* also be there eternally" (X,4;562).

In certain passages of *The Will to Power,* however, we can trace another attitude toward procreation, an attitude associated with the conception of will to power as appropriation. In these remarks we clearly see Nietzsche's driving motive as the desire to preserve in thought the unity and self-identity of that which grows and becomes more. Nietzsche is here exploring the fundamental dynamics of will to power through the activities of protozoa, which present these dynamics in their primitive, clarified outlines. Thus in the "protoplasm" that overwhelms and assimilates its food Nietzsche finds an image of primitive will to power, of which "'nourishment' is merely a derivative phenomenon" (*WP* 702). But when he ponders the phenomenon of propagation among amoebas Nietzsche is confronted with the inverse of the image of assimilation: here it is not a matter of the growing and becoming more of the selfsame but rather of procreation as splitting, falling apart, perhaps perishing as the self-identical. And when Nietzsche does not recuperate procreation as the "achievement of the individual" (680), he interprets it not as positive will to power but as a form of "expulsion" (*Ausstossung;* Kaufmann and Hollingdale translate this word as "excretion"), "the throwing off of ballast, a pure advantage" for the individual which preserves the outline of its *Einheit* in this way (653). Or he treats propagation as the result of weakness, "impotency": "A protoplasm divides in two when its power is no longer adequate to control what it has appropriated" (654); or, again, as an attempt to retain control in some form: "in order not to let go what has been conquered, the will to power divides itself into two wills (in some cases without completely surrendering the connection between its two parts)" (656). In all of these remarks we see a will to power that expresses itself as the opposite of self-surpassing, and procreation as a by-product of this will, or as a threat to it, or as a malfunction of it, but never as expressing the *essence* of will to power.

But in one remark, *WP* 655, written earlier than the others cited here, and in fact from the period of *Zarathustra* (1885), the interpreta-

---

image of masculine asceticism, the feedback loop by means of which animal vigor was prevented from spilling into the world. See also *Daybreak* 552, where Nietzsche describes ideal pregnancy in terms that balance between those of *Zarathustra* and those of the *Genealogy of Morals*.

tion of the same phenomenon appears to be the opposite: "The stronger . . . grows and in growing it splits itself into two or more parts. . . . The greater the impulse towards variety, differentiation, inner decay, the more force is present" (*WP* 655). Here we see the less frequent centrifugal moment of Nietzsche's thought, the valuation of decay and differentiation as expressions of overflowing energy (cf. *WP* 747 and 1015; *GS* 149; and especially *BGE* 256 and 262). Yet even here the contrast with the preceding remarks is not as great as it might seem, for here Nietzsche is contrasting the strength of that which grows and splits with the weakness of that which seeks "to become one with it." "The stronger, on the contrary, drives others away; it does not want to perish in this manner" (*WP* 655). Thus it is once again the autonomous, separate form of the individual that is being asserted, even in decay and death ("every living thing wants to die in its own way," Freud will say), as against a loss of individuality that would come not from division in this case but from fusion with a "weaker" that "presses to the stronger" in a way that sounds unmistakably like the action of a woman's love as Nietzsche represents that love.[11] The approach of the "weaker" threatens death to the "stronger": but now, by an interesting twist in Nietzsche's imagery, *sparagmos,* the tearing apart of the *Einheit* of the individual, becomes not the *consequence* of this approach but a desirable *alternative.* "The weaker presses to the stronger from a need for nourishment [it wants to consume the substance of the stronger: *omophagia,* the other half of the maenadic threat]; it wants to get under it, if possible to become one with it [Nietzsche appears to mean: in the way that a parasite "becomes one" with the host whose blood it sucks]. The stronger, on the contrary, drives others away; it does not want to perish in this manner; it grows and in growing it splits itself into two or more parts" (655).

Now we are confronted with an opposition not between being preserved and perishing but rather between two forms of perishing, and it become even more difficult to divide between self-surpassing and self-surpassing: the self-surpassing that Nietzsche evades and the one by means of which he evades it. Along this vector of Nietzsche's

[11] "In many cases of feminine love, perhaps including the most famous ones above all, love is merely a more refined form of parasitism, a form of nestling down in another soul, sometimes even in the flesh of another—alas, always decidedly at the expense of 'the host' " (*The Case of Wagner* 161).

thought, the superior individual is seen as something that is preserved only so that it can be expended, wasted, squandered. This is the most surprising and fascinating of Nietzsche's inversions of perspective: contrary to the argument of the *Genealogy of Morals,* he sees the victory of "the weak and underprivileged" in this perspective not as the negation of life but as a way life has of "preserving the type 'man'"; "otherwise," Nietzsche wonders, wouldn't "man . . . cease to exist?" Because it is the strong who are a threat to the continuation of life:

> History shows: the strong races decimate one another: through war, thirst for power, adventurousness, the strong affects: wastefulness—(strength is no longer hoarded, spiritual disturbance arises through excessive tension); their existence is costly. . . . They are races that squander. "Duration" as such has no value: one might well prefer a shorter but more valuable existence for the species. . . . We stand before a problem of economics. (*WP* 864)

A problem of economics indeed! Is it better to preserve the race or to squander it *in the right way?*

Here as everywhere in Nietzsche a central concept splits in two: "life" is that which is best continued by the weak, but also that which is best affirmed, made most valuable, by those who put an end to it: "The *enhancement* of the type fatal for the *preservation* of the species?" (*WP* 864).

Nietzsche here attempts something like a dialectical resolution of the conflict of forces we traced in the "The Hellenic Will," the conflict between the necessity that valuable individuals be nurtured and preserved and the necessity that the boundaries of their individuality be exceeded by the transcendent force of which they are only the manifestation and instrument. And with the same complex maneuver, Nietzsche reconciles his aristophilia, which in the *Genealogy of Morals* expresses itself at the limit as a preference for individualistic barbarism over civilization[12]—therefore as nostalgic primitivism, a dead end for

[12]"These bearers of the oppressive instincts that thirst for reprisal. . . . These 'instruments of culture' are a disgrace to man and rather an accusation and counterargument against 'culture' in general! One may be quite justified in continuing to fear the blond beast at the core of all noble races . . . but who would not a hundred times sooner fear where one can also admire than *not* fear but be permanently condemned to the repellant sight of the ill-constituted? . . . And is that not *our* fate?" (*GM* I,11;42–43).

thought—with the requirements of a more rigorous and comprehensive thought, according to which durable institutions are necessary for the advancement of the type "man." We can trace the movement of this maneuver in sections 37–44 of the "Skirmishes of an Untimely Man" in *Twilight of the Idols:*

First moment (IX,37). Nietzsche praises the "positive strength" of "strong ages, noble cultures" through the example of the Renaissance, "the last *great* age" because it was "lavishly squandering and fatal." Our own weak age is, by contrast, "accumulating, economic, machinelike" (540). Here accumulation, which Nietzsche elsewhere so often couples with appropriation, is not a sign of genuine will to power, which is now identified with "squandering."

Second moment (IX,39). Nietzsche condemns a present that "lives for the day . . . very irresponsibly" and praises "institutions . . . out of which a *future* grows" and "the will to tradition, to authority, to responsibility for centuries to come, to the solidarity of chains of generations" (543). Here accumulation, economy, a refusal to squander are the positive signs of health and a strong will, apparently in contradiction to what has been said in section 37.

Third moment (IX,44). Economy and accumulation are shown to be the necessary precondition for the right kind of squandering, squandering on the grandest scale. "Great men, like great ages, are explosives in which a tremendous force is stored up; their precondition is always, historically and physiologically, that for a long time much has been gathered, stored up, saved up, and conserved for them—that there has been no explosion for a long time." And then we get Nietzsche's favorite example: "Take the case of Napoleon" (547). On the next page Nietzsche continues: "The great human being is a finale [here the future ceases to matter; institutions and the "solidarity of chains of generations" (39;543) cease to matter, their *telos* is achieved]; the great age—the Renaissance, for example—is a finale. The genius, in work and deed, is necessarily a squanderer: that he squanders himself, that is his greatness. The instinct of self-preservation is suspended, as it were; *the overpowering pressure of outflowing forces* forbids him any such care or caution" (emphasis added).

This passage gives new meaning to the remark in *The Will to Power* that "a living thing wants above all to *discharge* its force" (650); here the discharge becomes total, catastrophic, a complete evacuation of the energy stored in the system. We find a similar statement in *WP* 877, where Nietzsche once again uses his favorite example: "The Revolution made Napoleon possible: that is its justification. For the sake of a similar prize one would have to desire the anarchical collapse of our entire civilization." Here is a challenging new turn to Nietzsche's partiality in favor of the exception, for now the sense of greatness as beleaguered life recedes into the background and the genius, elsewhere called fragile, becomes an "explosive" who threatens the whole.

The great man is the final cause, *toû heneka,* of the species, but now no longer as the form that caps a process of making but as the force that shatters all form. And it was always toward this shattering that the process tended, on behalf of this shattering that form formed itself. (Where is Heidegger's "grand style" now?)

This whole conception is a magnificent perversion of Nietzsche's own most courageous and generous thought, that "it is of the very essence of the rich spirit to squander itself carelessly, without petty caution, from day to day" (*WP* 77). This thought is developed in *Zarathustra* as the thought of the most life-affirming and self-overflowing economy, one that mirrors the profligate economy of nature insofar as a human being can mirror that inhuman economy. Nietzsche's valuation when he chooses the "rich spirit" as the most admirable part of the whole is of course partial, just as partial as the valuation that chooses the restricted form of "noble" economy, but what it values is the part of the whole that maintains an open circulation between itself and the whole; whereas the judgment that chooses the "nobility" of a restrictive economy that preserves-itself-while-surpassing-itself chooses a part that looks to *exploit* the whole, that maintains an impermeable boundary between itself and the economy of waste to which it belongs. This "restricted" version of nobility is an obvious evasion of the inevitable force of the grand economy, but the "explosive" version of nobility is a more complex case. This economy also, like the Zarathustran economy, spills itself endlessly, yet in and through this wastage there is still an attempt to profit in some absolute fashion, to turn loss to advantage, make the wastage of the whole redound somehow to the advantage of the privileged part even while it too perishes with the whole. If the great man squanders himself (and his whole civilization along with him), he does it for his own greater glory; his squandering has a meaning, and that meaning is an augmentation of his own greatness, which is proportionate to the size of the conflagration he creates. His substance goes out from himself in order to return to himself, even though he will no longer be there; he is a "posthumous person," like Nietzsche himself, one of those who might say "it is only after death that we shall enter *our* life and become alive, oh, very much alive" (*GS* 365).

Nietzsche thus takes cover from the vast, senseless, irrecuperable squandering of the grand economy in the image of the vast, well-formed, self-augmenting squandering of the great man. Controlled amounts of immense squandering, small doses of it one might say, to cure the nausea of illimitable and uncontrollable squandering: a sort of homeopathy. The illimitable squandering of nature makes no sense because it has no center and no goal: the squandering of the great man represents this in a way that sums it up and gives it a meaning. This meaning is always *dramatistic* for Nietzsche. Its earliest form is the sacrifice of the Dionysian/Promethean/Oedipean hero in *The Birth of Tragedy,* and the logic of this dramatism always remains that of Nietzsche's aristophilia. In "Schopenhauer as Educator" Nietzsche quotes approvingly Goethe's remark that "the *causa finalis* of the activities of men and the world is dramatic poetry" and that without this final cause the world and human activity are useless (*UM* III,5;160). And in the 1880s Nietzsche writes in a note that if man has "lost *dignity* in his own eyes to an incredible extent" in modern times, it is because he is no longer "the center and tragic hero of existence in general" (*WP* 18). Nietzsche wants to restore the centrality of such an image, man as Roman or Roman candle to inspire faith in life with his expensive fireworks, who like one of Shakespeare's heroes acts "in defiance *against* life and advantage"; "and if the hero perishes by his passion this precisely is the sharpest spice in the hot draught of his joy" (*D* 240).

The explosive hero is clearly the heir of the Dionysian hero who gets torn apart; there is definitely something Dionysian about him. That is why he appeals to Nietzsche. Also because he is *not* Dionysian in just the right way, like Nietzsche himself, who is Dionysian but refuses to let a woman tear him apart. Or like the artist, who is, like Napoleon, a squanderer, inheritor of "a capacity that has gradually been accumulated and now waits for an heir who might squander it" (*GS* 354). The artist too, like the great man, is filled with an overpowering pressure of outflowing forces, in his case "an extreme urge to communicate; the desire to speak on the part of everything that knows how to make signs—; a need to get rid of oneself, as it were, through signs and gestures; ability to speak of oneself through a hundred speech media—an *explosive* condition" (*WP* 811). This artist is "able to squander himself without becoming poor" (812), but there is one way he dare not squander himself. "The force that one expends in artistic conception is the same as that expended in the sexual act: there is only one kind of force. An artist betrays himself if he succumbs *here,* if he squanders himself *here:* it betrays a lack of instinct, of will in general; it can be a sign of decadence—in any case, it devalues his art to an incalculable degree" (815). Here too the artist parallels the great man, who also preserves his substance against woman and remains simply himself, self-identical and self-augmenting. Woman "wants someone who *takes,* who does not give himself or give himself away"; "woman gives herself away, man acquires more"; consequently, "faithfulness" is "not an *essential* element" of man's love (*GS* 363); to demonstrate this we have no less an exemplar than Napoleon. When his wife once questioned his fidelity Napoleon replied, "I have the right to answer all accusations against me with an eternal 'That's me'" (*das-bin-ich; GS* 23).

Nietzsche the artist, the one who believes that all power centers are momentary, that the tide of will to power perpetually overflows their limits, also finds that in relation to the question of "man and woman" there is in him "at the bottom," "really 'deep down'," "some granite of spiritual *fatum*" (*BGE* 231). When he speaks on this subject (or on any "cardinal problem," he says, but the question of man and woman is the only example he gives of a cardinal problem), there is "an unchangeable 'this is I' [*das bin ich*]" that does the speaking. "Das bin ich": the same words with which Nietzsche had told us Napoleon asserted his boundaries against his wife.[13]

[13]In *GS* 362, Nietzsche gives Napoleon credit for the fact that "the *man* has again become master over the businessman and the philistine—and perhaps over 'woman'"; he then proceeds immediately in the next remark to the declaration that "woman wants to be taken and accepted as a possession" and that man on the contrary is a possessor. Similarly, here in *Beyond Good and Evil,* after the opening echo of his tribute to Napoleon, Nietzsche goes on to tell us (among other, similar bits of wisdom) that man "must conceive of woman as a possession, as property that can be locked" (238). *Locking women up,* we know that this is what the Athenians did; and the great threat of Dionysus, as Euripides depicts it, was that he inspired an intoxication in the women so that they left their looms and rushed outdoors, where they indulged in the various excesses associated with the Bacchic cult (tearing the king to pieces, for example). The Greeks feared this women's liberation, and so did the noble Romans. "What the Romans feared above all was the orgiastic and Dionysian cult that afflicted the women of Southern Europe from time to time when wine was still new in Europe" (*GS* 43).

The remark about his "granite of spiritual *fatum*" is Nietzsche's prelude to his announcement that he will now "state a few truths about 'woman as such,'" with the understanding, he says, that these are "only—*my* truths" (*BGE* 231). We must admire Nietzsche's irony toward his own misogynistic or gynophobic feelings, the candor with which he presents the remarks that follow as nothing more than an index of his own economy—therefore as a *personal confession,* since we are invited to read this index as something that leads us to the depths of the hidden Nietzsche. Some pages earlier, somewhat discretely sequestered away from this section, so as not to be *too* obvious—but close enough so that anyone who pays attention can draw the conclusion—he has told us that "the degree and kind of a man's sexuality reach up into the ultimate pinnacle of his spirit" (*BGE* 75). Nietzsche thus in this remark authorizes us, invites us, to look for the trace of his erotic economy in all of his thought, to find the system of displacements, conversions, defenses, and sublimations by which his relation to *Eros* drives the unfolding of the intellectual structures he generates.

But there is scarcely a disguise in this remark about how he feels "deep down" with respect to "man and woman": Nietzsche is about as hard, as *a-tomos,* as one gets; he is granite. A few pages later we find out why it is necessary for a man to be granite: woman inspires pity and fear, and "with these feelings man has so far confronted woman, always with one foot in tragedy, which tears to pieces as it enchants" (*BGE* 239).

Erotic economization is here, as always in Nietzsche (and perhaps not only in Nietzsche), an index to the general question of economy, above all to the question of which macro-economy is operative at a given moment, the general economy or the restricted economy. The type of greatness that explodes carries the restricted economy, the economy of self-preservation, to its limit by carrying it at least in appearance beyond its limit. But structurally, in the system of the forces that animate Nietzsche's thought, *wherever we find the part accruing to itself the value of the whole,* even if it does so only in order to squander it, we know there is an attempt on Nietzsche's part to staunch the irrecuperable outflow of a yet more wasteful economy.

This largest and most indifferent economy is also called "becoming" or "time." The being of the whole is eternal becoming, and "becoming must appear justified at every moment (or incapable of being evaluated; which amounts to the same thing)" (*WP* 708). It is precisely because there is no center, no conclusion, no goal, no place of rest, that each moment of eternal becoming is as valuable as any other. There is no privileged locus of value; thus, we either affirm the whole or deny the whole, and because there is an absolute parity of moments, and they all imply one another, forming an unbreakable interlocking chain, to affirm or deny one moment of the whole is to affirm or deny the whole. "Have you ever said Yes to a single joy? O my friends, then you said Yes to *all* woe. All things are entangled, ensnared, enamored; if ever you wanted one thing twice, if ever you said, 'You please me, happiness! Abide, moment!' then you wanted *all* back. All anew, all eternally, all entangled, ensnared, enamored—oh, then you *loved* the world. Eternal ones, love it eternally" (*Z* IV,19;435). There is a curious sort of humility expressed in this conception. An absolute democratization or leveling of time, no moment worth any more than any other, yet each infinitely precious—as the souls of human beings are in Christian thought. Isn't this the conception of time expressed in the Gospel of John, that "most beautiful fruit of Christianity," as Nietzsche called it in the "The Hellenic Will"? The hour of eternal life is here *now* (*nûn estin*), says John.

But the essence of every moment as moment of becoming is its passage into the *next moment,* its cessation in total and absolute evacuation or discharge of itself into the immediately adjacent future-now. This process, which Nietzsche must affirm, is also what agonizes his being, it is what he images as the devouring of its children by time. The "primordial contradiction that is concealed in things" of which Nietzsche speaks in *The Birth of Tragedy* (IX;71) is fundamentally this agony of temporality that "all that comes into being must be ready for a sorrowful end" (XVII;104). Nietzsche never makes the theme of temporality explicit in *The Birth of Tragedy,* but in the "The Hellenic Will" Nietzsche describes becoming (*Werden*) as "eternal self-contradiction in the form of time." Time itself is the Dionysian drama and the Dionysian *sparagmos,* acted out in each moment of becoming: "Every moment devours the one that precedes it, each birth is the death of countless beings, generation, life, and murder are one" (282).

The will to power as the will to appropriation is the will of one moment to devour all the others, to become the totality and thus attain liberation from the chain of becoming: "'Nourishment—is only derivative; the original phenomenon is: to desire to incorporate everything" (*WP* 657). Nietzsche indulges here a fantasy of *infinite expan-*

sion, as though in the case of some monstrous cosmic protozoan: "My idea is that every specific body strives to become master over all space and to extend its force (—its will to power) and to thrust back all that resists its extension" (*WP* 636).

Is the appropriation and overwhelming of others simply the expression of the innocent desire for self-enjoyment or is it the vengeance against time of which Zarathustra speaks? *Becoming more* would mean, at the limit, *becoming safe,* raising oneself clean out of the endless chain of moments in the vast democracy of becoming. And if the great protozoan explodes on his way toward filling all of space, at least he carved and devoured an enormous slice of the pie before he burst.

The discharge of the now into the immediately adjacent future-now is the microprocess of the whole of becoming, the pathos of self-loss which is what Nietzsche also calls will to power, insofar as will to power is defined as self-surpassing in the other sense, as the will to create beyond oneself and die. Zarathustra's yes is the attempt to experience becoming not as a violation of the self but as its essential act, to "welcome very moment of universal existence with a sense of triumph" (*WP* 55) and thus experience it as the essence of self-enjoyment, whatever its determinate content (triumph, defeat, pain, or pleasure). It is in time, not in space, that the self expands, becomes more, simply because it occupies new expanses of time, infinite time that has plenty of room for everybody, that will gladly devour us all—and each new now that I occupy is infinite, it implies the whole, it contains eternity if only I know how to affirm it as such. (Once again I underline Nietzsche's proximity to the Gospel of John. Nietzsche's interpretation of Jesus and his teachings is very clearly based on John, and this interpretation sounds strangely like Nietzsche's affirmation of the eternally recurring moment: "The 'kingdom of God' is nothing that one expects; it has no yesterday and no day after tomorrow, it will not come in 'a thousand years'—it is an experience of the heart; it is everywhere, it is nowhere" [*Anti* 34].) We can read all of Nietzsche's descriptions of will to power as ways of reconceiving this fundamental pathos, as a metaphor for what Heidegger has called being-in-time (though Heidegger, too, tries to contain its infinite spillage). Overpowering and incorporating as exercise of physical force would then be a weak interpretation, a literal-minded reading, but still a reading, of the problem of temporality. When Nietzsche feels stronger he knows that everything he does do is, must necessarily be, self-enjoyment as spilling of self in each moment into infinite futurity, and that the name of this pathos, this genuinely ecstatic temporality, is neither being nor becoming nor will to power but Eros: *Es gibt nur eine Kraft.* He also knows it in his weaker moments, as we have seen, in the form of denial, as praise of the strength that can resist the spilling of self by erotic *Triebkraft.*

Nietzsche's image of the incorporative protozoan seduces his thinking along the lines of his anxiety and his desire. If the image is imaginatively effective, it is as an evocation of the most primitive sort of self-enjoyment; but it is clearly, in Nietzsche's own terms, only one example of self-enjoyment among many others of radically different kinds, for instance, the ascetic's self-torture, the *Rausch* of the animal in heat that doesn't care if it dies. The process of protoplasmic assimilation is a first approximation to the notion of will to power, but it is so as a *simpler* instance, not as a *smaller* one. The fuller thought of will to power would then proceed by complex transformations (transformations of will to power such as Nietzsche describes for us everywhere, for example, into love, into pity, into self-overcoming), and not by a simple spatial expansion of it. There is *no* series beginning with the amoeba's act of incorporation that ends in the incorporation of all being. Nietzsche's truth is an earthly truth, and there is one earthly truth that marks the limit of all aspiration and all conceptualization: "Body I am entirely, and nothing else" (*Z* I,4;146). This body will not bear infinitizing; on the contrary, it is finitude in its essence, or the essence of finitude, for the finitude of the body is the constitutive and inviolable condition of the subjection to temporality. If we liberate the dynamic that, in Nietzsche's fantasy of fulfillment as an infinite body, pushes the image of incorporation beyond its limits, and house this dynamic instead within the finite and mortal body, then it is clear that this dynamic, which would push on to infinity if it could, must find its only possible expression in the passage of the finite body beyond its limit, that is, in bringing forth new life and dying—preferably in the same act; thus the transcendent significance of orgasm, by which the male images to himself in the shudder of his own flesh the unsurpassable truth of flesh. Of course there is no necessary connection between orgasm and bringing forth or death, merely the imaginative possibility. And because it is only a possibility, one possibility among others, Nietzsche can slide along the surface of the same metaphor and arrive at another possibility that sounds much like the first and yet can accumulate all the forces that are in flight from the first. The orgasm of the great man is not into the future, not an emptying of the self outward but a kind of self-consumption, a using up of the accumulation from the past for which others have been sacrificed, countless others, so that all they accumulated is now his, he is the terminus, the grand conclusion ("The great human being is a finale" [*Twi* IX,44; 548]). He plays the central role, a role that essentially includes dying, but dying in the grand manner, dying like a man, not as having had his substance drained by a parasite or vampire—"the *imperium Romanum* . . . not buried overnight by a natural catastrophe, not trampled down by Teutons and other buffaloes, but ruined by cunning, stealthy, invisible, anemic vampires. Not vanquished—merely drained" (*Anti* 59)—or squandered in the dark with a woman, but as conscious, chosen, and above all as spectacular, as something out here in the open where the gods can watch, something the gods will *want* to watch.

8

Pity and Love

Nietzsche continually tries to cast the principle of corruption into the outside, to treat it as nonessential, as an accident that afflicts life rather than as something proper to its innermost interiority. Even Napoleon was corrupted; but Nietzsche hopefully conjectures that this was *only an accident,* the chance result of circumstance: "He himself was corrupted by the means he *had* to employ and lost *noblesse* of character. If he had to prevail among a different kind of man he could have employed other means; and it would thus not seem to be a necessity for a *Caesar* to become bad" (*WP* 1026). At the same time, by an inevitable countermovement, Nietzsche keeps finding the principle of corruption deep within the *sanctum* of health and strength. The masters are the seat of vigorous life, yet "the degeneration of the rulers and the ruling classes has been the cause of the greatest mischief in history! Without the Roman Caesars and Roman society, the insanity of Christianity would never have come to power" (*WP* 874). Most strikingly, Nietzsche concludes in *The Antichrist* that the "*most corrupt* kind of corruption," Christianity itself, did not simply attack Rome from another site, was not an alien Semitic bacillus, but that "the same kind of religion" had already been present "in its pre-existent form" in the Greece of Epicurus: the "*subterranean* cults" Epicurus fought "were exactly like a latent form of Christianity" (*Anti* 58).[1]

[1]Epicurus himself, whom Nietzsche credits as the opponent of crypto-Christianity, is described elsewhere in *The Antichrist* as "a *typical decadent.*" Epicurus's "fear of pain, even of infinitely minute pain— . . . can end in no other way than in a *religion of love*" (30). Every element that is set up as the antithesis of impurity itself succumbs to impurity in some other locale of Nietzsche's text.

What Nietzsche in *The Antichrist* excoriates as "Christianity" is precisely that underground phenomenon of Greek life that he had praised in *The Birth of Tragedy* as the Dionysian mysteries. These rites conceived "individuation as the primal cause of evil" (*BT* X;74) and imaged redemption from this evil in terms of the rebirth of Dionysus, which Nietzsche glossed as a return to the primal unity of eternally subsisting life; thus they shared with Christianity "the concept of guilt, punishment, and immortality" (*Anti* 58). In his later account of the Dionysian mysteries Nietzsche emphasizes their sexual character and speaks of "eternal life" as the life that continues "through procreation, through the mysteries of sexuality" (*Twi* X,4;561), but even though Nietzsche stresses the difference between the Dionysian and Christian mysteries, he remains uncomfortably aware of how closely related they in fact are.

Nietzsche's difficulty in keeping their significance distinct has been emphasized by René Girard, but it is not entirely accurate to say, as he does, that "Nietzsche . . . rejected the conclusion" at which nineteenth-century anthropology arrived, "that Judaism and Christianity are the same as any other religion with a sacrificial origin."[2] In fact, Nietzsche already alludes to the connection between the Dionysian ritual and Christianity in *The Birth of Tragedy*. Nietzsche tells us there that Dionysus, after his overthrow by aesthetic Socratism, "sought refuge in the depths of the sea, namely the mystical flood of a secret cult which gradually covered the earth" (XII;86). It is hard to imagine what cult Nietzsche could be referring to if not that of Jesus. Furthermore, if in *The Antichrist* Nietzsche does not make explicit that the cult of Dionysus was one of the forms of crypto-Christianity, this appears to be a conscious suppression. For in a note which is apparently a draft of the remarks published in *The Antichrist*, he describes the religions "combatted by Epicurus" as those of "the lower masses, the women, the slaves, the non-noble classes" and lists Dionysus as one of the deities worshipped by these masses. The lists in *The Antichrist* and in this note are tellingly parallel with the single exception: in *The Antichrist*, "Osiris . . . the Great Mother, . . . Mithras" (58); but in *The Will to Power*, "Isis, Mithras, Dionysus, the 'Great Mother.'" Among the beliefs involved in those religions Nietzsche lists "hope of a beyond," "the bloody phantasmagoria of the sacrificial animal (the mystery)," and "asceticism, world denial, superstitious 'purification'" (*WP* 196).

[2]René Girard, "Nietzsche and Contradiction," in *Nietzsche in Italy*, ed. Thomas Harrison (Saratoga, Calif.: Anma Libri, 1988), 63.

It is clear that Dionysus and the Crucified are uncomfortably close in significance, and Nietzsche must struggle to drive a wedge between them. Their difference "is *not* a difference in regard to their martyrdom—it is a difference in the meaning of it" (*WP* 1052): no to life in one case, yes in the other. But the difficulty in drawing the distinction sometimes drives Nietzsche to wrest the two apart so violently that he veers too far in the opposite direction from the one he wants to deny. At one extreme there is passivity, negation; at the other, violent, appropriative aggressiveness; in between, something hard to achieve that we might call active receptiveness. The structure by which Nietzsche veers from one extreme to the other in this case is one that is frequently repeated in Nietzsche's text.[3] The initial phenomenon with which he is concerned has two faces, in this case, Christ and Dionysus. The two faces look very much alike and are called by the same name—in this case, "martyrdom," "the bloody phantasmagoria of the sacrificial animal"; but the name could be, for example, "asceticism," "squandering," "suffering," or "spirituality," since in each case there is a strong version and a weak version of the same phenomenon. Now Nietzsche discards the weak version of the phenomenon in favor of what he identifies as the strong version; but then he is left with a strong phenomenon that continues to be marked as such by its relation to the discarded, weak phenomenon, thus:

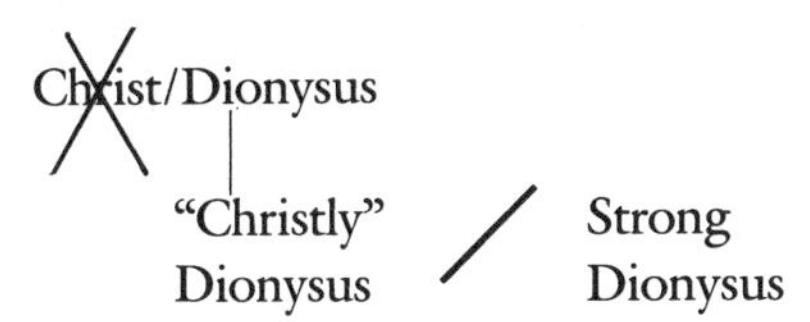

When Nietzsche is strongest, he knows how to think Dionysus not as such a duplicity but as something else altogether, as the unbounded, uncanny yes. But at other times he tries instead by a further purifying operation to drive out the residue within the strong phenomenon of what he perceives as passivity or weakness, and cultivate a culture of pure strength, thus:

[3]The phenomenon in Nietzsche's text that I analyze here was first described by Jacques Derrida in his reading of Rousseau. Derrida calls it the "principle of dichotomy which is repeated endlessly." "By a dichotomous operation that one must ever begin anew and carry further, Rousseau exhausts himself in trying to separate, as two exterior and heterogeneous forces, a positive and negative principle"; *Of Grammatology,* trans. Gayatri Chakravorty Spivak (Baltimore, Md.: Johns Hopkins University Press, 1976), 212; cf. 245–46.

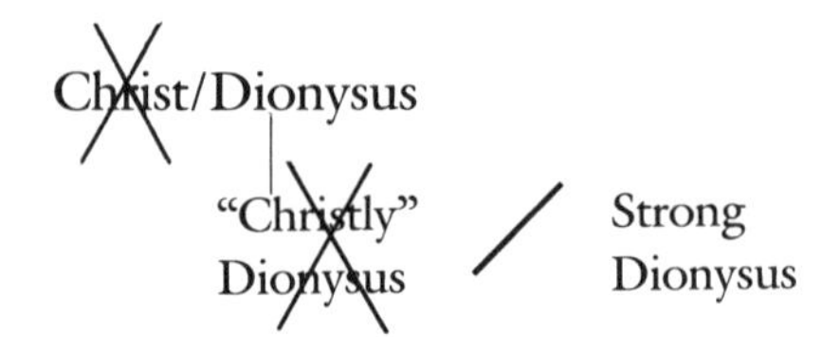

Now "Dionysus" becomes the name for the attitude that adopts the perspective of the conquerors and destroyers.[4]

A similar dynamic is involved in Nietzsche's various conceptions of the Dionysian hero. Because the Dionysian hero is a mask of the universal being, the being of all beings, he represents the whole by representing the pathos of becoming that each being alike must endure; but because he is a hero, a privileged or more valuable being, he represents the whole by accumulating within himself, summing up, the pathos of all the other, less valuable beings; he is the explosive hero who takes it from them and makes it his own: "The many distresses of all the small constitute a sum only in the feelings of powerful human beings" (*WP* 965).[5] In *The Birth of Tragedy* Nietzsche emphasizes the former structure, but there is already present in the emphasis on the hero the possibility of the latter, the possibility developed in the doctrine of genius of the unpublished "Hellenic Will."

The parallelism of genius and hero runs through all of Nietzsche's thought, and the link between the two is what makes it possible to read so much about Nietzsche's own economy in his remarks on the hero. The genius is just another sort of hero, another summing-up of the totality, and in fact the *greater* one since the hero can only sum up his own civilization, but the genius can conceivably include within himself all of human history.

[4]The degree to which Nietzsche's desire to "incorporate" all of history stands in dangerous proximity to the "Christly" is nowhere more explicit than in this remark from 1887–1888 (*WP* 218): "Our pre-eminence: we live in the age of comparison, we can verify as has never been verified before: we are in every way the self-consciousness of history. We enjoy differently, we suffer differently: our instinctive activity is to compare an unheard-of number of things. We understand everything, we experience everything, we no longer have in us any hostile feelings. Although we may harm ourselves by it, our importunate and almost amorous inquisitiveness attacks, unabashed, the most dangerous things.

"Everything is good—it requires an effort for us to deny anything. We suffer if we should happen to be so unintelligent as to take sides against anything—Fundamentally, it is we scholars who today best fulfill the teaching of Christ."

[5]The "powerful human being" thus substitutes for God as a "summarizing power": "Fortunately such a summarizing power [as God] is missing (—a suffering and all-seeing God, a 'total sensorium' and 'cosmic spirit' would be the greatest objection to being") (*WP* 708).

Once again, a double investment. We spoke earlier of the capacity for "incorporation" of history that "the most powerful and tremendous nature" would have, of its double sense as receptive and as aggressive. In *The Gay Science* Nietzsche expresses his ambition concerning this capacity in both senses. Here it is in the first sense, in one of the most *halcyon* passages in all of Nietzsche:

> If one endured, if one *could* endure this immense sum of grief of all kinds while yet being the hero who, as the second day of battle breaks, welcomes the dawn and his fortune, being a person whose horizon encompasses thousands of years past and future, being the heir of all the nobility of all past spirit—an heir with a sense of obligation, the most aristocratic of old nobles and at the same time the first of a new nobility [notice the contrast here with the great man who is purely and simply a *finale* and leaves exhaustion in his wake]— . . . if one could burden one's soul with all of this—the oldest, the newest, losses, hopes, conquests, and the victories of humanity; if one could finally contain all this in one soul and crowd it into a single feeling—this would surely have to result in a happiness that humanity has not known so far: the happiness of a god full of power and love, full of tears and laughter, a happiness that, like the sun in the evening, continually bestows its inexhaustible riches, pouring them into the sea, feeling richest, as the sun does, only when even the poorest fisherman is still rowing with golden oars! (*GS* 337)

And now here is the same ambition in the appropriative mood ("mood" here in something like a grammatical sense, as in "subjunctive mood"):

> "Oh, my greed! There is no selflessness in my soul but only an all-coveting self that would like to appropriate many individuals as so many additional pairs of eyes and hands—a self that would like to bring back the whole past, too, and that will not lose anything that it could possibly possess. Oh, my greed is a flame! Oh, that I might be reborn in a hundred beings!"—Whoever does not know this sigh from firsthand experience does not know the passion of the search for knowledge. (*GS* 249)

In both of these passages we see once again the absoluteness of Nietzsche's desire, his tendency to want to be all beings, occupy all of space, here in the forms of affect and cognition; but the desire expressed in the second passage is, so to speak, a contractive expansiveness compared to that expressed in the first.

Nietzsche's desire to be the whole takes yet one more form, that of nostalgia for a lost unity. This nostalgia is originally expressed in *The Birth of Tragedy,* but it survives the metaphysics of music and turns up once again in Nietzsche's writings on rhetoric, where the primal unity is now identified in terms of language:

> The will [to speak] . . . is nothing individual. If one would imagine a primal mythological being with a hundred heads, a hundred feet and a hundred hands, as the form of the primordial human being: this being would speak with himself, and when he noticed that he could speak with himself as with two, three, or even a hundred beings, he would let himself crumble into his parts, individual men, because he would know he could not entirely lose his unity: because this is not in space, like this multiplicity of a hundred men; on the contrary, when they speak the mythological monster experiences himself once again as a completely unified being [*ganz und eins*]. (Naumann, 10:294)

This theme also turns up several times in the writings on Empedocles to which David Krell has called attention. In a note from 1872—1873, Nietzsche writes that "the conviction that all living things are united testifies to the fact that there was once an *enormous living creature* of which we are fragments: . . . Everything was bound by love alone; . . . Such love was torn and split asunder by enmity"; similar remarks are in Nietzsche's lectures on Empedocles delivered in 1872, 1873, and 1876.[6]

It is as though Nietzsche's original nostalgia for a lost unity of all beings, his desire to be restored as a part to the whole, were invertible into the desire to *become the whole* by expanding to incorporate all the other parts. In either case, there is a restored totality. But, in one case, self-identity is retained; in the other, the self dissolves, its boundaries are permeated by the being of others, countless others, or the self explodes, is dispersed into an infinitude of bodies and roles.

Is Nietzsche an appropriator like Napoleon, or is he unhinged like

[6]David Farrell Krell, *Postponements: Woman, Sensuality, and Death in Nietzsche* (Bloomington: Indiana University Press, 1986), 42, 44.

an artist—at least, like a *modern* artist? For modern artists are very much like hysterics, indeed, "painfully like hysterical females" (*WP* 812). And Nietzsche gives this account of the hysteric:

> The hysteric is false—he lies from love of lying, he is admirable in every art of dissimulation—unless his morbid vanity plays a trick on him. This vanity is like a continual fever that requires narcotics and does not shrink from any self-deception, any farce, that promises momentary relief. . . .
> The absurd irritability of his system, which turns all experiences into crises and introduces the "dramatic" into the smallest accidents of life, robs him of all calculability: he is no longer a person, at most a rendezvous of persons and now this one, now that one shoots forward with shameless assurance. Precisely for this reason, he is great as an actor: all these poor will-less people whom doctors study so closely astonish one with their virtuosity in mimicry, transfiguration, assumption of almost any *desired* character. (*WP* 813)

This sounds like a description of what Derrida has called "the Nietzsches," all those discordant voices that shoot forward with shameless assurance in Nietzsche's text, heedless of whether or not they contradict each other.[7] But surely Nietzsche does *not* mean to describe himself as one of these "hysterics"? When he speaks of the hysterical modern artist, he is thinking of Wagner. Here, for example, is how Nietzsche speaks of him in *The Case of Wagner:*

> The problems he presents on the stage—all of them problems of hysterics—the convulsive nature of his affects, his overexcited sensibility [and so on] . . . all of this taken together represents a profile of sickness that permits no further doubt. *Wagner est une nevrose* [Wagner is a neurosis]. Perhaps nothing is better known today . . . than the Protean character of degeneration that here conceals itself in the chrysalis of art and artist. . . . Wagner is *The modern artist par excellence.* (V;166)

But now listen to his description in *Twilight of the Idols* of the "Dionysian state":

> In the Dionysian state . . . the whole affective system is excited and enhanced: so that it discharges all its means of expression at once and

[7]Jacques Derrida, "Interpreting Signatures (Nietzsche/Heidegger): Two Questions," in *Dialogue and Deconstruction: The Gadamer-Derrida Encounter,* ed. Diane P. Michelfelder and Richard E. Palmer (Albany: SUNY Press, 1989), 68.

> drives forth simultaneously the power of representation, imitation, transfiguration, transformation, and every kind of mimicking and acting. The essential feature here remains the ease of metamorphosis, the inability *not* to react (similar to certain hysterical types who also, upon any suggestion, enter into *any* role). . . . He enters into any skin, into any affect: he constantly transforms himself. (IX,10;519–20)

Isn't this Nietzsche? And isn't this why it's so hard to say who is speaking when "Nietzsche" speaks, who is "I" or "we" and who are "they" in his text? His experimentalism involves his whole self, which is entirely dissolved in the perspective of the moment, and thus ranges freely from the largest and most generous utterances to the meanest and most reactive, as though one voice knew nothing of the others. And this is how Nietzsche conceived the Dionysian state from the beginning: already in the famous passages of section 8 of *The Birth of Tragedy* Nietzsche described the poet as one who feels "the urge to transform himself and to speak out of other bodies and souls," and the chorus as a whole mass of people among whom this "artistic gift" which is "a surrender of individuality and a way of entering into another character" is "encountered epidemically." Even in the more sober *Course on Rhetoric* Nietzsche speaks of the orator's art as "imitative" and describes the orator as one who speaks "like an actor" from "the interior of the character of another person [*aus einer fremden Person heraus*]" (Musarion, 5:305).[8] This connection suggests the continuity between Nietzsche's thinking on rhetoric and on the Dionysian which has escaped Lacoue-Labarthe,[9] the substructure to the metaphysics of "music" which could persist after this metaphysics has been stripped away. What persists is a concern with the possibility of tran-

[8]The problem of representation in Nietzsche therefore does not primarily concern mental representation, *Vorstellung,* but rather impersonation. Impersonation, the properly Dionysian *mimesis,* is already identified by Plato in book 3 of the *Republic,* in a discussion that has tremendous resonance with *The Birth of Tragedy,* as mimetic contamination itself. To impersonate others is to speak with their voices, and there is thus *even in the epic* (here Plato is perhaps more discerning than Nietzsche) the element of self-loss or *Rausch* in those passages in which Homer ceases to speak in his own person and instead speaks as though he were one of his characters; once it gets started, this sort of thing can lead a man into an unlimited rapture of imitation. "The more debased he is the less will he shrink from imitating anything and everything. He will think nothing unworthy of himself, so that he will attempt, seriously and in the presence of many, to imitate all things, including . . . claps of thunder, . . . and the sounds of all instruments, and the cries of dogs, sheep, and birds" (*Republic* 3.373a–b).

[9]Philippe Lacoue-Labarthe, "Le détour," *Poetique* 5 (1971):53–76.

scending the boundaries of individuality by some sort of sympathetic sharing of subjectivity.

Nietzsche's tendency toward what he views as a form of hysteria, "painfully like" that of "hysterical females," this centrifugal movement that marks him as the opposite of what he most frequently characterizes as the exceptional or noble type: what sort of syndrome is it, what causes it?

In the writings from the period of *The Birth of Tragedy* Nietzsche characterizes the Dionysian experience as one that is capable of sharing in the *Urleid,* the primordial suffering of all the world, but he reserves the term pity (*Mitleid*) for the weaker, Apollo-mediated forms of identification with others (*KGW* III 1:23). In fact, in the famous passage in section 21 in which Nietzsche asks how one could "endure to perceive the echo of innumerable shouts of pleasure and woe in the 'wide space of the world night,'" he tells us that pity (*Mitleiden*) for the figures of the Apollonian illusion saves us from the shattering perception of the primordial suffering of the totality (*Urleiden*) (132–33). But this depreciation of what he calls pity is actually on behalf of an intensified form of the capacity to share the suffering of others: ordinary *Mitleid* is a pale reflection of Dionysian suffering.

Beginning with *Human All Too Human,* Nietzsche makes *Mitleid* one of the most persistent targets of his criticism, and often speaks as though there were in reality no such thing, as we have seen; he claims that it is our own suffering, aroused in a variety of ways, and not that of the other that afflicts us when we feel what is called pity (*D* 133). Nevertheless, alongside this trend there is another, equally as persistent, according to which Nietzsche continues to reserve the possibility of a rare and difficult act of imagination by which one could, after all, transport oneself sympathetically into the subjectivity of another. "In very rare cases—when the genius of skill and understanding (*Können und Erkennen*) merges with the moral genius in the same individual—we have . . . those pains that must be seen as the exceptions in the world: the extra-personal, transpersonal feelings, in sympathy with a people, mankind, all civilization, or all suffering existence" (*H* 157). Nietzsche is careful to add that "these feelings acquire their value through association with especially difficult and remote perceptions (pity per se is not worth much)." Thus we find here, despite the disappearance of the metaphysics of the *Ur-Eine,* a continued belief in profound forms of sympathetic identification that transcend the comparatively superficial phenomenon of *Mitleid.* Again: "The great lack of fantasy [*Phantasie*] from which [the ordinary man] suffers keeps him from being able to empathize with other beings [*hineinfühlen*] and he therefore participates in their vicissitudes and suffering as little as possible" (*H* 33). And: "Because of a lack of imagination (*Phantasie*) most princes and military leaders can easily appear to be harsh and cruel, without being so. *Egoism is not evil,* for the idea of one's 'neighbor' . . . is very weak in us; and we feel toward him almost as free and irresponsible as we do toward plants and stones. That the other suffers *must be learned;* and it can never be learned completely" (*H* 101).

Nietzsche even believes that we should learn to sympathize with animals. In "Schopenhauer as Educator" he declares that "more profoundly feeling people have at all times felt sympathy for the animals" (*UM* III,5;157). And in *The Wanderer and His Shadow* he says that

> many animals, through the way they look, sound, and comport themselves, inspire men *imaginatively to transport* themselves into them [*Hineindichten*—an interesting verb], and many religions teach that, under certain circumstances, the souls of men and gods may dwell in animals: for which reason they recommend . . . a reverential awe in traffic with animals in general. Even after this superstition has vanished, the sentiments it has given rise to continue to operate, mature and flourish.—As is well known, on this point Christianity has proved to be a barren and regressive religion. (57; cf. *H* 101)

Remarks such as these are continuous with the later remarks we have already canvased concerning Nietzsche's desire to sum up the experience of mankind in himself, his sense that "the isolation of the individual ought not to deceive us: something flows on *underneath* individuals" (*WP* 686). Two phenomena that look very much alike: on the one hand, *Mitleid* and, on the other, something called *Phantasie,* or a mental operation called *hineinfühlen* or *hineindichten,* which would be the true coin of which the other is the counterfeit. What Nietzsche names with these other names is therefore *true Mitleid,* the deep and genuine version of that which *Mitleid* usually names. And this true *Mitleid* is precisely that which afflicts Nietzsche from within, what he names as his greatest abyss and temptation. The form in which it afflicts him is not the weak form unconnected with "difficult and remote perceptions" but instead precisely the sort that feels too immediately and intensely the sufferings of others.

This pity that Nietzsche cannot bear, or can hardly bear, is almost indistinguishable from something he calls "love."

Here we arrive at the final turn in our exploration of Nietzsche's economy. Commentators on Nietzsche do not talk much about Nietzsche and love; yet love is one of the most frequently recurring words in *Zarathustra,* where Zarathustra also continually speaks of his loneliness (he is "the loneliest of all"—[Z III,4;276]) and, in certain crucial passages, of his own need for love and his resentment at not receiving it. Zarathustra calls pity his "deepest abyss" (III,2;269), but two pages earlier he says that "love is the danger of the loneliest; love of everything if only it is alive." Like pity, love is a permeability of the boundary of individuation or a pouring-out of the substance of the self. This pouring-out is figured in *Zarathustra* almost entirely in terms of love for humanity, and especially of the "higher men." But there are two sections in the second part in which another kind of love is in question. One "The Tomb Song," is only allusive: "O all you glances of love, you divine moments! How quickly you died"; "Scarcely as the gleam of divine eyes it came to me—passing swiftly as a glance" (*Z* II,11;222–23). The other, however, "The Night Song," which we touched on earlier, is quite explicit. I allow myself here to recall the merely biographical fact, if it is a fact, that this song, as Erich Podach puts it, "awakened within" Nietzsche in 1893, "when he was still wholly under the delight and magic and martyrdom of his friendship with Lou":[10] "A craving for love is within me," sings Zarathustra, "but I live in my own light; I drink back into myself the flames that break out of me. I do not know the happiness of those who receive. . . . A hunger grows out of my beauty: *I should like to hurt those for whom I shine*. . . . *Such revenge* my fullness plots: *such spite* wells out of my loneliness" (emphasis added; II,9;218).

In *Ecce Homo,* where Nietzsche poses as one who is entirely autonomous, he cites "The Night Song" in its entirety and exclaims that "nothing like this has ever been written, felt, or *suffered:* thus suffers a god, a Dionysus" (*EH* IX,8;308). But even though what Zarathustra describes is apparently a desire to be loved, the Nietzsche of *Ecce Homo* describes the song as Zarathustra's immortal lament "at being con-

[10]*The Madness of Nietzsche,* trans. Fritz August Voigt (New York: Putnam, 1931), 102.

demned by the overabundance of light and power, by his sun-nature, *not to love*" (emphasis added; IX,7;306). And it is true that there are ambiguities in "The Night Song"; even though it reads overwhelmingly like a cry for love, it withholds itself just enough to leave open Nietzsche's interpretation of it in *Ecce Homo*. "Oh, craving to crave!" Zarathustra exclaims at one point, as though he does *not* crave and only wishes he were less autarkic and could desire love.

So even at his moment of what looks like the most explicit erotic self-revelation, Nietzsche withholds himself just enough to create a shade of uncertainty. Still, it is astonishing that he could even once come this close to an explicit confession of his need for love—and that he should then, in *Ecce Homo,* repeat the confession or near-confession, even under the form of denegation ("lament at being condemned . . . not to love" equals "this does *not* express a craving for love"). But if Zarathustra only wishes he could love, why does he say "I do not know the happiness of those who receive"? Why does he say "such spite wells up out of my loneliness"?

In fact, in part 4 Zarathustra tells us some more about the economy of erotic ressentiment. He says the greatest sinner is the one who curses those who laugh, and he asks, "Does one have to curse right away, where one does not love? . . . And he himself simply did not love enough: else he would not have been so wroth that one did not love him" (*Z* IV,13;405). Here matters become more complicated: the inability to love does not exclude the demand to be loved, and in fact those who withhold their own love are most vengeful against others who will not love them.

There is one more scene in *Zarathustra* that resonates with these themes, the "Magician" scene with its song. Essential studies by Karl Reinhardt and David Krell[11] have shown how complex is Nietzsche's relation to this song, which was originally conceived as the lament of a woman in childbirth and eventually is put in the mouth of Ariadne as one of the *Dionysus Dithyrambs,* under the title "The Plaint of Ariadne." These writers suggest that Nietzsche's own voice speaks in this song in ways that reveal his most profound pathos, his tendency toward the "voluptuousness of the martyr" which confounds the distinctions between active and passive, strong and weak, and even male and female on which Nietzsche usually insists.

[11]Karl Reinhardt, "Nietzsche's Lament of Ariadne," *Interpretation* 6 (1977): 204–24; Krell, *Postponements*.

Who warms me, who loves me still?
Give hot hands!
Give a heart as glowing coals!
. . .

Thus I lie
Writhing, twisting, tormented
With all eternal tortures,
Hit
By thee, cruelest hunter
Thou unknown *god*!

Hit deeper!
Hit once more yet!
Drive a stake through and break this heart!
. . .

No! Do come back
With all thy tortures!
To the last of all that are lonely,
Oh, come back!
(*Z* IV,5;364–67)

But the magician who utters these words in *Zarathustra* is only posing as the afflicted one implied by his utterance, here conceived as the "ascetic of the spirit," in order to deceive Zarathustra. The magician is afflicted with a compulsion to mimicry which sounds much like Nietzsche's own:

> You always have to be equivocal [Zarathustra reproaches the magician]—tri-, quadri-, quinquevocal. And what you have now confessed, that too was not nearly true enough or false enough to suit me. . . . You would rouge even your disease when you show yourself naked to your doctor. In the same way you have just now rouged your lie when you said to me, "I did all this *only* as a game." There was *seriousness* in it too: you *are* something of an ascetic of the spirit. (368)

The self-reflexive complexity of Nietzsche/Zarathustra's reproach should be apparent, especially when we recall what Zarathustra has earlier said to his disciples: "But what was it that Zarathustra once said to you? That the poets lie too much? But Zarathustra too is a poet. Do you now believe that he spoke the truth here? Why do you believe that?" (*Z* II,17;239). Here I am concerned only with the fact that the structure "Magician/compulsive mimic who is undecidably both an ascetic and not an ascetic" is also the structure of the textual Nietzsche whose outlines we have been tracing, and that when Zarathustra hears the magician's lament this is what he says, *as reported by the magician:* "You *believed* in my distress [the magician says to Zarathustra] when you held my head with both your hands; I heard you moan, 'He has been loved too little, loved too little'" (IV,5;368). We know the magician is a liar, but we have no reason to think he is misreporting in this case. After all, he is citing Zarathustra's own words back to him; a lie would make no sense here. And yet, why are the words not reported when Zarathustra speaks them? Why are they only reported by a notorious deceiver? Once again, Nietzsche reveals himself only by placing his revelation in a slightly disconcerting obscurity.

"The great poet dips *only* from his own reality," Nietzsche says, and then gives his own *Zarathustra* as an example: "When I have looked into my *Zarathustra,* I walk up and down in my room for half an hour, unable to master an unbearable fit of sobbing" (*EH* II,4;246). The dominant pose in *Ecce Homo* is of mastery and self-control, and the final words of Zarathustra's that Nietzsche stresses are "become hard!" (IX,8;309), but Nietzsche melts when he reads his own book, he sobs uncontrollably, he can't help it. Why? He doesn't tell us.

When Zarathustra holds the magician/ascetic's head in his hands Zarathustra moans, "He has been loved too little, loved too little"; as though this were one avatar of Nietzsche grieving over another avatar of Nietzsche.

Is this too ingenious a suggestion, one too dependent on a certain modern way of interpreting texts? Consider, then, what Schopenhauer says about the ultimate nature of weeping, in a passage from book 4 of *The World as Will and Representation* which Nietzsche must have known, considering that it comes in the middle of Schopenhauer's account of the nature of love and *Mitleid,* the very account that Nietzsche constantly criticizes, explicitly or implicitly. Schopenhauer has just identified *Mitleid* with *agapé* and contrasted it with the "selfishness" of *Eros,* and now he makes the following remarks which profoundly confuse the distinction he has just made while in some ways going deeper into the understanding of *Mitleid* than Nietzsche, who is so contemptuous of Schopenhauer's doctrine (e.g., *D* 133), ever goes:

> Weeping is by no means a positive manifestation of pain, for it occurs where pains are least. In my opinion, we never weep directly over pain that is felt, but always only over its repetitions in reflection. Thus we pass from the felt pain, even when it is physical, to a mere mental picture or representation of it; we then find our own state so deserving of sympathy that, if another were the sufferer, we are firmly and sincerely convinced that we would be full of sympathy and love to help him. Now we ourselves are the object of our sincere sympathy; with the most charitable disposition, we ourselves are most in need of help. We feel that we endure more than we could see another endure, and in this peculiarly involved frame of mind, in which the directly felt suffering comes to perception only in a doubly indirect way, pictured as the suffering of another and sympathized with as such, and then suddenly perceived again as directly our own; in such a frame of mind nature finds relief through that curious physical convulsion. Accordingly, *weeping is sympathy with ourselves,* or sympathy thrown back to its starting-point. It is therefore conditioned by the capacity for affection and sympathy, and by the imagination. Therefore people who are either hard-hearted or without imagination do not readily weep. . . .
>
> . . . That we are moved to tears not by our own sufferings, but by those of others, happens in the following way; either in imagination we put ourselves vividly in the sufferer's place, or we see in his fate the lot of the whole of humanity, and consequently above all our own fate. Thus in a very roundabout way, we always weep about ourselves; we feel sympathy with ourselves. This seems also to be a main reason for the universal, and hence natural, weeping in cases of death. It is not the mourner's loss over which he weeps; he would be ashamed of such egoistical tears, instead of sometimes being ashamed of not weeping. In the first place, of course, he weeps over the fate of the deceased; yet he weeps also when for the deceased death was a desirable deliverance after long, grave, and incurable sufferings. In the main, therefore, he is seized with sympathy over the lot of the whole of mankind that is given over to finiteness. In consequence of this, every life, however ambitious and often rich in deeds, must become extinct and nothing. In this lot of mankind, however, the mourner sees first of all his own lot, and this the more, the

more closely he was related to the deceased, and most of all therefore when the deceased was his father.[12]

Yet it isn't obvious what there is in the song that could lead Zarathustra to draw the conclusion that the magician has been "loved too little." The magician does call himself "the loneliest" (which is of course Zarathustra's own title), but that is just one, almost incidental, moment of the song. The dominant note is the ambivalence of the plea to an invisible god, the combination of desire to be free of him ("Away! Away!") and of desire to have him continue his tortures ("No! Do come back/*With* all thy tortures!"). This combination of pleasure and pain aroused by means of the fantasy of a divine agent is the voluptuousness of the martyr which had fascinated Nietzsche at least since *Human, All Too Human* ("when [the saint] yearns for visions, conversations with the dead, or with divine beings, it is basically a rare form of voluptuousness that he desires, perhaps that voluptuousness in which all others are wound together in one knot" [*H* 142]). In the *Genealogy of Morals* he analyzed the structure of this reflexive cruelty in relation to the man of bad conscience who "ejects from himself all his denial of himself . . . as God . . . as torment without end" (II,2;92), though in these remarks he is silent about the element of voluptuousness involved. Is Zarathustra suggesting by his response to the magician that this transcendental masochism is caused by lack of love?

There is such a thing as an absolute desire for love, a desire as absolute as that which indulges the fantasy of infinite expansion, and which no human love can satisfy. The desire to be loved limitlessly is the inverse or passive correlate of the desire to appropriate all of space,

[12]*The World as Will and Representation,* vol. 1, trans. E. F. J. Payne (New York: Dover Publications, 1969), 376–78. Schopenhauer's analysis here is somewhat elliptical and gives the impression of arguing in a circle: our ability to sympathize with ourselves depends on our "capacity for love and sympathy"—apparently for others. But then when we sympathize with the suffering of another, it is really our own suffering we sympathize with. But Schopenhauer has provided the elements of a more powerful analysis when he tells us that "we pass from felt pain . . . to a mere mental picture or representation of it" (first step), and then seeing our own suffering as we would see that of another (second step), we sympathize. Here would be the point at which sympathy originates, in what is neither simply a self-relation nor simply the relation to another, but in which the representation of the self is seen *as though* it were that of another. The relation to the representation of another is thus not the origin of sympathy but the *mediating image* by which sympathy originates in a self-reflection. It would then follow without confusion that sympathy for another's suffering involves "the turning back . . . on to our own individuality," as Schopenhauer describes it in the next section (378).

a passive appropriativeness, limitless receptivity to the outflowing of another being. And there has been at least one man who manifested this absolute desire. Who? It *isn't* Nietzsche; rather, Nietzsche's antithesis, the negative Dionysus of the Jews:

> It is possible that underneath the holy fable and disguise of Jesus' life there lies concealed one of the most painful cases of the martyrdom of *knowledge about love:* the martyrdom of the most innocent and desirous heart, never sated by any human love; *demanding* love, to be loved and nothing else, with hardness, with insanity, with terrible eruptions against those who denied him love; the story of a poor fellow, unsated and insatiable in love, who had to invent hell in order to send to it those who did not *want* to love him—and who finally, having gained knowledge about human love, had to invent a god who is all love, all *ability* to love—who has mercy on human love because it is so utterly wretched and unknowing. Anyone who feels that way, who *knows* this about love—*seeks* death. (*BGE* 269)

Does Nietzsche not know this about love? Manifestly, he does. So he is not entirely unlike Jesus; he has the same knowledge, but perhaps not the same desire?

The paragraph just cited stands at the end of a remarkable section of *Beyond Good and Evil* in which Nietzsche unmasks his own myth of the great man with a coldness and penetration I do not think he achieves anywhere else in relation to this subject. Let us read the section as a whole and try to locate Jesus within this fuller context.

Nietzsche begins by confronting the paradox that so often arises in his work: "The corruption, the ruination of the higher men, of the souls of a stronger type, is the rule." But this time Nietzsche recognizes that this corruption is not an unfortunate accident, something from outside that unaccountably overwhelms what is per se great and valuable, but that great men in the sense in which he has mythologized them *do not exist:*

> Who knows whether what happened in *all great cases so far* was not *always* the same [emphasis added]: that the crowd adored a god—and that the "god" was merely a poor sacrificial animal [notice the deflated Dionysian imagery here]. Success has always been the greatest liar[!]—and the "work" itself is a success; the great statesman, the conqueror, the dis-

> coverer is disguised by his creations, often beyond recognition; the "work," whether of the artist or the philosopher, invents the man who has created it. . . . "Great men," as they are venerated [presumably, Caesar and Napoleon included], are subsequent pieces of wretched minor fiction. (*BGE* 269)

Nietzsche here includes the whole gamut of greatness, from the "conqueror" to the "artist" and "philosopher." Now he proceeds to speak of the example of poets, with the implication that what is true of them is true of all other great men: "Those great poets, for example—men like Byron, Musset, Poe, Leopardi, Kleist, Gogol (I do not dare mention greater names, but I mean them)—are and perhaps must be men of fleeting moments, enthusiastic, sensual, childish, frivolous, . . . with souls in which they usually try to conceal some fracture; often taking revenge with their works for some inner contamination" (269).

Nietzsche's parenthetical remarks are strangely coy; does Nietzsche mean greater poets or greater men of another type? Why does he not "dare" mention them? Why is he using only *poets* as examples? Can Nietzsche even now not quite bring himself to be perfectly explicit concerning the hollowness of his idols of political power? Is Nietzsche one of these poets? He doesn't say; but if he is not, he would have to be the exception to "all great cases so far," and he doesn't say that, either. And now his thoughts start to turn in the direction that will lead to Jesus. These sensual, childish, inwardly damaged, vengeful men quite naturally soak up something that flows *boundlessly* toward them from women, something that is here first called "pity" and then "love":

> It is easy to understand that *these* men should so readily receive from woman—clairvoyant in the world of suffering and, unfortunately, also desirous far beyond her strength to help and save—these eruptions of boundless and most devoted *pity*. . . . Woman would like to believe that love can achieve *anything*. . . . Alas, whoever knows the heart will guess how poor, stupid, helpless, arrogant, blundering, more apt to destroy than to save is even the best and profoundest love! (*BGE* 269)

This is where Nietzsche's remarks about Jesus come in: Jesus, who, like Nietzsche, realizes the inadequacy of human love, imagines a divine love to replace it. The crucial point is that Jesus here acquires an exemplary significance he does not have elsewhere in Nietzsche because he is introduced here as a member of the set "great men," as the culmination of the series, the one who exemplifies at the limit the desire that shows itself in a less absolute form in others.

Jesus' demand for love is extreme, and in an earlier remark in *Beyond Good and Evil* Nietzsche attributes the most extreme demand for love to the *most subtle and appropriative* man; this desire in fact determines his "order of rank":

> Regarding a woman, . . . those men who are more modest consider the mere use of the body and sexual gratification a sufficient and satisfying sign of "having," of possession. Another type, with a more suspicious and demanding thirst for possession, . . . wants subtler tests . . . to know whether the woman . . . gives up for his sake what she has or would like to have. . . . A third type, however, does not reach the end of his mistrust and desire for having even so: he asks himself whether the woman, when she gives up everything for him, does not possibly do this for a phantom of him. *He wants to be known deep down, abysmally deep down,* before he is capable of being loved at all; he dares to let himself be fathomed. (emphasis added; *BGE* 194)

This is how the man who stands highest in the order of rank, the one who is most ambitious in his possessiveness—thus, it follows, the one with the greatest *will to power* in erotic matters—wants to be loved. He demands that the soul of the woman touch him "abysmally deep down," where his noble soul stands preserved behind all its masks. The trouble is, as Nietzsche tells us in remark 269, there is *no such love,* at least not from a woman; even her "best and profoundest love" fails to see the man as he truly is; this inadequacy of all human love is what led Jesus to imagine a god who is all love.

Not that women don't *try;* they really would like to give the man this boundless outpouring that he demands; in fact, it is of the essence of the female that she should love in this way: "What woman means by love is clear enough: total devotion [*Hingabe*] (not mere surrender [*Hingebung*]) with soul and body, without any consideration or reserve, rather with shame and horror at the thought of a devotion that might be subject to special clauses or conditions" (*GS* 363). This unconditional outpouring of self, expenditure without reserve, is the very *telos* of femininity, the perfection of woman's being; its complement is the restricted economy of the male who withholds his being from her so that he can accumulate hers:

> Man, when he loves a woman, wants precisely this love from her and is thus himself as far as can be from the presupposition of feminine love. Supposing, however, that there should also be men to whom the desire for total devotion [Nietzsche clearly means here the desire to *give* such devotion] is not alien; well, then they simply are—not men. A man who loves like a woman becomes a slave; while a woman who loves like a woman becomes *a more perfect woman*. (*GS* 363)

But what is Nietzsche saying?! A woman *perfects herself* by giving herself over to the appropriative desire of a man "who *takes,* who does not give himself or give himself away; on the contrary, he is supposed to become richer in 'himself'—through the accretion of strength, happiness and faith given him by the woman who gives herself" (*GS* 363). But we remember this about the "perfect woman" in *Ecce Homo:* "They all love me. . . . Fortunately, I am not willing to be torn to pieces: the perfect woman tears to pieces when she loves" (III,5;266). What Nietzsche in *The Gay Science* and *Beyond Good and Evil* pictures as the absolute desire of the most appropriative man, his ultimate possessiveness, is also that which most threatens a man's integrity, his self-possession. The remark in *Ecce Homo* is not an aberration; it follows from an analysis of pity/love which Nietzsche consistently holds to, according to which it is *the appropriative mode of the weak.* "When we see somebody suffer, we like to exploit this opportunity to take possession of him; those who become his benefactors and pity him, for example, do this and call the lust for a new possession that he awakens in them 'love'; and the pleasure they feel is comparable to that aroused by the prospect of a new conquest" (*GS* 14). "Pity is the most agreeable feeling among those who have little pride and no prospects of great conquests; for them easy prey—and that is what all who suffer are—is enchanting. Pity is praised as the virtue of prostitutes" (*GS* 13). Thus, if a man could totally possess the woman by possessing all her love, a love which would penetrate to the bottom of his being, she would *possess him.*

The greatest desire thus desires what it also most fears; appropriation undoes itself. This result is woven into the essence of the drive to appropriation, for if *all* will is will to incorporate the other and there is no end to it, then all incorporation necessarily undoes itself because what it incorporates will always itself be in its essence incorporativeness. The strong says "Yield!" and the weak says "Take me!" and in being taken snares the strong. "The weaker presses to the stronger from a need for nourishment; it wants to get under it, if possible to become one with it" (*WP* 655); "Enrollment, so as to satisfy the will to power in a larger whole: submission, making oneself indispensable and useful to those in power; love, as a secret path to the heart of the more powerful—so as to dominate him" (774); "Woman's love and sympathy—is there anything more egoistic?" (777). But the process doesn't end here. If the one who pities tries to incorporate the sufferer, the sufferer is trying to take the substance of the pitier: "The pity that the spectators . . . express consoles the weak and suffering, inasmuch as they see that, despite all their weakness, they still *have* . . . the *power to hurt*" (the power called "the right of the masters" in the *Genealogy of Morals*); "The thirst for pity is a thirst for self-enjoyment, and at the expense of one's fellow men" (*H* 50). Finally, even the action of the most appropriative, the Caesar, may be viewed as an enrollment in a larger whole: "Among the strongest, richest, most independent, most courageous," will to power appears as "instinctive self-involvement with a great quantum of power to which one is able to give direction: the hero, the prophet, the Caesar, the savior, the shepherd" (note the homogenization of the Caesar and savior types). And Nietzsche makes explicit the connection with that he has said about sexual love: "Sexual love, too, belongs here: it desires to overpower, to take possession, and it *appears* as self-surrender" (*WP* 776).

Nietzsche says sexual love *appears* as self-surrender, as though this were mere phenomenon, and overpowering, appropriation were the reality; but if now there is no difference between Jesus, Caesar, and a woman in love, if appropriation takes the form of surrender and surrender is really appropriation, will to power truly is best understood as a pathos. If that which incorporates is incorporated by what it incorporates ad infinitum, then appropriation or incorporation would be identical with the limitless spilling of the self.

Nietzsche *knows* this; it is what he knows most deeply, and sometimes says or implies. It is also what he goes endless bypaths to evade, this absolute *reciprocity* of the leveling process of appropriation. Nietzsche asserts that there must be *rank order,* there must be one who takes, accumulates, becomes more, and is not taken, so that there will be a goal, a consummation, for an otherwise aimless, meaningless human life. Does he ever entirely free himself of those entirely traditional sentiments about ***merely animal*** life that he expresses in "Schopenhauer as Educator"?

> To hang onto life madly and blindly, with no higher aim than to hang on to it; not to know that or why one is being so heavily punished but, with the stupidity of a fearful desire, to thirst after precisely this punishment as though after happiness—that is what it means to be an animal; and if all nature presses towards man, it thereby intimates that man is necessary for the redemption of nature from the curse of the life of the animal, and that in him existence at last holds up before itself a mirror in which life appears no longer senseless but in its metaphysical significance.
>
> . . . The tremendous coming and going of men on the great wilderness of the earth, their founding of cities and states, their wars, their restless assembling and scattering again, their confused mingling, mutual imitation, natural outwitting and downtreading, their wailing in distress, their howls of joy in victory—all this is a continuation of animality: as though man was to be deliberately retrogressed and defrauded of his metaphysical disposition. (*UM* III,5;157–58)

This endless dispersal of the substance of humanity can only be brought to a halt by an aim *upward,* an aim at a goal, an end: the saint, the hero, the artist who gives us a "clear and finished picture" (160) of this life.

In terms of the economics of love described by Nietzsche in *The Gay Science* 363, what has to be avoided because it violates the essence of maleness and femaleness is a reciprocal human love in which the male would flow so to speak *horizontally* (rather than upward), without reserve, toward the female, as she toward him, because this would be *nothingness,* there would be nothing left, no one to preserve being as each spilled toward the other, both would cease to exist: *horror vacui,* the nausea of spilling into a void. "A woman's passion in its unconditional renunciation of rights of her own presupposes precisely that on the other side there is no equal pathos, no equal will to renunciation; for if both partners felt impelled by love to renounce themselves, we should then get—I do not know what; perhaps an empty space?" (*GS* 363). This is the pathetic fate of mortal love; phttt! nothing left. This is what Plato and the saints say; that is why divine and ideal loves are necessary. Nietzsche agrees: "Here and there on earth we may encounter a kind of continuation of love in which this possessive craving of two people for each other gives way to a new desire and lust for possession—a *shared* higher thirst for an ideal above them. But who knows such love? Who has experienced it? Its right name is *friendship*" (*GS* 14).

Always the same themes, and not just in Nietzsche; wherever there is the desire for meaning and the search for something more durable than the pointless pouring-forth of life, there will usually also be the distinction between the human and the animal, fear of the female who disperses one's substance, and loathing of the corruption of the body.[13] The link is not exactly, as Krell suggests, between "woman, sensuality, and death," because there is no one thing we can call "death": and in some ways those who most loathe corruptibility are readiest to die, all those heroic young men, for example, who hasten resolutely toward death as to a lover's bed. Nietzsche, too, loves the idea of a certain kind of death: "To die proudly when it is no longer possible to live proudly. Death freely chosen, death at the right time, brightly and cheerfully accomplished amid children and witnesses:

[13]On these themes, see my reading of *Heart of Darkness* in "Conrad's Mortal Word," *Critical Inquiry* 12 (Summer 1986): 720–40. As for Heidegger, where is he to be located in all this? He is mostly silent on these subjects, hardly a word about *Eros* and the female to be found anywhere. But here is one telltale link in the chain, a scent that puts us on the trail of Heideggerean *piety:* "Being is the ether in which man breathes. Without this ether, he would descend to the mere beast and his whole activity to the breeding of beasts"; *Schelling's Treatise on the Essence of Human Freedom,* trans. Joan Stambaugh (Athens: Ohio University Press, 1985), 98. Similarly, Heidegger recoils from what he sees as the consequence of Nietzsche's having "dispatched to oblivion" the "*essence* of truth": "All that is left is the solitary superficies of a 'life' that empowers itself to itself for its own sake"; *Nietzsche,* vol. 3, trans. Joan Stambaugh, David Farrell Krell, and Frank A. Capuzzi (San Francisco: Harper and Row, 1987), 176–77. If Heidegger here means life in general, as I take it he does, he is recoiling from the idea of *the totality of life* "all by itself," all alone, as an individual person might be alone. This is indeed the ultimate fear of the transcendentalizing thinker, apparently even as resourceful a one as Heidegger. Concerning this distinction between man and the beasts, Derrida writes that "a powerful and ample chain from Aristotle, at least, to our day, it binds ontotheological metaphysics to humanism. The essential opposition of man to animal—or rather to animality, to an univocal, homogeneous, obscurantist concept of animality—always serves the same interest there. . . . Of the three wounds to anthropic narcissism, the one Freud indicates with the name Darwin seems more intolerable than the one he has signed himself. It will have been resisted for a longer time"; *Glas,* trans. John P. Leavey, Jr., and Richard Rand (Lincoln: University of Nebraska Press, 1986), 27. Derrida comments on Heidegger's relation to the questions of sexuality and animality in "Geschlecht: Difference sexuelle, difference ontologique," and "La main de Heidegger (Geschlecht II)," both in *Psyché: Inventions de l'autre* (Paris: Editions Galilée, 1987); see also *Of Spirit: Heidegger and the Question,* trans. Geoffrey Bennington and Rachel Bowlby (Chicago: University of Chicago Press, 1989).

then a real farewell is still possible, as the one who is taking leave is still there [a terrible irony in this; did Nietzsche know about his illness, did he suspect that long before his death he would no longer *be there?*]; also a real estimate of what one has achieved . . . drawing the sum of one's life [always the emphasis on *adding it all up* in one sum!]" (*Twi* IX,36;536–37). But then there is that other phenomenon that Nietzsche loathes, which is the essence of *ugliness,* the creeping death that assaults from within, as Christianity assaulted the *imperium Romanum,* as the principle of weakness always assaults strength, draining its substance. Wherever the woman is depreciated and pushed away, there always lurks this terror of the worm of corruption, of the irresistible, autonomous tide of other-than-life that life carries within it but which must be bounded off, defined as that which supervenes from outside, that which is most fundamentally alien to life. Nietzsche tells us it is the "deepest instinct of the species" to hate the "decline of the type" implied by the putrescence at the root of ugliness: "Every suggestion of exhaustion, of heaviness, of age, of weariness; every kind of lack of freedom, such as cramps, such as paralysis; *and above all, the smell, the color, the form of dissolution, of decomposition* [emphasis added]—even in the ultimate attenuation into a symbol [so this putrescence can be anywhere, in symbolic form]—all evoke the same reaction, the value judgement 'ugly.' . . . It is the deepest hatred there is" (*Twi* IX,20; 526–27).

In the face of these threats to his self-possession, Nietzsche recoils, contracts, throws up boundaries and barriers, idealizes health and strength and manliness; but also, as we know, in another, countermovement of his economy it is what he wants to embrace and to teach us how to embrace (though perhaps, as Krell suggests, this embrace, though constantly approached, is indefinitely postponed). As against Plato's ideal beauty that is the ultimate refuge for mortality, ultimate storehouse of the substance of a *psyche* that would otherwise be squandered, Zarathustra says "Where is beauty? Where I must will with all my will; where I want to love and perish that an image [*Bild*] may not remain a mere image [does this allude to the act of procreation?]. Loving and perishing [*Lieben und Untergehen*]: that has rhymed for eternities. The will to love, that is to be willing also to die. Thus I speak to you cowards!" (*Z* II,15;235). And those who lack the will to love and die are called "emasculated" (*entmannt*).

There is for Nietzsche no single formula for the law of being; the law of being opens out its expression into new forms depending on circumstances and also on a kind of rhythmicity or law of alternation. "I am"—"I expand, I become more"—"I bring forth": so we could name three major expressions of the law of being as it expands into its most capacious form. At the limit of these circles, inscribed within them as their *internal* limit, is Dionysus—"I go under."

The Aristotelian metaphysics of life, with its division between the vegetative, sensitive, and intellectual souls, gives us a clue as to the articulation of the law of being in sentient life, but it is structured according to an idealizing impulse and thus conceives consciousness, representation, and volition as the outermost circle, the *telos* of the unfolding of *psyche*. The division between, on one side, the vegetative and animal souls and, on the other, the intellectual soul, fixes permanently for Western thought the supposedly undeniable and absolute boundary between animal and human, as though the articulations of the law of being must observe the boundary between these two major biological articulations. The boundary Aristotle draws seems one of the most basic facts of the world: there are plants, then there are animals, then, on the other side of an ontological abyss that divides these realms of being, there are humans. Yet in fact the Aristotelian articulation falsifies something that was clearly known to Plato, that is in fact one of Plato's central ideas: *the most essential is something we share with the animals*. It is Eros, the drive to bring forth beyond oneself. And yet Plato's Eros, though it is shared by the animals, is in fact the *Triebkraft* that constitutes their animality, essentially aims at the transcendence of animality. "I bring forth" must not, for Plato, be inhabited by "I go under"; "I bring forth" is interpreted as *in its essence* the desire to *transcend death*. But for Nietzsche "I bring forth" is constituted in its essence by "I go under"—"I die," "I will, I desire my own death"—which is enclosed in the innermost core of the will to bring forth. "The will to love [*Wille zur Liebe,* the phrase resounds strikingly in a Nietzschean context], that is to be willing also to die."

This is no ordinary desire, because it is the desire of what I cannot help but get, and also of what, if I were not so absolutely incapable of escaping it, I would escape. This is what confounds the structure of desire as we are ordinarily inclined to analyze it; it is what forces Nietzsche and Freud to develop their analyses of the paradoxal structure of the death drive. Nietzsche calls it *amor fati*.

The ambivalences, chiastic reversals, double investments, and so on that we have traced in Nietzsche's text follow from the paradox of this *telos* that is the undoing of all teleology.

9

The Will of the Ring

Napoleon or ascetic knower: what they share in common is a *fatum* made of granite, the knowledge that they are inviolably themselves, that their boundary of identity holds good. "Know thyself" was the word of Apollo inscribed at Delphi, and Nietzsche tells us that this was the law of "the delimiting of the boundaries of the individual," so that self-knowledge is for Nietzsche the essential bulwark against Dionysian "self-oblivion" (*BT* IV;46). Therefore, he can equate self-knowledge functionally with Spartan (mutatis mutandis, Napoleonic) militarism: "The *Doric* state and Doric art are explicable only as a permanent military encampment of the Apollinian" (47), they are a means of keeping up a rigid boundary against the Dionysian tide.

But in another mood Nietzsche believes that this self-knowledge is illusory, that "we are unknown to ourselves, we men of knowledge"; "for us the law 'Each is furthest from himself' applies to all eternity" (*GM* Preface,1;15). Seen in this perspective, the stance of knowledge and self-knowledge would be not the antithesis of Dionysian rapture but its final intensification, the culmination of forgetfulness in which, like Archilochus asleep among Dionysus and the maenads (*BT* V), the individual dreams himself as knower and forgets that he is dreaming, most enfolded within the Dionysian rapture when he is farthest from it.

The will to knowledge tries to hold the self and all of life within the field of conscious purview, the boundaries of which would be the encompassing container of the self; but what necessarily overflows the field is the motion of the life that drives that self, that drives the will to knowledge and the movement of containment. When Nietzsche turns the screw of self-knowledge far enough, turns the will to truth against itself, asking what the truth is about this will, he discovers that it is the will to overcome life, urge, and desire, to take power over the most fundamental conditions of life—but that this too is life, urge, and desire, and that "such a self-contradiction as the ascetic appears to represent, 'life *against* life' is, physiologically considered . . . , a simple absurdity" (*GM* III,13; 120). And now the illusion of self-mastery comes undone, we see that there is *nothing but life,* that there is no getting outside it, that the knower too is only its path and footprint and that the drive within him will overflow his boundaries and spill itself into an infinity of new forms.

Nietzsche cannot get outside this oscillation, but he can represent it allegorically, can tell us what it feels like to be involved in this constant unstable movement between the perspective of the knower who tries to contain himself and all of life and the rapture of will or desire which is the motion of that life within and without the one who would try to grasp it. Nietzsche expresses what this dizzying oscillation feels like in the image of life as a woman whom he loves and cannot master, in the two "Dancing Song" sections of *Thus Spoke Zarathustra.*

Everyone knows about Zarathustra's whip, the one the old woman tells him to carry whenever he goes to women (*Z* I,18;179), but almost everyone forgets what happens to this whip. It turns up in "The Other Dancing Song" when Zarathustra encounters life once again, who teases him and draws him toward her but runs away and will not let him catch her. Finally, Zarathustra exclaims, "I am verily tired of always being your sheepish shepherd. You witch, if *I* have so far sung to you, now you shall cry. Keeping time with my whip, you shall dance and cry! Or have I forgotten the whip? Not I!" (III, 15;338). But in fact life's response immediately deprives Zarathustra's gesture of all its apparent force. "Covering up her delicate ears," she says to him, "O Zarathustra, don't crack your whip so frightfully! After all, you know that noise murders thought—and just now such tender thoughts are coming to me." "You know that noise murders thought"—this is one of the most consistent notes in Nietzsche's work, always the praise of quiet and the unraised voice. Zarathustra himself had earlier said to the fire hound: "Believe me, friend Hellishnoise: the greatest events—they are not our loudest but our stillest hours. Not around the inventors of new noise, but around the inventors of new values does the world revolve; it revolves *inaudibly*" (II,18;243).

In "Schopenhauer as Educator," Nietzsche had complained of the ruin of great human beings and said that even the strongest are worn down, "they breathe heavily and their voice can easily become too loud" (*UM* III,3;138); and later in the same paragraph he regretted the "loud, too loud triumphing" of Schopenhauer when he finally acquired readers. In the *Gay Science,* "Anyone with a very loud voice is almost incapable of thinking in subtleties" (216); in the *Genealogy of Morals,* "A spirit that is sure of itself . . . speaks softly" (III,8;110); in *Beyond Good and Evil,* "the genius of the heart who silences all that is loud and self-satisfied" (295; cited in *EH* III,6;268). So when life reproaches Zarathustra for making noise with his whip, Nietzsche's text as a whole resonates in harmony with her protest, which thus clearly undercuts the blustering ideology of masculine dominance that the whip symbolizes. We hear no more of the whip; in the end the woman life and the man Zarathustra, who love each other but can never quite come together, look at each other and over the green meadow and weep: "But then," says Zarathustra, "life was dearer to me than all my wisdom ever was" (*Z* III,15;339).

"The Other Dancing Song" concerns the profound ambivalence of this love of life which Zarathustra declares. Zarathustra's faithfulness to life is in doubt. "O Zarathustra, you are not faithful enough to me. You do not love me nearly as much as you say; I know you are thinking of leaving me soon" (*Z* III,15;338); but this is because Zarathustra fears that life is no dependable object for his love. "Whatever I create and however much I love it, soon I must oppose it and my love," life had said to him earlier (II,12;227), and now she warns him that "If your wisdom ever ran away from you, then my love would quickly run away from you too" (III,15;338). Zarathustra's ascetic wisdom is the rival of whom life is jealous, it is what keeps him from trusting too much in life, and only because he holds himself back from life in this way does life continue to love him; yet it is also this mutual distrust that keeps Zarathustra and life from loving each other "from the heart" (338), so that they continually approach each other and run away from each other and finally weep together. An ordinary tale of love, in other words, the tale of beings who desire to be assured of the fullness of the turning-toward and pouring-out-toward them of the being of the other but who reserve themselves in the absence of such assurance, yet are drawn toward the other precisely by the other's evasiveness, since they fear nothing so much as the fullness of the other's presence—perhaps precisely because this presence must necessarily remain a presence that always might (and eventually must) fail, and that therefore wounds all the more with the force of an ineradicable residue of unfaithfulness the nearer and more present it becomes, threatening to tear the unwary lover to pieces. "I fear you near, I love you far," Zarathustra says to life, "your flight lures me, your seeking cures me" (337).

But these are no ordinary lovers, or at least life is not; life is what is closest to Zarathustra, what if he can never master and appropriate, he cannot get away from either, that which he says yes to even when he most says no ("Deeply I love only life—and verily, most of all when I hate life" (*Z* II,10;221]).

For Nietzsche *amor fati* means that he throws himself into the abyss of an infinitely self-implicating oscillation, and if we have heard too much of late about abysses, it's worth bringing up again here, because who would have thought that Nietzsche, of all people, would image his surrender to the abyss (is this only an image?) as his love for a woman? When he looks into life's eyes, Zarathustra says in "The Dancing Song," he seems to be "sinking into the unfathomable": "Into your eyes I looked recently, O life! And into the unfathomable I then seemed to be sinking. But you pulled me out with a golden fishing rod; and you laughed mockingly when I called you unfathomable" (*Z* II,10;220). Life laughs at him and tells him he is being like all the other men who go around projecting onto her all their own sententious notions: "Thus runs the speech of all fish," she says, "what *they* do not fathom is unfathomable. But I am merely changeable and wild and a woman in every way, and not virtuous" (220). This is a masculine view of women if there ever was one, even if it is put in the woman's mouth; but in "The Dancing Song," this most enraptured passage in all of Nietzsche's work, there is none of the coldness and self-withholding that constitute the mood of Nietzsche's misogyny: here the charm of life's ironic play with him transcends any distinction of surface and depth, and what matters is the intoxication of life, the forgetfulness of desire.

Zarathustra's wisdom consequently becomes jealous of his love of life. Wisdom is the competitor for Zarathustra's devotion, love of wisdom is what would pull Zarathustra away from his attachment to life; but Zarathustra is giving himself up to desire, forgetting his wisdom. "You will, you want, you love—that is the only reason why you *praise* life" (*Z*II,10;221), his wisdom angrily reproves him. But in the rapture of this scene Zarathustra sees through the distinction between wisdom and life, sees that wisdom is life, too.

> Then I almost answered wickedly and told the angry woman the truth; and there is no more wicked answer than telling one's wisdom the truth.
>
> For thus matters stand among the three of us: deeply I love only life—and verily, most of all when I hate life. But that I am well disposed toward wisdom, and often too well, that is because she reminds me so much of life. She has her eyes, her laugh, and even her little golden fishing rod: is it my fault the two look so similar? (221)

What is perhaps most astonishing about this song is the tone Nietzsche achieves in speaking of things that elsewhere he speaks of in such different tonalities: wisdom and the feminine. Derrida has made us acutely aware of the structure of veiling/unveiling of the truth-as-female that operates in Nietzsche's text:[1] in "The Dancing Song" this imagery is applied to wisdom-as-female, but then the whole complex is inscribed within the playful, ironic, rapturous exchange between Zarathustra's voice and this other voice which is in one sense also his, which he ventriloquizes, but which in another sense ventriloquizes him.

> And when life once asked me, "Who is this wisdom?" I answered fervently, "Oh, yes, wisdom! One thirsts after her and is never satisfied; one looks through veils, one grabs through nets. Is she beautiful? How should I know? But even the oldest carps are baited with her. She is changeable and stubborn; often I have seen her bite her lip and comb her hair against the grain. Perhaps she is evil and false and a female in every way; but just when she speaks ill of herself she is most seductive."
>
> When I said this to life she laughed sarcastically and closed her eyes. "Of whom are you speaking?" she asked; "no doubt, of me. And even if you are right—should *that* be said to my face? But now speak of your wisdom too."
>
> Ah, and then you opened your eyes again, O beloved life. And again I seemed to myself to be sinking into the unfathomable. (*Z* II,10;221)

Life is the true subject, the one who speaks through Zarathustra and for that matter through Nietzsche too. Consequently, when "thus I willed it" is spoken, the character of the "I" that wills is transformed in

[1] Jacques Derrida, *Spurs: Nietzsche's Styles,* trans. Barbara Harlow (Chicago: University of Chicago Press, 1978).

the speaking, the "I" that existed the moment before expands, opens wide, receives the compelling surge of its own life which also overflows its boundaries, and when now "I" and "yes" are uttered, who is it that speaks? There is no unbounded yes without this Dionysian *Rausch* in which the precious one who has been so jealously preserved is infinitely spilled and somehow, from another center of force, another I speaks the affirmation. Dissociative, perhaps hysterical phenomenon.[2]

We leave aside the fact that "The Dancing Song" has a dramatic context, and a quite significant one. Zarathustra, the loneliest one, sings the song to some pretty dancing girls who dance with Cupid while he sings; and when the song is finished and the girls abandon Zarathustra, he becomes very sad and wonders what good it does him to continue living. We especially ignore the further resonances of the theme of dancing girls in this book, the reference to men who watch "wicked, dancing, naked girls" in the fourth part (IV,15;413) and, a little later on, the sadomasochistic eroticism of the magician's song

[2]R. Hinton Thomas, *Nietzsche in German Politics and Society, 1890–1918* (Manchester: Manchester University Press, 1983), 138–39, points out the clear parallel between Nietzsche's relation to life in the two dancing songs and his relation to Wagner's music. In a passage of *Human, All Too Human* (134), Nietzsche had described the effect of Wagner's "unending melody" as similar to walking gradually into the sea and giving oneself up to the watery element. Wagner's art involves a "decay of rhythm" and thus is unable to give proper form to music, which itself has an "all too feminine nature" that requires the discipline of rhythm. Then, in *GS* 368 Nietzsche comments that his foot "resents" Wagner's music and "rebels" against it; "my foot feels the need for rhythm, dance, march." The way one yields to Wagner's music, Thomas remarks, is similar to the way Zarathustra feels when he looks into life's eyes; and the way he tries to impose rhythm on life with his whip parallels the way Nietzsche tries to bring rhythmic order to Wagner's music. Thomas's suggestion is rich with possibility, but his conclusion is that the use of the whip by Zarathustra therefore represents a triumph of self-overcoming by which decadence is vanquished. Laurence Lampert also tries to justify the use of the whip, arguing that it "provides . . . the new measure that binds even Life by giving her a tempo or a time to keep, the time of eternal return. He does not whip Life into submission by imposing some virtue on her that is not her own . . . ; he considers her ways and wills their eternal return"; *Nietzsche's Teaching: An Interpretation of Thus Spoke Zarathustra* (New Haven: Yale University Press, 1986), 239. Both Thomas and Lampert thus try to acquit of machismo a passage that will not admit of acquittal; but they ignore the subsequent passage in which Nietzsche provides his own criticism of the whip, the passage in which life causes Zarathustra to drop his noisy whip because it "murders thought." What Thomas's observations show is actually an additional connection between the Dionysian and the Wagnerian, and the degree to which Nietzsche's resistance to Wagner's music is intertwined with his fear of women and of Dionysian self-loss. This intertwining lies completely outside Heidegger's field of vision when he approvingly comments, regarding *WP* 838, that "in opposition to 'the complete dissolution of style' in Wagner, rules and standards, and above all the grounding of such, are here demanded clearly and unequivocally"; *Nietzsche,* vol. 1, trans. David Farrell Krell (San Francisco: Harper and Row, 1979), 130.

with its metaphoric dancer whose leg has been nibbled off (IV, 16;420). After all, Zarathustra does *not* pursue the girls, he is resigned to his loneliness (even though, as he says in "The Night Song," it does get to him sometimes), and what he has to work out is the problem that remains for him *even in his loneliness* of a certain self-relation that necessarily passes through a perfidious outside. If the artist, the philosopher, and the ascetic priest attempt to reflect themselves back to themselves by making a detour through a false outside, Zarathustra's dilemma is the one that condemns all such attempts to failure: even though he is all alone, in his innermost innerness dwells this authentic outside he calls life. He *is* his life, and yet he isn't. Or, rather, he is identical with life, but life is not identical with him. He will cease to be, and life will go on and will not even miss him. Therefore, inevitably, life must be imaged as a woman. Yet this woman is also Nietzsche "himself": the other center of force from which Nietzsche/Zarathustra's "I" can speak its great affirmation finds utterance as a woman's voice. When Nietzsche/Zarathustra most ecstatically or hysterically affirms the annihilation of the bounded form of his ego, he speaks from outside himself in a woman's voice, speaks to himself as to a woman whom he loves, allows himself completely to let himself go, falls into the abyss of her eyes, runs after her, weeps with her.

But "The Other Dancing Song" does not seem to be quite as ecstatic as the first one. There are strains between the lovers, and Zarathustra may not be quite so wholehearted in his relation to the woman, life, as it looks at first sight, even if we accept Lawrence Lampert's interpretation of the secret he whispers in her ear:

> "You think, O Zarathustra, I know it, of how you want to leave me soon."
>
> "Yes," I answered hesitantly, "but you also know—" and I whispered something into her ear, right through her tangled yellow foolish tresses.
>
> "You *know* that, O Zarathustra? Nobody knows that." (*Z* III,15;339)

And then they look at each other and weep together. What does Zarathustra whisper in her ear? Lampert thinks it must be the secret of eternal recurrence: "His answer to her final words—'You want to leave me soon!'—affirms his mortality: 'Yes,' he will leave her soon. However, this necessity is not a refutation of life, for his 'Yes' is followed by a 'but'—'But you also know . . . ,' and this 'yes . . . but' suggests that the whispered words are some variant of the phrase, 'I will eternally return.'" And Lampert tells us that, as Nietzsche says in *Ecce Homo,* this is "the highest affirmation of life that can ever be achieved."[3]

But life does not say that Zarathustra must die because he is mortal, she accuses him of *wanting* to leave her, and soon. Zarathustra has said that the will to love is also the willingness to die, but here *wanting to die* seems to take on its more usual coloring of an evasion of the death implied in love. What is evoked here is the whole problematic of asceticism, of an economy that preserves itself by destroying itself, that leaves life so that life will not leave it. And if what Zarathustra says next is that he will eternally return, does this really mean, or simply mean, that Zarathustra loves life just as she is, as Lampert, and Nietzsche also, claims? Does this acceptance not annul itself? To love life just as it is is to accept that we do *not* return, that the precious wine or salve of our being is spilled once and for all; what a curious double flow is set up when one says, "not only do I accept that I die once and for all, but I accept it so wholeheartedly that I am willing to do it over and over for all eternity." So if *that* is what Zarathustra says to life after "The Other Dancing Song," it is certainly not the simple declaration of love Lampert thinks it is. And then, too, why would life and Zarathustra weep together immediately thereafter? Is this how lovers act who know they will always be reunited after every parting?

We could read this scene as the navel or deepest self-representation *en abyme* of Nietzsche's text, the moment in which, set within a context that allegorizes Nietzsche's relation to life in erotic images, Nietzsche/Zarathustra declares the unspeakability of a knowledge that cannot know itself, that is only knowledge so long as it does not know that at its core it is rapture, and when it becomes enraptured forgets the ascetic will that would restrict the self to the perspective of the knower. And if someone who calls himself "Nietzsche" thought afterward that he had a formula by which to express what he did not and could not have written, no one can fill in the blank that will always remain *in the text* concerning what it is that Zarathustra whispers in life's ear, and which life says nobody knows.

Still, if the hand that wrote those words did not declare the eternal recurrence, it does seem as though there might have been at the moment of nondeclaration something like the repression of an impulse to

[3]Lampert, *Nietzsche's Teaching,* 238.

declare it—to escape the abyssal oscillation of life into which Zarathustra falls as into the eyes of a woman, by declaring the *movement of return* from all falling—because in the immediately following section Nietzsche sings his song to eternity. Lampert tells us that this is the marriage song of Zarathustra and life, Zarathustra having rechristened life as "eternity." "All joy wants eternity," sings Zarathustra, and in "The Seven Seals" he expands on this: "Never yet have I found the woman from whom I wanted children, unless it be this woman whom I love: for I love you, O eternity! *For I love you, O eternity!* (Z III,16;340).

Lampert's interpretation is very plausible and makes satisfying sense of the link between "The Seven Seals" and the preceding section. If "eternity" means "eternal recurrence," when Zarathustra says he loves eternity he means that he affirms life just as it is, including the fact of mortality, and thus rejects the life-denying transcendentalism that wants to get away from the mortal body. I do not want to quarrel with this reading; I do not disagree with it, so far as it goes. But the pattern of Nietzsche's psychodialectic makes it questionable whether that is *all* that is going on here, whether here as elsewhere Nietzsche has not created a linguistic structure that will allow the simultaneous flow of contradictory investments. When Zarathustra declares that eternity is the only woman from whom he wants children he echoes once more the transcendental doctrine of *Eros* of the *Symposium,* a doctrine of transcendance of the mortal body which involves avoidance of the female who bears mortal children. Of course we know that Nietzsche is the anti-Platonist par excellence, that Zarathustra comes to preach the evangel of the mortal body, and so on. So he *cannot* mean here what his utterance, at least on its face, clearly says. On the other hand, nothing is more deeply rooted in the totality of Nietzsche's text than the gynophobia that would motivate just such a meaning.

But "The Seven Seals" is only a rehearsal for the dithyramb with which Zarathustra brings his teaching to a close, "The Drunken Song" of the fourth part. Here Zarathustra reiterates the desire for eternity, articulating it in a way that makes more apparent the ambiguity of the meaning of the eternal return.

We pass over the first few sections of "The Drunken Song," as immensely interesting and worthy of comment as they are, and begin with section 8, in which Zarathustra attains the height of his rapture and pronounces the exordium to the final movement of his dithyramb.

"What am I? a drunken sweet lyre—a midnight lyre, an ominous bell-frog that nobody understands but that *must* speak, before the deaf, you higher men" (*Z* IV,19;434). In section 9, he goes on:

> You vine! Why do you praise me? Did I not cut you? I am cruel, you bleed; what does your praise of my drunken cruelty mean?
>
> "What has become perfect, all that is ripe—wants to die"—thus you speak. Blessed, blessed be the vintager's knife! But all that suffers wants to live: Woe! Woe entreats: Go! Away, woe! But all that suffers wants to live, that it may become ripe and joyous and longing—longing for what is farther, higher, brighter. "I want heirs"—thus speaks all that suffers; "I want children, I do not want *myself*."
>
> Joy, however, does not want heirs, or children—joy wants itself, wants eternity, wants recurrence, wants everything eternally the same.

The tensions in the language of this passage, both internal and contextual, are extraordinary. There is a straightforward sense here, and also something that destabilizes that sense. Those who suffer want things to be different than they are, they cannot affirm the now as it is; the ripe and joyous are those who say yes even unto death. This is the consistent sense we could extract from the passage. But as in "The Seven Seals," into this satisfyingly closed formula there intrude disturbing resonances. Zarathustra had earlier addressed this to the despisers of the body: "I say unto you: your self itself wants to die and turns away from life. It is no longer capable of what it would do above all else: to create beyond itself. . . . So your self wants to go under" (*Z* I,4;147). But in "The Seven Seals" he himself repudiated the women who might bear him children, and now he repudiates even the *desire* to procreate. Whereas earlier in *Zarathustra* and also in the *Genealogy of Morals* we are told that those who suffer turn against life, here it is the sufferers who want to live and procreate and the joyous ones who want to die. Furthermore, there is a curiously ambiguous distribution of suffering here. The joyous one, the vine which is the opposite of the sufferer, is the object of "drunken cruelty" and blesses the knife that makes it bleed. This image of masochistic enjoyment is not exactly the *opposite* of the image of suffering. Nietzsche is once again invoking the form of voluptuousness which flowers most luxuriantly in the ascetic and the martyr, or in Dionysus Zagreus (for whom the bleeding vine is a metonymy).

There is thus a disturbingly untidy mixture of forces in this passage. Of course it remains possible to reconcile the apparent contradictions. Masochistic enjoyment is not the opposite of suffering; but masochism, as suffering that says yes, is the opposite of suffering that says no. In section 10 Zarathustra says that "pain too is a joy" and declares that to say yes to a single joy is also to say yes "to *all* woe," because "all things are entangled, ensnared, enamored" (*Z* IV,19;435). So, technically, joy that wants *itself,* recurrence, "everything eternally the same," encompasses *all things,* is the unbounded yes and amen that has no opposite; suffering that wants heirs would be a mere partiality that has failed to affirm the whole and thus looks for redemption in children. But in order to extract this meaning in its theoretical purity we would have to shut our ears to the resonance of the "no to children, yes to myself" that is uttered here, and the connection between this utterance and, for example, Nietzsche's description in the *Genealogy of Morals* of the philosopher's ascetic refusal of marriage so that he can save all his animal vigor for himself.

Section 11 is the climax of Zarathustra's rapture, as he pours out an effusion on the nature of joy which is the most ecstatic expression in Nietzsche's work of the nature of self-enjoyment.

> All joy wants the eternity of all things, wants honey, wants lees, wants drunken midnight, wants tombs, wants tomb-tears' comfort, wants gilded evening glow.
>
> *What* does joy not want? It is thirstier, more cordial, hungrier, more terrible, more secret than all woe; it wants *itself,* it bites into *itself,* the ring's will strives in it; it wants love, it wants hatred, it is overrich, gives, throws away, begs that one might take it, thanks the taker, it would like to be hated; so rich is joy that it thirsts for woe, for hell, for hatred, for disgrace, for the cripple, for *world*—this world, oh, you know it!
>
> You higher men, for you it longs, joy, the intractable blessed one—for your woe, you failures. All eternal joy longs for failures. For all joy wants itself, hence it also wants agony. O happiness, O pain! Oh, break, heart! You higher men, do learn this, joy wants eternity. Joy wants the eternity of *all* things, *wants deep, wants deep eternity.* (*Z* IV,19;435–36)

Even though Nietzsche speaks here of the thirst for *world,* the pathos he describes is not easy to distinguish from that of the ascetic or martyr. "Spirit is the life that itself cuts into life," Zarathustra had said in the second part (II,8;216); and these words had been ironically echoed back to him by the conscientious in spirit in the fourth part (IV,4;363), in such a way that the repetition seemed to imply a critique of the ascetic element in Zarathustra's teaching. But here, at the height of Zarathustra's rapture, the formula recurs with "joy" in the place of "spirit," joy "wants *itself,* it bites into *itself.*"

In one sense, Zarathustra's affirmation here seems to be the most open and capacious in Nietzsche's work because it accomplishes the full inclusion of the negative that we have seen Nietzsche repeatedly evade through the strategy of excluding inclusion: it is *primarily* the negative to which joy says yes, including "cripples" and "failures" and all forms of agony. Go back and reread the *Genealogy of Morals* with this passage in mind; what are we to make of strength and health and the conquering barbarian in the light of what Zarathustra now says?

And yet this affirmation is also the most absolutely self-enclosed or self-recuperating.

This internal or micro-economy of Nietzsche/Zarathustra's is echoed in the structure of the macro-economy, the grand economy of the whole, the rhythm of which is eternal recurrence. Eternal recurrence is supposed to be the key to everything else in Nietzsche, the "thought of thoughts," says Heidegger, which "grants supreme lucidity and decisiveness to beings at every moment" and captures "Nietzsche's fundamental metaphysical position."[4] Our concern is, however, with the character of the metaphysician's investment in his metaphysics, and from this point of view what glares at us concerning the doctrine of eternal recurrence is its structural availability for double investment. On the one hand, as Heidegger says, it is the thought that is hardest to bear; but on the other hand, it is the *most economical thought,* the most consoling one, the one that recuperates absolutely all of the squandering that goes on in the grand economy of the whole. Nietzsche confesses this in one note: "To me . . . everything seems far too valuable to be so fleeting: I seek an eternity for everything: ought one to pour the most precious salves and wines into the sea?—My consolation is that everything that has been is eternal: the sea will cast it up again" (*WP* 1065). The eternal recurrence expresses the self-enclosedness of the grand economy, its flow that does not dissipate into an outside because any possible outside is part of its inside and so it always

[4]Martin Heidegger, *Nietzsche,* vol. 2, trans. David Farrell Krell (San Francisco: Harper and Row, 1984), 147, 5.

recovers all expenditures, remains inviolably and eternally identical with itself, "a firm, iron magnitude of force that does not grow bigger or smaller, that does not expend itself but only transforms itself; as a whole, of unalterable size, a household without expenses or losses, but likewise without increase or income" (*WP* 1067). Conceived in this way, the grand economy is not wasteful and eternal recurrence is not so unbearable after all; it mirrors the economy of the ascetic who always flows back into himself.

When Zarathustra says that joy "wants *itself,* it bites into *itself,*" he says that "the ring's will strives in it." This ring is the image of both eternal recurrence and of the, let us provisionally say, narcissistic will to self. In the second part Zarathustra had told his disciples, "Your virtue is what is dearest to you. The thirst of the ring lives in you: every ring strives and turns to reach itself again" (*Z* II,5;206). And when his animals recite to him the doctrine of eternal recurrence they say, "Everything parts, everything greets every other thing again; eternally the ring of being remains faithful to itself" (III,13;329). "Eternally . . . faithful to itself": the only faith that cannot be broken.

Everything is contained in the self-reflection of a single being who can never go outside himself, for whom there is only the endless transit away from himself/back to himself of his own going out and going under, an eternal, internal spillage with a double flow that remains always open to the strategic recuperations of double investment.

Am I saying that Nietzsche is wrongly or culpably incapable of going outside himself? No, for two reasons.

First, because what I have tried to show is that even if Nietzsche does run away by this duplicitous movement away/toward, he also knows that there is no escape, that this whole complex structure of pipes and conduits by which he keeps pouring his outflow into himself is fated to move inexorably toward the irrecuperable spillage that it is the means for evading.

Second, because it is not clear that there is anything besides what we call narcissism, which therefore ceases to mean what it would mean if it had any antithesis. Certainly Freud, who in the essay "On Narcissism" tries to distinguish narcissistic love from some *other* kind that would not ultimately be the return-to-itself of a subjectivity, falls into self-contradiction and confusion and fails to make the distinction;[5] on the

[5]"Freud's description of different types of love choices, whatever their diversity or complexity, leaves no doubt, however, on one point: the prevalence of narcissism, if not in every libidinal relation at least in every *love* relation, in the sense of passion: that state of loss of self

contrary, what he shows is the opposite of what he tries to show. But even narcissistic subjectivity in its strictest sense is condemned to the detour through another and to an internal fracturing that disables any simple self-appropriation. Nietzsche is right, everything begins and ends in self-enjoyment, even if you spill yourself into infinity there is nobody else but you who feels it and somehow the ring closes even when it breaks open, perhaps most of all when it breaks open.

When the eternal recurrence is first announced in *The Gay Science,* when the demon comes to announce it, to explain that you will have to live this life over and over "innumerable times more," with "nothing new in it" but always the same pains and joys in every minute detail, why is it that he comes "into your loneliest loneliness" to announce it? Isn't it because it is *this,* the loneliest loneliness itself into which the demon comes, and not the repetition of specific events of suffering, that is the essence of the unbearability of the eternal return, so that when Nietzsche/Zarathustra thinks of reliving his life innumerable times what he thinks of is the eternity of an absolute solitude where no human voice ever reaches? "For me—how should there be any outside-myself? There is no outside. But all sounds make us forget this; how lovely it is that there are sounds" (*Z* III,13;329). In *The Gay Science,* Nietzsche describes in the most graphic and disturbing terms what his solitude feels like (modestly casting it in quotation marks, as though the sentiment belonged to someone else; but the someone else is one of the "posthumous people," a set to which Nietzsche too belongs): "The estrangement, the cold and quiet of the grave around us—this whole subterranean, concealed, mute, undiscovered solitude that among us is called life but might just as well be called death" (365). And in a fragment from a decade earlier which Krell calls "astonishing," titled "Oedipus Talks of the Last Philosopher with Himself," the philosopher is the only human being left in the world, with only his own voice for company.

> No one talks to me other than myself, and my voice comes to me as the voice of a dying man. With you, beloved voice, with you, the last vapor-

---

that he calls *Verliebtheit.* This is clear notably in the description of object-choice in men"; Jean Laplanche, *Life and Death in Psychoanalysis,* trans. Jeffrey Mehlman (Baltimore, Md.: Johns Hopkins University Press, 1976), 77–78.

> ous remembrance of all human happiness, let me tarry just an hour more. With your help I shall deceive myself about my loneliness; I shall lie my way into society and love. For my heart refuses to believe that love is dead, cannot bear the terror of the loneliest loneliness: it compels me to talk, as though I were two.[6]

An economy that pours itself out endlessly into itself, therefore preserves itself even as it squanders itself because there is only itself from alpha to omega. But the price of this self-preservation is eternal, absolute solitude.

"I am one thing, my writings are another matter," Nietzsche says in *Ecce Homo,* but nobody calls this distinction into question to the degree that he does. "Ecce" is a deictic, it means right here, present before our eyes, behold the man himself. And then we get mostly an account of his books.[7] And this account itself constitutes another of his books, the only one that is physically present when we read its "ecce," so that it announces itself as though it were saying "I, this book here, am the man whom I conjure you to behold," either the man idealized, eternalized (insofar as books are eternal), so that "after death" he becomes "alive, oh, very much alive," this posthumous man, or else simply as all that is left of the man, the echo of a voice.

Has there ever been a more cunning project of self-representation? Nietzsche does not say "here I am, look at me, I display my portrait to you"; he leaves everything to be inferred from hints, allusions, tones of voice, from the structure of the masks he wears when he speaks, not the man himself but his traces. And yet these traces project the strange illusion of a being of infinite pathos whose pathos is that he cannot quite become real, a being of flesh and blood. He remains a kind of phantasm or ghost who does not inhabit the text but *haunts* it: "Example: one reaches out for us but gets no hold of us. That is frightening. Or we enter through a closed door. Or after all the lights have been extinguished. Or after we have died" (*GS* 365). What makes this phantasm disturbing is that it seems to be the "real" Nietzsche, the only Nietzsche that ever managed to come into being, as though this were not only all that is left of him but also all there ever was.

[6]David Farrell Krell, *Postponements: Women, Sensuality, and Death in Nietzsche* (Bloomington: Indiana University Press, 1986), 39–40.

[7]Cf. Hugh Silverman, "The Autobiographical Textuality of Nietzsche's *Ecce Homo,*" in *Why Nietzsche Now?,* ed. Daniel O'Hara (Bloomington: Indiana University Press, 1981), 141–51.

And yet these same texts that inscribe Nietzsche's pathos also warn us incessantly about the snares and self-deceptions of pity, about how it is a means for appropriating the sufferer, how it makes "smaller" the "worth and will" of the one pitied (*GS* 338), and so on. And then, somewhat sobered by these considerations, I remind myself that Nietzsche's writings aren't a man, or a ghost either, and if they constitute the wiring or plumbing of an "economy" the only libido that runs through these wires or tubes as I read is my own.

APPENDIX

The Birth of Tragedy Reconstructed

The Birth of Tragedy is practically the hinge between Romanticism and everything that is post-Romantic, including Nietzsche's own later work. Nietzsche's discussion here focuses on the classical reference-points of what is called Romanticism (Rousseauistic primitivism, recourse to a transcendental subject, doctrines of genius and inspiration, idealization of the Greeks, antipathy to the rationalization of nature, etc.), and the structure of its fundamental distinctions is deeply influenced by Schiller's definition of the "naive" and "sentimental," concepts which, Nietzsche declares in a manuscript note, he means to "heighten" (*steigern*) so as to correspond to the metaphysics of will and illusion (Musarion, 3:337). Here, then, is romanticism at the limit, about to boil over from forces which, contemporary interpreters in the wake of Paul de Man tell us, were already there in the texts of the arch-Romantics themselves, though largely ignored or repressed by commentators. Thus Tilottama Rajan finds in Schiller's analysis of "sentimentality" a "post-modernist concern with representation" because Schiller "sees the ambivalent character of emotions like desire and nostalgia as registering linguistically in a fracturing of the sign."[1]

But how can *The Birth of Tragedy* be used as an exhibit or example in the case of Nietzsche and Romanticism when its own internal articulation is now more in question than ever? The challenging deconstructions of this book by de Man and Philippe Lacoue-Labarthe make it impossible merely

[1]Tilottama Rajan, "Displacing Post-Structuralism: Romantic Studies after Paul de Man," *Studies in Romanticism* 24 (Winter 1985): 457. Rajan argues, however, that Schiller "sees the text phenomenologically as the language of self" not "the self post-structurally as a text."

to gesture at *The Birth of Tragedy* as though what it says stands still for us to refer to.[2] Of course one could merely gesture at the readings of Lacoue-Labarthe and de Man, as though the results of these readings could now function as reliable stand-ins for *The Birth of Tragedy* "itself."

The alternative would be to challenge these readings, a task that would for several reasons be long and involved. First, because of the notorious complexity of *The Birth of Tragedy* "itself," even apart from any critical methodology one might bring to it, the labyrinthine crossings and returns of its argument that baffle any summary that tries to be faithful to the nuance and apparent contradiction on major points that we find there. Second, because we must deal with the unpublished materials surrounding this text, both the rhetorical writings from the period following its publication and the drafts and collateral materials connected with the published text. Both Lacoue-Labarthe and de Man have argued that these unpublished writings make explicit what deconstructive reading finds implicit in the published text. One might immediately feel that these writers display a curiously nondeconstructive confidence in the stability and trustworthiness of unpublished, as opposed to published, writings; nevertheless, it is by no means easy to reply to the arguments grounding their recourse to the manuscripts. Finally, because to challenge these readings is to interrogate not only *The Birth of Tragedy* and the relevant unpublished writings but also the style and presuppositions of the critical methodology used by these critics, one form of what is called "deconstruction." In fact, these readings would be, given their authors and dates of provenance, not examples but archetypes, defining exemplars of literary deconstruction. Since de Man's essay in turn points to *The Birth of Tragedy* as an "exemplary model" that sheds light on what he calls the "aberrant" view of Romanticism (a view based on metaphor and genetic sequence) against which he is arguing (101–2), we find ourselves up to the neck in exemplarity.

The answer to the question of what *The Birth of Tragedy* really says (or what it says and what it enacts) depends in part on the assumptions that we bring to it regarding what Romanticism is; but this answer will then be evidence for our definitions of Romanticism. And the way in which Lac-

[2]Paul de Man, "Genesis and Genealogy (Nietzsche)," in *Allegories of Reading: Figural Language in Rousseau, Nietzsche, Rilke, and Proust* (New Haven: Yale University Press, 1979), 79–102; henceforth cited as "deM." Philippe Lacoue-Labarthe, "Le détour," *Poetique* 5 (1971): 53–76; henceforth cited as L-L.

oue-Labarthe and de Man answer both of these interimplicated questions depends on their sense of what the method of deconstruction is.

Let us therefore begin with a consideration of this method.

Now, by no means are the method or results of these two essays entirely homogeneous. De Man's essay is bolder, more obviously programmatic, more significant in its implications (which go far beyond Nietzsche studies); Lacoue-Labarthe's is more nuanced and dialectical, and much more careful in its attention to the detail of the unpublished material. De Man's essay, written later, relies on Lacoue-Labarthe's and attempts to move beyond it. Whereas Lacoue-Labarthe concludes that Nietzsche's study of rhetoric after *The Birth of Tragedy* ultimately "forces the abandonment" of the text's entire project (74), de Man argues that Nietzsche's rhetorical *practice* already, within *The Birth of Tragedy,* calls directly into question those elements of "logocentrism" and "melocentrism" that Lacoue-Labarthe thinks are only equivocally treated there.

Nevertheless, despite these differences there is substantial agreement between the two essays on the fundamental issues. Nietzsche in *The Birth of Tragedy* is driven by a desire for presence or the in-itself, which he calls Dionysus or the will. The Dionysus-Apollo split is the "simple difference of presence with its opposite" (L-L, 72) or the distinction between "appearance and its antithesis," or "between metaphorical and proper language" (deM, 91). Already by the time of *The Birth of Tragedy,* as the unpublished papers show, Nietzsche had taken the "decisive step" in breaking with Schopenhauer by denying that the ultimate reality is knowable (L-L, 67), yet in the published text he clings ambiguously to Schopenhauer's claim that "music is the unmediated image of the will [*unmittelbares Abbild des Willens*]," a claim that inscribes Nietzsche's difficulty since, as de Man says, the notion of an "unmediated representation" is a "logical absurdity" (96). Nietzsche is thus caught in the classic philosophical dilemma as this dilemma is known to deconstruction. He wants a transcendent reality (Dionysus) to be made present, and he distinguishes this reality from a realm of "good" representation (Apollo) which is metaphysically inferior but nevertheless validated because it serves to make Dionysus present. There is furthermore a realm of "bad" representation (Euripidean realism) which is the decay of good (Apollonian) representation and has no relation whatever to Dionysus. But in fact everything is infected with the badness of representation, and Dionysus can never be present, as Nietzsche himself concludes in the writings on rhetoric adduced by Lacoue-Labarthe, and as is already legible on the rhetorical level of *The Birth of Tragedy,* according to de Man.

This is a textbook deconstruction if there ever was one, an open and shut case, and *The Birth of Tragedy* seems to lend itself to this operation in the most convenient way—especially according to de Man, who declares it "hermeneutically satisfying" (101) to have his interpretation confirmed by Nietzsche's manuscript remarks.

But is this really *The Birth of Tragedy* that has been deconstructed, or some other text constructed for the purpose of deconstruction? Constructed according to the following principles.

1. The terms of the analysis are wielded with a surprising confidence in the stability of their meaning that contrasts sharply with the skepticism about the terms of the text analyzed. This is particularly true of de Man, who deploys canonical distinctions between metaphoric and literal language, presence and absence, reality and appearance, as though these terms had some fixed meaning that could be referred to with a minimum of concern for contextual shifts. It will be objected that de Man knows all too well how questionable these categories are, that it is the metaphysical tradition and not de Man that is mystified by them, that he uses them as if they were in quotation marks, and only in order to reveal the contradictions hidden within them. I reply that the process of citing metaphysical concepts is no less problematic than that of using them, and quotation marks raise questions as to *who* is being cited and whether the citation is accurate, faithful to context, and so on (a question that comes to a head when it is a matter of a quotation that has been translated from another language, interpretively translated, or perhaps mistranslated, as we shall see).

2. The articulations of the target text are treated as though they could all be reduced to a series of bipolar oppositions which could themselves all be ranged under the heading of a master bipolar opposition: presence/absence or Dionysus/Apollo. The question of whether there could be articulations heterogeneous to such a series is not even considered.

3. The text is viewed from a middle distance, more closely and probingly than has commonly been the case heretofore, but not nearly as closely as possible. From this distance, fissures in the text become visible; yet the fissures occur between unities of meaning (appearance/reality, Dionysus/Apollo). A closer look might reveal *fissures within these unities,* so that nothing called "Dionysus" would appear that could simply (with "little difficulty," as de Man says [91]) be equated with presence, truth, literal

meaning, and so on. Thus the look from the middle distance would credit Nietzsche with having created unities that a closer look would show he never succeeded in creating, and perhaps did not try to create; and would do so in order to provide itself with the oppositions that it could submit to a canonical process of deconstruction.[3]

To look more closely and reveal these further fissures in the text would be to reconstruct *The Birth of Tragedy*. In place of a text that says one thing and rhetorically enacts one other thing, we would have a text with a multiplicity of strata and a variety of claims, such that the relation of one to the other could not be summarized at one bound. This does not necessarily mean that there is nothing here to deconstruct. But first we need to put together the more comprehensive texture of the text and its context which would be the material for a more comprehensive deconstruction, one that would respect the specificity of the articulations attempted by Nietzsche as well as those that he borrowed and revised. "Subject," "consciousness," "representation" and so on are not concepts that can be simply *referred to;* they are conceptual structures that are differently reconstituted every time their context shifts, both the macrocontext of the history of philosophy and the microcontext of specific texts such as *The Birth of Tragedy* and the relevant manuscripts.

Yet it must be said that none of what follows in this essay would have been written without the acute stimulus provided by Lacoue-Labarthe and de Man. De Man in particular is such a devilishly intelligent misreader, his assault on the text so frustratingly close-textured, that replying to his argument proves the most demanding kind of test of a reader's attention. Both Lacoue-Labarthe and de Man bring into sharp focus the necessity of dealing in careful detail with philosophical problems raised by *The Birth of Tragedy* which would otherwise slip by with only casual reference—if, for example, one tried to get an orientation toward the questions they raise by perusing the four hundred pages of the otherwise remarkably thorough study of *The Birth of Tragedy* presented by Silk and Stern.[4]

[3]There are, however, other models of deconstruction that do not take such oppositions for granted. Bernard Pautrat had already in 1971 shown that Nietzsche never tries to think of Apollo as simply exterior to Dionysus or of language as simply exterior to music, but that the Dionysian is ordered by a structure of "internal doubling, to which we must give the name of difference in general"; *Versions du soleil: Figure et systeme de Nietzsche* (Paris: Editions du Seuil, 1971), 118. Although I follow a different route through Nietzsche's texts, my method and results are, I think, compatible with Pautrat's.

[4]M. S. Silk and J. P. Stern, *Nietzsche on Tragedy* (Cambridge: Cambridge University Press, 1981).

It is true, as Lacoue-Labarthe has pointed out, that already by the time of *The Birth of Tragedy* Nietzsche had begun to distance himself from Schopenhauer's conception of the will, and that this movement is reflected ambiguously in *The Birth of Tragedy*. Lacoue-Labarthe does not explain exactly where that ambiguity lies, but one could point to the fact that before the introduction of the long quotation from Schopenhauer in section 16, Nietzsche avoids using the term "will" in its metaphysical sense, preferring instead terms such as "primal unity" and "ground of being." I notice only one use of "will" in what looks like its universal, metaphysical sense (in section 3), and it comes with quotation marks, so that it looks like a metaphoric usage. Furthermore, in at least three places in the early sections Nietzsche has removed the word "will" which he had used in the corresponding passages of an early draft called *The Dionysian Worldview*.[5] Thus *Zug des Willens* in section 1 of the draft (50) becomes *Zug der Natur* in section 2 of *The Birth of Tragedy* (29). And whereas in *The Dionysian Worldview* the will is twice imaged as the agent acting through the Dionysian and Apollonian tendencies (II;58 and III;62), in *The Birth of Tragedy* (IV;38) Nietzsche speaks of the "common goal" (*gemeinsame Ziel*) of the two drives without positing an agent that acts through them. Yet following the quotation from Schopenhauer, there are a number of references to the metaphysical will (e.g., "will in its omnipotence," XVI;104; "universal will" [*Weltwillens*], XVII;104, 107; "insatiable will"]*gierige Wille*], XVIII;111).

This striking shift in Nietzsche's terminology seems to lend support to the suspicions aroused by the deconstructive readings. Nietzsche apparently tried to write the metaphysical will out of *The Birth of Tragedy* but found, on arriving at section 16, that he could not do it. Section 16 is the point at which he begins the transition from the Greeks to the "analogous phenomena of our own time," and in making this transition Nietzsche reveals that it is in fact in these phenomena that "the origin" of his "insight" into the Dionysian birth of tragedy is found. This insight is a *deduction by analogy* from certain arguments of Schopenhauer's, a deduction that Nietzsche lays bare in the crucial penultimate paragraph of section 16. Schopenhauer provides the doctrine that music is "the immediate language of the will," and that the listener of music is stirred to produce verbal and imagistic representations that serve as determinate

[5]All citations of *The Dionysian Worldview* are from III 2, and all citations of the German text of *The Birth of Tragedy* from III 1, of *KGW*.

embodiments of that which music expresses "in the universality of mere form" (*BT* XVI;102, cited from *WWR,* 1:262–63).[6] Nietzsche takes this schema and pushes it to its limit by arguing that if ordinary music gives birth to ordinary symbolic image, then music "at its highest stage" must give birth to the "most significant example"; that is, Dionysian music gives birth to "*tragic* myth" (*BT* XVI;103).

This deduction, which provides the basic form of Nietzsche's whole argument in *The Birth of Tragedy,* is rooted so firmly in Schopenhauer that Nietzsche now quotes several pages from the *World as Will and Representation* to support his point. The problem is that along the way Nietzsche is forced to include just that aspect of Schopenhauer's argument about which he apparently has the most doubt. There are two intertwined aspects to the Schopenhauerian doctrine of music that Nietzsche here cites. One concerns how music is "related to image and concept" (101) (i.e., as universal form to determinate example); the other, which grounds the first, concerns the notorious relation of music to the "will itself." Nietzsche has avoided speaking of the (metaphysical) will up to now, but at this point he finds he cannot make the connection he needs with Schopenhauer and Wagner unless he adduces "this most important insight of aesthetics," produced by Schopenhauer and confirmed by Wagner, that music is "an immediate copy (*unmittelbares Abbild*) of the will itself" and therefore represents "what is *metaphysical,* the thing in itself" (100). Once he has done this, there is no longer any point in not speaking of the will, and henceforth Nietzsche does in fact do so. Not, however, without one last compunction about what he is doing. After he finishes adducing the Schopenhauerian doctrine of the relation between music and will, Nietzsche gives us a signal concerning his reservations. He says, "From these facts, intelligible in themselves, *and not inaccessible to a more penetrating examination,* I infer . . . " (emphasis added; 103). The "more penetrating examination," then, would be the one we can excavate from the unpublished notes, and *The Birth of Tragedy* as we know it retains the traces of Nietzsche's ambivalence about Schopenhauer's account.

Haven't I just helped to demonstrate that the arguments of Lacoue-Labarthe and de Man concerning *The Birth of Tragedy* are substantially

[6]References to the English translation of Schopenhauer are to *The World as Will and Representation,* trans. E. F. J. Payne, 2 vols. (New York: Dover Publications, 1969); here and henceforth cited as "*WWR.*" References to the German texts are to *Sämtliche Werke,* ed. Eduard Grisebach, corrected printing prepared by Ernst Bengmann, 6 vols. (Leipzig: Philipp Reclam, 1920); henceforth cited as "*SW.*"

correct? So it seems—but we have not yet moved close enough to the text. We must now begin the process of desynonymization of the terms according to which *The Birth of Tragedy* is articulated, beginning with Dionysus. What does "Dionysus" really name in *The Birth of Tragedy?* It is a significant subtlety that not the name "Dionysus" but instead the *adjective* "Dionysian" plays the leading role: that is how the word is first introduced (along with "Apollonian") and that is the predominant use throughout. There is a Dionysian art, and there is a Dionysian state (which Nietzsche calls "physiological") (*BT* I;33) that corresponds to this art. This state is that of *Rausch,* "rapture," which Kaufmann perhaps somewhat misleadingly translates as "intoxication."[7] There is also what is called a "Dionysian reality" (VII;59), presumably the true metaphysical reality (though we will shortly have to qualify this presumption), but to call this reality Dionysian is not to identify it with Dionysus. It is Dionysian because it is the world *symbolized by* Dionysus and accessible only to those who are in the state of Dionysian *Rausch.* When Nietzsche personifies the metaphysical principle he still does not call it "Dionysus" but instead the "Dionysian world-artist" (I;37).

There is thus a series of things referred to as "Dionysian" for a variety of reasons. The *state* is Dionysian because it enables the perception of Dionysus; the *art* is Dionysian because it is a product of this state, or because it produces *representations of* Dionysus; the reality, however, is called Dionysian because it is the reality *represented by* Dionysus. The Dionysian state and the Dionysian art are very far from the Dionysian reality, as is visible from the fact that when the satyr chorus projects the presence of Dionysus "himself," we are already in the realm of "Apollonian" image (*BT* VIII;64).

It is easy to confuse Dionysus with the Dionysian reality because he is said to be the "real stage hero" (*BT* VIII;66) behind all the protagonists of tragedy, the being who really acts and suffers behind all the masks. But the suffering of the "one truly real Dionysus" is that engendered by the "the state of individuation" (X;73), and the state of individuation is the falling-away from the unity of the transcendental reality, the *Ur-Eine.*

[7]This is a state that will continue to play a crucial role in Nietzsche's thought and may be the connecting thread between its early and late manifestations, as well as the properly *Romantic* kernel out of which all his thought, early and late, unfolds.

Thus Dionysus communicates on one side of his signification with the transcendental unity and on the other side with the fragmented world of phenomenal individuals. He is not a representation in the same sense as the tragic hero is; in relation to the phenomenon of the tragic hero, Dionysus is the nonphenomenal reality that the phenomenon represents. But in relation to the transcendental unity, the "Dionysian world-artist," Dionysus is the representation of the encasing of transcendental life within the restrictive boundaries of individual form, with everything that implies: above all, the transience of all individual form, the suffering that follows from the fact that "all that comes into being must be ready for a sorrowful end" (*BT* XVII; 104). Dionysus thus belongs to that special category of representation called *myth,* which, as "most significant example" (XVI;103) or as "highest spiritualization and ideality" (XVII;105) of the symbolic image, is *image at the limit,* the determinate particular expanded as far as it will go toward universality.

Myth is the mediation between the determinate image of tragedy and the universal or contentless form of music, and Dionysus as interpreted by Nietzsche would be the name of this essential character of the representationality of myth. The dismemberment of Dionysus by the Titans would represent the true nature of mythic representation because it is the image that represents the *agony of the determinate image,* its explosion and dispersal as it reaches its limit and then expires in its attempt to represent the unrepresentable universality. The Dionysian fate of Prometheus is thus also that of the sign that strives for a universal signification: "In the heroic effort of the individual to attain universality, in the attempt to transcend the curse of individuation and to become the *one* world-being, he suffers in his own person the primordial contradiction that is concealed in things" (*BT* IX;71). And if we wanted to read *The Birth of Tragedy* as the parable of its own failure to make present the absolute presence, here is where we could find such a moral stated with the greatest clarity.

But we have barely begun our inventory of the resources or recourses of this text—or of the deconstructive charges laid against it.

We have seen so far that there is some wavering in *The Birth of Tragedy* over whether to call the metaphysical principle "the will," that the metaphysical reality is not identical with Dionysus, and that "the Dionysian" is itself articulated into several distinct manifestations. All of this would call for some modification in the expression of the arguments of Lacoue-Labarthe and de Man, but does not as yet touch their central claim: that Nietzsche still clings, in this text, to Schopenhauer's doctrine that music is the "immediate copy" of a metaphysical presence that Schopenhauer calls the will, and that Nietzsche had already rejected precisely this doctrine of Schopenhauer's metaphysics, having taken the "decisive step" (L-L, 67) between 1870 and 1871, when he declared that the will itself was *not* the ultimate reality, only "the most universal form of appearance of something that is for us otherwise completely undecipherable" (Musarion, 3:341). If Nietzsche *really thought,* in private, that the *Ur*-presence was "completely undecipherable," then it seems he could not have thought that music or anything else could be its adequate "mirror."

Once again, we must look more closely at Nietzsche's words. In the first place, is it really so clear what Nietzsche is saying in the sentence cited by Lacoue-Labarthe? For if the will is in fact an appearance of the undecipherable, the undecipherable does manifest itself and is, if not decipherable, at least not entirely out of relation to appearance.[8] At first sight Nietzsche seems to be disagreeing here with Schopenhauer's doctrine that the metaphysical being is will and is immediately present in us and immediately known by us as will (*WWR,* 1:110–11). But even if will were not *consubstantial* with primal being, it could still be a *representation* of that being. The idea of a "form of appearance" of an "undecipherable" is not an easy one to interpret, and we should hesitate to take its meaning for granted in the way Lacoue-Labarthe does.

The remark on which we have been focusing is from the "Music and Tragedy" fragment of spring 1871, and de Man has seized on a later passage in this same text to make a more complicated claim. De Man argues that *The Birth of Tragedy* rests on the claim that the "essence" labeled Dionysus must be able to "function as origin" in order for *The Birth of Tragedy* to "unfold its symbolic story," but that precisely this is denied by Nietzsche in a manuscript remark which consequently "could never have stood in the final version if *The Birth of Tragedy* had to survive as text" (deM, 101). Here is Nietzsche's remark: "One could object that I myself have declared that the 'Will' receives an increasingly adequate symbolic expression in music. To this I reply, in a

[8]But beyond this, it might even be *decipherable* through the appearance of will. If we read *übrigens* as meaning "otherwise," then Nietzsche does not say it is undecipherable but that it is *otherwise,* apart from the will, undecipherable—which seems to leave open the possibility that in the will at least we *might* be able to read its nature.

sentence that summarizes a basic principle of aesthetics: *the Will is the object of Music, but not its origin*" (Musarion, 3:344; de Man's translation). Setting aside de Man's unallowable assumption that the will in this passage can be unproblematically equated with Dionysus,[9] let us say that what Lacoue-Labarthe and de Man demonstrate by their quotations is that for Nietzsche the will is neither the ultimate reality *nor* the origin of music.

But what exactly does this prove? Does it show that there has been a reversal or rupture in Nietzsche's thought? Or does it merely show that Nietzsche has been rearranging his terms in order to refine the articulation of what remains, in the sense directly relevant to these attempted deconstructions, the "same" structure? Are not Lacoue-Labarthe and de Man here overly confident in the stability of the meanings of perhaps highly mobile terms?

In the first place, the remark cited by Lacoue-Labarthe far from reinforcing de Man's point actually undermines it. For if "will" is no longer the name for the absolute presence, then *it is nothing to de Man's point that Nietzsche should now deny that the will is the origin of music.* At the same time, the remark cited by de Man shows that Nietzsche is trying to hold on to that dictum of Schopenhauer's about which both Lacoue-Labarthe and de Man say he is the most ambivalent in *The Birth of Tragedy.* So long as Nietzsche identified the will with the primordial reality, he had severe doubts about how music or anything else could be its adequate representation, since, as we see in the notes from winter 1870–1871, Nietzsche repeatedly concludes that there is no way back to the *Ur-Eine* for us. Yet once he declares that the will is *not* the *Ur-Eine* but only its form of appearance, the way is clear for him to reassert that music is the unmediated image of the will, though now "will" is taken in a sense that is perhaps no longer rigorously Schopenhauerian.[10] And in fact that is what he says, though de Man

[9]De Man does say that Dionysus is "not identical with the Will," and defines him more precisely as the *possibility of appearing* of an "essence" (100). De Man does not make clear what he means by this, and his illustrative quotation only garbles the issue (see n. 19 here for an analysis of de Man's quotation). In the remarks that follow, to which I refer above, he drops the distinction, whatever it might have been, between Dionysus and the will, and speaks as though the will in the manuscript passage just is Dionysus.

[10]I say "perhaps" because Schopenhauer suggests in volume 2 of *WWR* a conception of the will that may not be as far from this idea of Nietzsche's as one might think. In the first supplement to book 2, entitled "On the Possibility of Knowing the Thing in Itself," after speaking of the "act of will" as the phenomenon "in which the thing in itself appears in the very thinnest of veils," Schopenhauer says that the question may still be raised of "what that

does not notice it, in the very remark de Man cites. Nietzsche says there that "the Will is the object of music"—that is, the object imitated or represented by music. If it is not absolutely clear here that this is what he means, he makes it perfectly explicit two pages later: "The 'will' as most primordial form of appearance is the object of music: in which sense it [i.e., music, the pronoun is *sie*] can be called the imitation (*Nachahmung*) of nature, but of the most universal form of nature" (Musarion, 3:346).

Furthermore, Nietzsche reaffirms that music is in fact *rooted in,* though it does not *represent,* the absolute reality, the "undecipherable." The will is not the origin of music because music "rests in the womb of that power which under the form of the 'will' generates (*erzeugt*) a universe of vision out of itself: *the origin* (*Ursprung*) *of music lies beyond all individuation,* a proposition that after our discussion of the Dionysian is self-evident" (Musarion, 3:345). This is also what Nietzsche says in *The Birth of Tragedy:* "The Dionysian . . . is the . . . source of music" (XXIV;141).

The remarks in the unpublished notes appear to be the "more penetrating examination" to which Nietzsche alludes in section 16 of *The Birth of Tragedy*. Music remains, as *The Birth of Tragedy* declares, the "general mirror of the universal will" (107), only "will" is now not absolute being but its form of appearance; and absolute being remains precisely what de Man denies, the *origin* of music. Nietzsche desynonymizes, as de Man does not, the notions of "object represented" and "origin," "will" and "Dionysian reality," and this desynonymiza-

---

will, which manifests itself in the world and as the world, is ultimately and absolutely in itself; in other words, what it is, quite apart from the fact that it manifests itself as *will,* or in general *appears,* that is to say, *is known* in general. This question can *never* be answered, because, as I have said, being-known of itself contradicts being-in-itself, and everything that is known is as such only phenomenon. But the possibility of this question shows that the thing-in-itself, which we know most immediately in the will, may have, entirely outside all possible phenomenon, determinations, qualities, and modes of existence which for us are absolutely unknowable and incomprehensible, and which then remain as the inner nature of the thing-in-itself, when this, as explained in the fourth book, has freely abolished itself as *will,* has thus stepped out of the phenomenon entirely, and as regards our knowledge, that is to say as regards the world of phenomena, has passed over into empty nothingness. If the will were positively and absolutely the thing-in-itself, then this nothing would be *absolute,* instead of which it expressly appears to us there only as a *relative* nothing" (*WWR,* 2:198). It is a question how precisely Nietzsche had in mind all the nuances of Schopenhauer's thought, thus whether he himself knew how little "rupture" there was between his speculations on this score and Schopenhauer's doctrine.

tion preserves rather than destroys the overall structure of his argument in *The Birth of Tragedy*. The analysis is subtler, more refined, but represents a development from Schopenhauer's dictum rather than a "rupture."

It is time to reject a fundamental assumption of the readings of Lacoue-Labarthe and de Man. This assumption, which has so far dictated the form of our inquiry, is that the crucial problem in *The Birth of Tragedy* is the problem of representation, and that this problem is to be conceived in terms of the relation between a copy and an original. Nowhere in either Lacoue-Labarthe's essay or de Man's do we find a careful examination of just what Nietzsche means by "representation," as though the problem were self-evident and essentially simple in structure; hence de Man's confident declaration that the notion of an "unmediated representation" is a "logical absurdity" (96), as though an "unmediated representation" were supposed to mean a representation that makes *immediately present* what it represents. Yet Schopenhauer when he introduces his discussion of music in *The World as Will and Representation* tells us quite explicitly that music is the copy of an original which by its nature can itself never be representation (*wesentlich nie Vorstellung seyn kann*) nor be mentally represented without mediation (*nie unmittelbar vorgestellt werden kann; SW,* 1:339). (Payne translates the latter phrase as "can . . . never be directly represented" [*WWR,* 1:257]; Haldane and Kemp as "can never . . . be directly presented as idea.")[11] Thus when Schopenhauer declares that music is "immediately" the image of the will (*unmittelbar Abbild des Willens selbst ist; SW,* 1:346), he does not at all mean the absurdity de Man ascribes to him; by "immediate image" he means simply that music is, unlike the other arts, not a *representation at two removes,* not a representation of the Platonic or species ideas, but a representation of the original which the Platonic ideas also copy.[12]

[11] Arthur Schopenhauer, *The World as Will and Idea,* trans. R. B. Haldane and J. Kemp (Garden City, N.Y.: Dolphin Books, 1961), 332.

[12] Above the particularity of the individuals, according to Schopenhauer, are the timeless forms of ideas (*Ideen*) of whole species of things, which Schopenhauer identifies with Plato's ideas. The more objective types of art arouse the knowledge of these ideal forms through the representation of individual things; the ideas themselves are the "adequate objectivity" of will in which the "full objectification" of the will takes place (secs. 45–51). Whenever the subject becomes lost in pure contemplation of any one of the ideas, he perceives the entire "world as idea" and is raised above all mere individuation and the subject-object split. But

Music can be an immediate image because it is a *universal form* (*allgemeine Form*). We cannot begin to understand anything about the problematic of representation in the Schopenhauerian/Nietzschean metaphysics of music if we do not grapple with this fundamental notion of universal form.[13] According to Schopenhauer, all the other arts are restricted to the representation of "particular things" (*einzelner Dinge; SW,* 1:339), but music, like geometrical figures and numbers, though it is itself "perceptible and thoroughly determined," (*anschaulich und durchgängig bestimmt;* 345) represents the movements of feeling "always in the universality of mere form, without the material" (*in der Allgemeinheit blosser Form, ohne den Stoff;* 346).

It should be clear how inadequate any bare distinction between presence and absence or original and copy must be to deal with the notion of universal form. If they are not adjusted to deal with the problem of universality, these distinctions necessarily make Nietzsche's arguments look obscure and paradoxical, because they can apply in their bare simplicity only to the representation of things or, at best, of Platonic ideas. The will, though it is the *Ding an sich,* is not a thing but rather the universal being of all things. De Man confuses the matter badly when he tells us that the *Ding an sich* is "the entity as substance" (90), an Aristotelian formula that has no application to Schopenhauer's use of the term. The *will* as *Ding an sich* is transcendent being in the strongest sense, the "innermost essence, the kernel, of every particular thing and also of the whole" (*WWR,* 1:110), and is free of all the predicates which apply to individual things. "It is itself one, yet not as an object is one . . . [nor] as a concept is one . . . but . . . as that which lies outside time and space, outside the *principium individuationis*" (113).

---

nevertheless, the ideas are still not the will itself but only its mirroring or "objectification"; they serve as a *mediation* between the metaphysical will itself and the particularity of phenomena. Thus the objective arts "objectify the world indirectly only by means of the Ideas," but *music* represents neither phenomena nor ideas but the will itself.

[13]Even Pautrat misses the significance of this concept. He attributes the superiority of music over language to the fact that music is sonorous, whereas language is tied to visible image (*Versions du soleil,* 60). But this distinction, all too convenient for a certain kind of deconstruction, cannot account for Nietzsche's condemnation of the new dithyramb. This is still sonorous, but it is only a "wretched copy of the phenomenon" (*BT* 17;107) and fails to achieve the universality of true music. Pautrat proceeds to overturn his own reading on this topic, so his overall argument is not affected by this omission; yet it is a significant inaccuracy in that portion of Pautrat's reading that presents itself as faithful to the manifest content of Nietzsche's text.

This is not to say that the deconstructive critique of presence is beside the point here. On the contrary. But it cannot be a simple operation, for deconstruction would here have to take account of the specific transformations by which presence is subtilized from substance into pure form. A really rigorous reading would thus have to take into account the most sophisticated versions of such a subtilization, for example Wittgenstein's version in the *Tractatus* (and we might keep in mind that Wittgenstein was the *other* great philosopher whose youth was steeped in Schopenhauer).

Nietzsche's entire argument concerning the relation between music and language depends on this distinction between universal form and particular example, and Lacoue-Labarthe's discussion of Nietzsche's theory of symbolism is flawed by the absence of any mention of it.[14] It is not true, for instance, that "Nietzsche uses without distinguishing between them (*indifferement*) two terms, *Symbol* and *Gleichnis*" (L-L, 68). Wherever relevant in *The Birth of Tragedy* Nietzsche restricts *Gleichnis* to a technical Schopenhauerian usage according to which the word denotes the particularity of a determinate example in its non-universality, specifically as opposed to the formality of the universal.[15] The Schopenhauerian doctrine on this score is quoted in section 16, where the particular case is carefully defined in its relation of "example" to the generality of musical form (102–3), and Nietzsche ob-

[14]De Man's very strong claim at the conclusion of his chapter "Rhetoric of Tropes" that Nietzsche's valorizations in *The Birth of Tragedy* "can be reversed at will" (118) arises at least in part from the same omission. De Man translates a remark from 1871 as follows: "We have therefore an exactly reversed relationship. . . . For [the ancients] the world of representation was clear; for us, it is the Dionysian world we understand" (117). But in the space of de Man's ellipsis Nietzsche characterizes the ancients as closer to the *Gleichnissartigen des Bildes,* which means something like "the similitude-like character of the image," and the "Dionysian world" of the moderns as the *Allgemein-Dionysischen,* "universal-Dionysian." Thus even if Nietzsche ponders a certain reversal here, the underlying opposition of Dionysian universality and the particular *Gleichnis* is preserved. Furthermore, it must always be kept in mind how much in flux Nietzsche's ideas are in these notes. On the next page, he appears to change his mind about what he has just said about the ancients: "It's completely erroneous to say that the Greek world was characterized by the plastic, the modern by music. The Greek had much rather the complete unification of Dionysian and Apollonian." This is of course just what he says in *The Birth of Tragedy*. De Man mysteriously cites this remark from the unnumbered proofs of the, at that time, as yet unpublished Colli-Montinari edition (where they now appear in *KGW,* III 3: 320–21), but it is actually available in the Musarion edition (3:360–61), which de Man cites elsewhere.

[15]Thus when in section 21 Nietzsche draws "the contrast of the phenomenon and the thing-in-itself," his loose manner of expression must be cashed in in terms of the fuller analysis that takes account of the mediating distinction between universal form and particular *Gleichnis* or instantiation.

serves this technical distinction throughout *The Birth of Tragedy*. Thus in section 5 he describes the Apollonian dream image (which mirrors the first, musical copy of the will) as an *einzelnes Gleichnis oder Exempel*. (*KGW* III 1:40). Kaufmann obscures the distinction when he translates *Gleichnis* here as "symbol" (49). In the last two paragraphs of section 6 Nietzsche repeatedly refers to the Apollonian *Bild* as a *Gleichnis*. Here again, Kaufmann's translation obscures the distinction Nietzsche is making, especially when he has Nietzsche confusingly say that because music "symbolizes a sphere . . . prior to all phenomena," all phenomena are, "compared with it, merely symbols" (55). Nietzsche's distinction here is between music as *Symbol* and phenomena as *Gleichnis*. He then proceeds to speak of language as *Symbol* of phenomena, but he has made clear that it is only *Gleichnis* of music. (Golffing, otherwise often unreliable, actually does a better job here, rendering *Gleichnis* as "similitude" and "mere analogy" in order to retain the contrast with "symbol.")[16]

This schema does not lend itself easily to a reduction to the terms of de Man's epochal critique of the Romantic symbol. The Apollonian dream image or *Gleichnis* is a sort of synecdoche, since ontologically it participates in the reality that it renders visible (being, like everything else, a manifestation of will); yet qua representation it is an inferior mode, a mediated representation or representation at two removes (therefore similar to de Man's "allegory"). Music, however, which is not mere similitude but symbol of the thing-in-itself, is only a *form without a content;* thus, unlike the Romantic symbol, it does not make present a "plenitude." And to complicate matters further, the very secondariness or mediacy that makes the dream image or *Gleichnis* inferior to music is regarded along another axis of interpretation as the ultimate goal or *telos* of the *Ur*-being precisely because it is a *mere appearance of mere appearance* (*BT* IV;45).

Now, form, *eidos,* has been since Plato and Aristotle the philosophic medium par excellence, the medium of transition between the world of contingent, transitory presence and that of Absolute Presence. But the essence of that Absolute Presence has characteristically been defined as mind or intellect. Within the context of such an intellectualizing metaphysics the deconstructive schema on which Lacoue-Labarthe

[16]*The Birth of Tragedy and the Genealogy of Morals,* trans. Francis Golffing (Garden City, N.Y.: Doubleday Anchor Books, 1956), 46.

and de Man rely may find some purchase once we adjust it for the problem of universality. But there is a further complication when, as for both Schopenhauer and Nietzsche, universal form turns out to be not the harmonious form of *nous* (mind) but of endless striving, suffering, and contradiction. Such a conception threatens the boundaries of the classical definition of transcendent presence in a radical fashion, despite the persistence of distinctions between the phenomenon and thing-in-itself. It is no accident that Nietzsche tries to reinterpret the form of will as a scale of quantities of pleasure and displeasure (a question to which we return below); this step follows almost inevitably from Schopenhauer's break with the metaphysics of *nous*.

And what of the *unconscious*? Amazingly, neither Lacoue-Labarthe nor de Man notice how radically the emergence of the unconscious in Schopenhauer affects the terms of the problematic of representation. Consider, for example, the following remarks by de Man:

> What Nietzsche calls, following Schopenhauer, the "Will" is still a subject, a consciousness capable of knowing what it can and what it can not tolerate, capable of knowing its own volition. The self-representing faculty of the will is a self-willed act; in music, the will wills itself as representation. Schopenhauer's definition of music as being the "unmediated image of the will [*unmittelbares Abbild des Willens*]" rests in the power and the authority of the will as subject. (96)

De Man here entirely assimilates the terms of *The Birth of Tragedy* to a simplified schema of conscious agency and representation-for-consciousness. This assimilation is facilitated by de Man's entire failure, here or anywhere else in his essay, to respect the distinction between the individual will, which though not a "conscious agent" makes use of consciousness,[17] and the transcendent will, which does not.[18] The

[17]Consciousness is a mere *mechane,* a tool or instrument for "preserving the individual and the species, just like any organ of the body" (*WWR,* 1:152).

[18]De Man's remarks cited immediately above confuse the phenomenal and metaphysical will so subtly that they are susceptible to being read as though he were clearly aware of the distinction and were only drawing its consequences. If so, de Man would be saying that "what Nietzsche calls the 'will' is also the phenomenal subject as which it shows itself, a consciousness [etc.]. . . . In music, the metaphysical will wills itself as representation through the agency of the phenomenal subject through which it creates this music. Schopenhauer's definition of music as 'unmediated representation' of the metaphysical will rests in the power and authority of that will itself as the True Subject that is the real origin of music." But if we read de Man's comments in this way (which takes a lot of reading), the

distinction between a transcendent and an empirical will is deeply rooted in metaphysics; yet we must not overlook the way in which the agency of the unconscious enters Schopenhauer's text under cover of this distinction.

Nietzsche, like Schopenhauer, uses the word "will" in a way that is not exactly ambiguous but whose inflections do not always call attention to themselves. Schopenhauer says that there is only one will, which is "present whole and undivided in everything in nature" (*WWR*, 1:129); but phenomenal individuals are deluded by the veil of individuation and imagine themselves separate from all other beings. Consequently, instead of perceiving the unity of the one will, they lose themselves in the conflictual world of nature and suffer from the constant urgings of their (deluded) wills. Thus when Schopenhauer speaks of "will" sometimes he means the metaphysical whole which is will and sometimes he means its expression or refraction as "phenomenon" in individual beings. Although the two are *in substance* one and the same, the individual will is a modification of the metaphysical will and has different descriptive characteristics. Only by turning away from our own will and viewing the will in its totality do we achieve "objectivity" and the quieting of our own will (*WWR*, 1, secs. 34–35).[19] Because de Man treats the Schopenhauerian transcen-

---

conclusion to which he is building does not follow. He concludes that Nietzsche undermines the authority of his own voice through his "negative valorization of representational realism and the private lyrical voice (in section five)" (97). De Man's argument here shows that he is not in fact taking account of the distinction between the private voice and the true poetic voice that follows from the distinction between the phenomenal will and the true subject, which Nietzsche made in that same section 5 to which de Man refers. What Nietzsche argues there is that the lyrical voice is *not* private, the lyric *not* subjective. De Man's remark that Nietzsche has argued "against the subjectivity of the lyric" (98) is subtly ambiguous and *could* yield that meaning, but in view of his earlier remark about "negative valorization" of the lyrical voice, it more clearly suggests that Nietzsche has *derogated lyricism* and therefore undermined his *own* voice when it turns lyrical in *The Birth of Tragedy*. Since Nietzsche has in fact not at all derogated lyricism, he is perfectly consistent in trying to speak with the true lyrical voice, the voice of the true subject. He validates the lyric voice as Dionysian and thus attempts to validate his own position as (at times lyrical) spokesman for the Dionysian "point of view."

[19]When Nietzsche disagrees with Schopenhauer over the question of the lyric poet, he still relies on this schema of Schopenhauer's. Schopenhauer had argued that the lyric poet's consciousness is filled with "the subject of the will, i.e., *his own volition* [emphasis added] . . . as an affect, a passion, a moved state of mind . . . the remembrance of . . . personal ends"; consequently, according to Schopenhauer, lyric poetry is colored by "subjective mood, the affection of the will" (cited by Nietzsche, *BT* V;51). Nietzsche argues that the object contemplated by the lyric poet is not his own willing *as* his own, but as objectified, as separate from himself, so that his own passion is able to serve as similitude (*Gleichnis*) or

dent will as a conscious subject, he both misreads and mistranslates the passage from Nietzsche's notes in which he claims to find the "true rebuttal" of Schopenhauer which Lacoue-Labarthe had missed. Here is the passage as de Man presents it:

> Intelligence is justified in a world of aims. But if it is true that our aims are only a sort of rumination of experiences in which the actual agent remains hidden, then we are not entitled to transfer purposeful systems of action [*Handeln nach Zweckvorstellungen*] into the nature of things. This means that there is no need to imagine intelligence as capable of representation. Intelligence can only exist in a world in which mistakes can occur, in which error reigns—a world of consciousness. In the realm of nature and of necessity, all teleological hypotheses are absurd. Necessity means that there can only be one possibility. Why then do we have to assume the presence of an intellect in the realm of things?—And if the will cannot be conceived without implying its representation, the "will" is not an adequate expression for the core of nature either. (Musarion, 3:239; translation by de Man, 100)

---

representative image through which he may see the "basis of things": "this self is not the same as that of the waking, empirically real man, but the only truly existent and eternal self" (50).

We are now in a position to interpret an obscure passage in section 6 which is quoted by de Man (100–101) in a badly misleading context. Nietzsche says (in de Man's translation) that "the very nature [*ihrem Wesen nach*] of music excludes that it be the will" because will is "in essence the nonaesthetic"; the truth is rather that music "appears as" the will (*BT* VI;55). These remarks follow directly from the earlier ones concerning the will of the lyric poet. Nietzsche tells us that he is here referring to will "in Schopenhauer's sense," a remark which is open to misinterpretation since, as we have seen, there are *two* major senses of will in Schopenhauer. But Nietzsche goes on to specify that he means the particular sense which he had discussed in section 5: it is a nonaesthetic "frame of mind" which is in question, thus the subjective disposition of an individual (and not the metaphysical will). Thus music cannot *ihrem Wesen nach* be will for the same reason the suffering man cannot be poet—because will, in the sense operative here, is mere subjectivity, a phenomenon of individuality. (Incidentally, Golffing's translation garbles Nietzsche's point here by unaccountably transferring "ihrem Wesen nach" to the *will*. Thus we get Nietzsche saying that music cannot represent "the essential nature of the will," which suggests that it is the metaphysical will that is in question.)

When he says that music "*appears as* will," moreover, Nietzsche is not speaking of music itself but, as he specifies earlier in the paragraph, of the way that music manifests itself "in the mirror of images and concepts"—that is, in its translation by the poet into language. The poet, inspired by music, attempts to express in words the impressions evoked by the music. In these words music "appears as will"; that is, the poet linguistically represents the "agitations of passion," creating a verbal equivalent (inadequate as it necessarily is) of the appearance of music. Once again it is a question of the example or similitude that symbolizes a universality.

In fact, this passage is practically a paraphrase of Schopenhauer, who certainly did not hold that representations of a goal (*Zweckvorstellungen*) needed to be injected into "the nature of things." Concerning nature, Schopenhauer says that

> we see at once from the instinct and mechanical skill of animals that the will is also active where it is not guided by any knowledge. . . . Their action here takes place without motive, is not guided by the representation [*Vorstellung*]. . . . Representation as motive is not a necessary and essential condition of the will's activity. (*WWR,* 1:114)

Concerning the will itself, he says that

> every will . . . has an object, an aim of its willing; what then does it ultimately will, or what is that will which is shown to us as the being-in-itself of the world striving after? Like so many others, this question rests on the confusion of the thing-in-itself with the phenomenon. (163)

> In fact, absence of all aim . . . belongs to the essential nature of the will in itself, which is an endless striving. (164)

According to Schopenhauer's metaphysics of will, the world is *Vorstellung* of the will only in relation to the existence of representing creatures in the world. Before the arising of such creatures, the will works "in the dark," as "blind urge," though in the necessary unfolding of its "tendency" it works with "infallible certainty" (even as Nietzsche tells us that "in the realm of nature, of necessity" there is only one possibility and no mistakes occur, which is why no *Vorstellungen* are necessary). But as soon as "the brain or a larger ganglion" develops, "*the world as representation* . . . stands out at one stroke" and "the world . . . shows its second side" (*WWR,* 1:150).

In fact, in the passage de Man cites, Nietzsche appears to be arguing against his *own* suggestion in remark 59 of the same manuscript that "the Kantian-Schopenhauerian idealists" had failed to recognize the working of an *Ur*-intellect in nature, below the level of consciousness (Musarion, 3:235). In remark 62 he had suggested that this *Ur*-intellect was "essentially representation of purpose"—that is, that unlike thought in which will and the representation of the goal are two separate things, the *Ur*-intellect needed no representation to view but was itself, in its essence, the representation of its own purpose. In the remark cited by de Man he seems to retreat from the ascription of an *Ur*-Intellect to nature, and thus to return to a more Schopenhauerian position. As for the final sentence of de Man's quotation, which seems to suggest that *there* at least Nietzsche is denying that the will can be represented: de Man has mistranslated. Nietzsche does not say "without implying *its* [*seine*] representation" (as de Man says) but instead "without implying *a* [*eine*] representation." That is, the representation in question is not the representation of will but the representation *by* the will of its goal, its holding of a *Vorstellung* of its *Zweck* before itself. That this is the type of representation intended in this remark is apparent from the remarks leading up to this one. Nietzsche is saying "if the concept 'will' implies that the will must view a *Vorstellung* of its goal, then 'will' is the wrong term for the core of nature"—but Schopenhauer had already denied that *Vorstellungen* of a goal had anything to do with the will.

The proliferation by Nietzsche of contradictory perspectives on unity and the *Ur*-being should make us hesitate to take any one of them too literally. If he personifies this being in some places, he implies that it is impersonal and aimless when he speaks of the "spasms of the agitations of the will" (*BT* XIV;118); if unity with nature is introduced as Dionysian in section 1, in section 3 the "oneness of man with nature" is "naive" and "Apollonian" (43); most important, if suffering and contradiction are described as the primordial state of original unity, they are then ascribed to the tearing apart of this unity, the state of individuation. In view of these and other contradictions, we can and should accept the text's repeated warnings concerning the inadequacy of the verbal *Gleichnis* and relegate all the talk about the *Ur*-being to the realm of allegorical similitude. Nietzsche tells us explicitly that the experiences of a "unity leading back to the heart of nature" are only a "metaphysical comfort" (VII;59), one form of artistic "illusion" among others (XVIII;109–10). This is not something said only once and "contrary to all earlier claims," as de Man argues (99); once we learn to distinguish the various stages of "the Dionysian" it is clear that the aspect of illusion enters in as soon as the Dionysian cult becomes Hellenized.

If we subtract the metaphysical allegory from Nietzsche's talk about the Dionysian, we are left with descriptions of various *experiences of* and *reactions to* "the Dionysian." There appears to be operating here an early form of Nietzschean "perspectivism," and perhaps one compatible with the manuscript remark that defines the will as the "most universal form of appearance." What does it mean, then, to say that the will is the form of appearance of that which does not itself appear?

Nietzsche clearly understands the disproportion between transcendent being and all determinate beings. Transcendent being cannot manifest itself as *a* being or as an affection of a being.

We could interpret Nietzsche's remark as his *transcendental-phenomenological reduction,* his way of bracketing the question of being-in-itself in favor of the question of the structure of the appearing of being. The will is the name of the receptiveness to the world of an embodied being, the name of the way in general in which the world registers on a being capable of sensation. The scale of this receptiveness is the scale of pleasure and displeasure; Nietzsche's phenomenology is one of *quantities* of these sensations and not of forms, for, although the will is the *form* of appearing, "the strivings of the Will express themselves as pleasure or unpleasure and in this exhibit only quantitative differentiation" (*KGW* III 2:64, cf. Musarion, 3:341–42). Nietzsche's phenomenology should perhaps, then, be called an "aesthesiology." Transcendent being, however, is so to speak *off the scale;* it does not register on our sensorium. But even if it is not directly knowable, there is one thing we can know about it: it is the limit of individuation, the totality or nothingness out of which individuals come and which swallows them up again.

This *limit of individuation,* which is the only irreducible kernel of Nietzsche's allegory in *The Birth of Tragedy,* is not itself capable of being represented, yet there is, phenomenologically or aesthesiologically, something that corresponds to it as its effect or affect: it is the passage to the limit of sensation, its extreme, ultimate intensification along both dimensions to the point that pleasure and displeasure cease to be distinguishable and a rupture of the scale occurs. This is the *excess* of nature (*BT* IV;46), the Dionysian *Rausch* the expression of which is said to be music.

Once again, there is a deceptive simplicity of substance implied by a term that is actually complex in reference: there is a substructure to "music" that goes beyond the question of music.

On the one hand, not all music counts as music in the sense relevant to *The Birth of Tragedy,* for the "psalmodizing" of the Apollonian harp player (V;46) does not count, nor does the "tone painting" of the New Dithyramb (XVII;107); on the other hand, music manifests itself initially, in the orgiastic Dionysian, as what is *not* music, as "*piercing shrieks*" (V;46). Nietzsche's most extensive discussion of this phenomenon in *The Birth of Tragedy,* in section 3, moves ambiguously from speaking of the cry to speaking of music, as though the two were the same phenomenon, something which in *The Dionysian Worldview* he explicitly asserts: "When does the language of gesture no longer suffice? When does Tone become Music? Above all in the Will's states of the most extreme pleasure and displeasure, . . . in the transport [*Rausch*] of feeling: in the cry [*Schrei*]" (*KGW* III 2:67).

Not only does Nietzsche slide ambiguously between music and shrieking, but he throws in "the entire symbolism of the body," gesture and dance, elements that in *The Dionysian Worldview* he was careful to distinguish from and subordinate to musical *Ton* but which here are introduced as the underlying tremors out of which music emerges: first there is "the whole pantomime of dancing, forcing every member into rhythmic movement. Then the other symbolic powers suddenly press forward, particularly those of music" (*BT* II;40).[20] Nietzsche is indeed evoking the greatest immediacy possible, but not as representation: it is a matter of the *communication of force.* The Dionysian *Rausch* is a state in which the "nearness" of a presence "speaks through forces" (*redet durch Kräfte*), shows itself as "forces, merely felt, and not condensed into images" (*BT* VIII;66–7; *KGW* III 2:60); and these forces are those of the excess (*Uebermass*) of the life surge that ruptures the boundaries of individuality. These same forces that express themselves as tremors of the body in the Dionysian celebrants express themselves as the "musical mood" of the lyric poet of section 5. Nietzsche says that the Dionysian musician is "pure primordial pain and its primordial re-echoing" (*BT* V;50), and this state, which is what Nietzsche calls, in Schiller's phrase, the "musical mood" (49), is what is "copied" in the form of music. Nietzsche's terminology creates some ambiguity in these key paragraphs, but from the main premises and overall struc-

[20]Cf. *Will to Power* 809: "The more complete phenomenon is always the beginning: our faculties are subtilized out of more complete faculties. But even today one still hears with one's muscles, one even reads with one's muscles." Farther on he adds, "One never communicates thoughts: one communicates movements, mimic signs, which we then trace back to thoughts."

ture of his account, it is clear that poetry is generated not out of music as a sonorous phenomenon but out of music as the poet's musical *mood* that precedes verbalization: a sort of transcendental music or unheard melody that would thus be the *pure form* of music. (The alternative would be to suggest what is obviously not true: that the lyric poet *composed a melody* first, and only then the poem.) This is, of course, just what Nietzsche had said in the title of the first edition of his book, which was not *The Birth of Tragedy Out of Music* but *The Birth of Tragedy Out of the Spirit of Music.*

The essence of Dionysian music is thus, to speak a Heideggerean language, *nothing musical;* Dionysian music expresses what the Dionysian cry expresses, the pathos of the rupturing of individuated being. That is why although Nietzsche keeps trying to find the essence of music in the "incomparable power of harmony," in the end it is in musical *dissonance* that he discovers the Dionysian essence of music, as the element that figures, within music, the failure of music to give form to the experience of the irretrievable loss of all form.[21]

There is thus not so much distance between what Nietzsche says about rhetoric and what he says about music. Lacoue-Labarthe cites section 3 of the "Course on Rhetoric" to show that Nietzsche's analysis of rhetoric contains an inversion of the fundamental order of *The Birth of Tragedy* according to which music engenders the image (L-L, 64), but Lacoue-Labarthe's reading seems to be an artifact of his interpretive machine. Here are the lines in question from Nietzsche:

> The power [*Kraft*] which Aristotle calls rhetoric, which is the power of picking out and exploiting, for each thing, what is effective and makes an impression, that power is at the same time the essence of language: language refers as little as does rhetoric to what is true, to the essence of things; it does not mean to instruct, but *to transmit to others a subjective excitation and apprehension* [emphasis added]. The language-forming man does not lay hold of things or events, but of excitations [*Reize*]: he does not hand over sensations [*Empfindungen*] but only copies [*Abbildungen*] of sensations. The sensation which is aroused by a nervous excitation does not lay hold of the thing itself: this sensation is represented exter-

[21]This privileging of dissonance over harmony is already present in the notes from winter 1870–1871 in which Nietzsche speaks of "the reality [Realität] of dissonance as opposed to the ideality of consonance" (Musarion, 3:319).

nally by an image [*Bild*]: but it is a question how, in general, an act of the soul [*Seelenakt*] can be represented by a sound-image [*Tonbild*]. (Musarion, 5:298)

And from the *Philosophenbuch,* there is the following: "Initially, to transpose a nervous excitation into an image [apparently, the *Seelenakt* of the above citation]! First metaphor! Then again to transform the image into an articulate sound! Second metaphor!" (Musarion, 6:79).

Lacoue-Labarthe wants to see in these remarks a neat reversal of the earlier doctrine: whereas in *The Birth of Tragedy* music engendered image, here image engenders sound (L-L, 72). But there is no justification for equating the internal "image," the sensation as which an excitation of the nerves is interpreted, as an "image" in the sense in which imagery is called "Apollonian" in *The Birth of Tragedy.* For the realm of "acts of spirit" by which nervous excitations are interpreted includes *all the sensory modalities,* including sound, as Nietzsche says in a very early remark also translated by Lacoue-Labarthe: "We do not know things in themselves and for themselves, only their images [*Abbild*] upon the mirror of our soul. . . . Color and sound do not belong to things, but to the eye and the ear" (L-L, 133). So there is in these remarks no sequence of (Apollonian) image to (Dionysian) sound (notice Lacoue-Labarthe's equivocation on "sound," too, as though sound were simply equivalent to music);[22] there is only a sequence of inner experience, whether visual, sonorous, or other, to outward expression of that experience.

The problem with Lacoue-Labarthe's reading of this passage, as of his entire reading of Nietzsche on rhetoric, is the way in which he focuses on the ontological and epistemological questions of language to the exclusion of another question that profoundly agitates Nietzsche himself. When Nietzsche writes, in the passage cited above, that language "transmits" (*übertragen*) to others "a subjective excitation and apprehension," Lacoue-Labarthe sees only the loss of relation to the object apprehended, its *Übertragung* into an element alien to it in which its essence is lost. This is undoubtedly a crucial question for Nietzsche, but it is not his only one and perhaps not his dominant one. It could be argued that his more urgent concern is with the problem of

[22]In contrast to Lacoue-Labarthe, Pautrat offers a beautifully subtle analysis of sonority and its complex relations to music and language; *Versions du soleil,* 94–107.

Übertragung from one subjectivity to another of precisely the *subjective character* of the apprehension that is transmitted. In that case, the movement from *The Birth of Tragedy* to the texts on rhetoric would be best understood not as a rejection of the object (music) concerning which Nietzsche had spoken in the earlier text, but as a reflection on the medium in which Nietzsche had tried to transmit his *subjective apprehension* of that object, in light of his dissatisfaction with the success of the transmission.[23] The Dionysian phenomenon is itself, as we have seen, a propagation of forces (*Kräfte*), forces that are communicated "epidemically" (*BT* VIII;64) among the rapt devotees. Nietzsche in *The Birth of Tragedy* had tried to become the "Dionysian bird" with its "ecstatically luring call" (XXIV;139) that would propagate the Dionysian force to his readers; but this of course was to attempt precisely what his own argument claimed to be impossible: to generate music (that is, the musical Dionysian *mood*) by means of language.

The longing Nietzsche manifests in *The Birth of Tragedy* is not for some problematic divinity but for the Dionysian melding of whole masses of human beings, the breaking down of all the "rigid, hostile barriers" that separate human beings so that the "union between man and man" can be "reaffirmed" (I;37). And this longing persists across the shift in medium from music to language, for the myth of a primal unity which is tied to music in *The Birth of Tragedy* is restated in linguistic terms in the 1873–1875 notes on "Reading and Writing":

> All intercourse [*Verkehr*] among men is based on this: that each is able to read the interior of the soul of the other; and the common language is the sonorous expression of a common soul. The more profound and sensitive [*inniger und zarter*] that intercourse becomes, the richer the language is, which grows or declines with this universal soul. Speaking is at the bottom a questioning of my fellow man concerning whether he has the same soul as I. (Naumann, 10:392)

> The will [to speak] . . . is nothing individual. If one would imagine a primal mythological being with a hundred heads, a hundred feet and a

[23]Cf. *Philosophy in the Tragic Age of the Greeks,* chap. 3: "And just as for the dramatist words and verses are but the stammering of an alien tongue, needed to tell what he has seen and lived, what he could utter directly only through music or gesture, just so every profound philosophic intuition expressed through dialectic . . . is the only means for the philosopher to communicate what he has seen. But it is a sad means; basically a metaphoric and entirely unfaithful translation" (44–45).

> hundred hands, as the form of the primordial human being—this being would speak with himself, and when he noticed that he could speak with himself as with two, three, or even a hundred beings, he would let himself divide into his parts, individual men, because he knew he could not entirely lose his unity—because this is not in space, like this multiplicity of a hundred men; on the contrary, when they speak the mythological monster experiences himself once again as a completely unified being [*ganz und eins*]. (Naumann, 10:294)

Later on Nietzsche will shrink from nothing so much as from the contact of masses of humanity, yet the root phenomenon that produces the Edenic longing expressed in these early texts persists all the way to the end. This phenomenon is the strange *permeability of Nietzsche's boundary of individuation*. Nietzsche feels, hears, and imagines the affect, pushed to its limit, of all humanity and of the whole history of humanity; like Prometheus "he suffers in his own person the primordial contradiction that is concealed in things" (*BT* IX;71) and aspires to the capacity to endure the totality of this contradiction, to be "the Atlas for all individuals, carrying them on a broad back" (72). If Nietzsche at the time of *The Birth of Tragedy* claims to hear the agony of a world of desire and ecstatic suffering in music and this is, as de Man suggests, a ridiculous claim to make about music, it is not at all ridiculous if we read it (as we should read all of Nietzsche, as Nietzsche tells us we should read him) as a revelation about Nietzsche himself, about his capacity to hear. Here is the passage ridiculed by de Man:

> Suppose a human being has thus put his ear, as it were, to the heart chamber of the world will and felt the roaring desire for existence pouring from there into all the veins of the world . . . how could he fail to break suddenly? How could he endure to perceive the echo of innumerable shouts of pleasure and woe in the "wide space of the world night," enclosed in the wretched glass capsule of the human individual, without inexorably fleeing toward his primordial home? (*BT* XXI;127)

Now compare the above passage to the following one from *The Gay Science:*

> Anyone who manages to experience the history of humanity as a whole as *his own history* will feel in an enormously generalized way all the grief

> of an invalid who thinks of health, of an old man who thinks of the dreams of his youth, of a lover deprived of his beloved, of the martyr whose ideal is perishing, of the hero on the evening after a battle that has decided nothing but brought him wounds and the loss of his friend. But if one endured, if one *could* endure this immerse sum of grief of all kinds. . . . (337)

Nothing but Nietzsche's writing style has changed in the interval between these two passages: the later passage, which is more to our taste in its "concreteness," tallies up the same "immense sum of grief," to which Nietzsche, like his Greeks, is so "uniquely susceptible" (*BT* VIII;59).

This sensitivity, this permeability of his boundary of individuation, his tendency to melt into the "enormously generalized" grief of an entire creation, is what the later works call *pity,* one of Nietzsche/Zarathustra's two great dangers, the recoil of which is *nausea,* the same overwhelming awareness, but without sympathy, of the existence of a whole universe of unredeemed beings, the horror of a vast meaninglessness. What is so remarkable about Nietzsche's pity is the universality of its scope; it is a whole world of passion and suffering that he hears clamoring and to which he must in some way shut his ears (whether by artistic illusion as in *The Birth of Tragedy* or by "becoming hard," as repeatedly in the later work). "I know . . . that I need only expose myself to the sight of some genuine distress and I am lost. And if a suffering friend said to me, 'Look, I am about to die; please promise to die with me,' I should promise it; and the sight of a small mountain tribe fighting for its liberty would persuade me to offer it my hand and my life" (*GS* 338). Nietzsche's myths of primal communion and its loss are the "subjective correlative" of this permeability of his boundary of individuation because they explain *pity as nostalgia.* That is, if Nietzsche feels so immediately vulnerable to suffering the passion and pain of all humanity, it must be, mythically speaking, because it is all *one* pain, the pain of a single being who suffers from division and from the longing to be reunited.[24]

[24]Cf. the notes from winter 1870–1871, in which Nietzsche repeatedly stresses that the subject of all suffering is the one will, and that "all pain is one and the same" (Musarion, 3:325). When Nietzsche speaks of the will as the subject of pain, he seems to be thinking in a different register than when he calls it the "form of appearance."

Pity and nostalgia. Do I make Nietzsche sound too Romantic, too Rousseauistic? The matter is not so simple. On the one hand, it is true that Nietzsche recognizes these impulses as something to be opposed and controlled; it could even be said that his career-long opposition to Romanticism is his opposition to these impulses. On the other hand, according to the reading I am here proposing this Romanticism would not be something *external* to Nietzsche's project but something that works it from within, as what has to be opposed so strenuously because it is so intimate, so proper to Nietzsche's own economy.

The Birth of Tragedy, like all of Nietzsche's work, is the allegory of this economy (but Nietzsche tells us that *every* philosophy is such an allegory, "the personal confession" and "unconscious memoir" of its author). And if we read it as such, it is clear that the entire work with its images of primal unity and primal division allegorizes one simple and irreducible recognition: "All that comes into being must be ready for a sorrowful end" (XVII;104). Near the beginning of his essay Nietzsche describes the Dionysian cry as "a yearning lamentation for an irretrievable loss [*unersetzlichen Verlust*]" (II;40), and this description is closely echoed in the characterization of the elegy in section 19. Here Nietzsche, once again drawing on Schiller's account of "the sentimental," invokes Schiller's distinction between idyll and elegy: "Nature and the ideal, [Schiller] says, are either objects of grief, when the former is represented as lost, the latter unattained; or both are objects of joy, in that they are represented as real. The first case furnishes the elegy in its narrower signification, the second the idyll in its widest sense" (XIX;117). Nietzsche then condemns the "cheerfulness" of the idyll as against the "elegiac sorrow of an eternal loss [*ewigen Verlust*]" (118).

Nietzsche never comments on the correlation of Dionysian lamentation and elegiac sorrow, but his characterization of the two in so nearly the same words makes the connection clear. The Dionysian lamentation is elegiac sorrow in its most extreme form, and the Apollonian image, which imposes the illusion of form and meaning, or the deeper ("Dionysian") illusion of a consolatory return to unity, palliates for the rapt viewer the unbearability of the Dionysian force, which is the *force of mourning.*

The problem of representation in *The Birth of Tragedy* can only be fully understood in relation to the problem of mourning, a problem concerning which, we know, de Man had important things to say—

though not in relation to Nietzsche. If there is in de Man's work, as Jacques Derrida has claimed, "an insistent reflection on mourning" and a meditation on "bereaved memory"[25]—and I think there is—then why does de Man so utterly ignore the presence of these themes in *The Birth of Tragedy?* Isn't all of *The Birth of Tragedy* concerned with the problem of giving a face and a voice, or faces and voices, to an absent, deceased, or voiceless entity, an entity called Dionysus, who is a figure not of any particular deceased being but of decease in general, of all that is already dead or all that lives as already affected by its future death, and thus a sort of transcendental elegy whose figure is *prosopopeia?*

So there is another reading de Man might have done of this text and rather strangely did not even approach. Perhaps the recent revelations concerning de Man's wartime journalism give us some clue as to why he did not.[26]

Nietzsche is, with Rousseau, the writer who has been most susceptible to political/ideological appropriation, and *The Birth of Tragedy,* with its appeals to Wagner and the German *Volk* and its evocation of phenomena of mass hysteria, is only too remindful of the era of Nazism. Could this not account for the coldness of de Man's reading, his utter refusal to listen to the "ecstatic call" of the "Dionysian bird"? I think the present essay adds to the evidence that de Man's later work was rooted in opposition to the types of doctrine, and the styles of thought behind them, to which he himself at one time (to a degree we do not yet know) succumbed.

[25]Jacques Derrida, *Memoires for Paul de Man* (New York: Columbia University Press, 1986), 22.

[26]See Paul de Man, *Wartime Journalism, 1939–1943,* ed. Werner Hamacher, Neil Hertz, and Thomas Keenan (Lincoln: University of Nebraska Press, 1988), and *Responses: On Paul de Man's Wartime Journalism,* by the same editors and publisher (1989).

Index

Library of Congress Cataloging-in-Publication Data

Staten, Henry, 1946–
Nietzsche's voice / Henry Staten.
p. cm.
Includes bibliographical references and index.
ISBN 0–8014–2500–X (cloth : alkaline paper).—ISBN 0–8014–9739–6 (pbk. : alkaline paper)
1. Nietzsche, Friedrich Wilhelm, 1844–1900. I. Title.
B3317.S675 1990
193—dc20 90–55131